Disability and Difference in Global Contexts

Disability and Difference in Global Contexts

Enabling a Transformative Body Politic

Nirmala Erevelles

To Alicia

Wishing you the very best as change agent!

palgrave
macmillan

First published in hardcover in 2011 by PALGRAVE MACMILLAN® in the United States—a division of St. Martin's Press LLC, 175 Fifth Avenue, New York, NY 10010.

Where this book is distributed in the UK, Europe and the rest of the world, this is by Palgrave Macmillan, a division of Macmillan Publishers Limited, registered in England, company number 785998, of Houndmills, Basingstoke, Hampshire RG21 6XS.

Palgrave Macmillan is the global academic imprint of the above companies and has companies and representatives throughout the world.

Palgrave® and Macmillan® are registered trademarks in the United States, the United Kingdom, Europe and other countries.

ISBN: 978–1–137–57732–0

The Library of Congress has cataloged the hardcover edition as follows:

Erevelles, Nirmala, 1965–
    Disability and difference in global contexts : enabling a transformative body politic / NirmalaErevelles.
        p. cm.
    ISBN 978–0–230–10018–3
        1. Sociology of disability. 2. Disabilities—Philosophy. 3. People with disabilities. 4. Historical materialism. I. Title.

HV1568.E74 2011
305.9'08—dc23   2011019473

A catalogue record of the book is available from the British Library.

Design by Newgen Knowledge Works (P) Ltd., Chennai, India.

First PALGRAVE MACMILLAN paperback edition: January 2016

10 9 8 7 6 5 4 3 2 1

This book is dedicated to my family
My Husband
Robert M. Young (1968–2010)
My Daughter
Maya Mildred Young
&
My Parents
The Late Antony Joseph Erevelles and Mabel Erevelles

CONTENTS

ACKNOWLEDGMENTS

THIS BOOK WAS WRITTEN UNDER THE MOST DIFFICULT OF circumstances. I received the contract for writing this book during the time my husband was receiving treatment for brain cancer, and I was only able to finish it after he passed away on January 31, 2010. Thus, it was only inevitable that the process of writing this book was filled with emotional highs and lows, starts and stops, tears and laughter, hope and deep despair. Writing this book has therefore become a collective process with so many people to thank for helping me make it this far.

First and foremost I want to thank my teachers at Syracuse University, who were the first people to teach me to think critically and radically about disability: Steven J. Taylor, my advisor who always believed in me, Sari K. Biklen, who counseled me through all the ups and downs in graduate school, and my teachers Robert Bogdan, Hank Bersani, Diane Murphy, Douglas Biklen, and Priti Ramamurthy who influenced my thinking in so many ways. I also want to thank the special education graduate student cohort, who challenged my thinking in creative ways.

Second, I want to thank my colleagues at both Auburn University and the University of Alabama. At Auburn University, I would like to thank my colleagues Jim Kaminsky, Kimberly L. King Jupiter, Judy Lechner, Renee Middleton, Holly Stadler, Ivan Watts, and Patty Whang, for mentoring me in my first job and enabling me to venture out into "radical" projects even though I was untenured at that time. At the University of Alabama, I owe immense gratitude to Stephen Tomlinson, Natalie Adams, John Petrovic, Doug McKnight, and Becky Atkinson, who as amazing colleagues not only kept academia exciting, but also covered my classes, took over dissertation committees, released me from meetings so that I could take care of my husband, and supported my work. Your intellectual and personal solidarity is much appreciated. I also appreciate the solidarity of my colleagues Brittney Cooper, Sara Childers, Dave Dagley, Aaron Kuntz, Utz McKnight, Cecil Robinson, and Jerry Rosiek among others. To the staff members in the ELPTS department at the University Of Alabama, Edward

Guy, Laura Ballard, Donna Smith, Angela Kelly, and Margie Carroll, a very warm thank you for all the work that you did for me with a ready smile. And to my amazing doctoral students who have sustained my passion for teaching and radical thinking in a difficult context, a warm thank you. Thank you Josh Burford, Daniel Dickens, Puneet Gill, Louis Ginocchio, Ingie Givens, Robert Hayes, Elizabeth Hendrix, Anne Kanga, Kathy Kinslow, Sikharini Majumdar , Carlton McHargh, Rachel McWhorter, Dymaneke Mitchell, Roland Mitchell, Andrea Minear, Jeena Owens, Tasha Parrish, Alison Schmitke, Noelle Witherspoon, and Gerald Wood—the list goes on. Teaching nurtures thinking and your thoughtful questions always inspired me to think harder. For those of you I have not mentioned here, note that it was an oversight that is much regretted.

To my amazing colleagues and friends at the Society of Disability Studies and the Disability Studies in Education Special Interest Group (SIG) at the American Educational Research Association, just knowing you all was an amazing educational and personal experience. I have learned so much from each one of you. Thank you Julie Allan, Liat Ben Moshe, Pamela Block, Susan Burch, Fiona Kumari Campbell, Eli Clare, David Connor, Scot Danforth, Lennard Davis, Stephen Drake, Phil Ferguson, Beth Ferri, Jim Ferris, Anne Finger, Ann Fox, Leslie Freeman, Susan Gabel, Deborah Gallagher, Anita Ghai, Carol Gill, Dan Goodley, Beth Haller, Alison Kafer, Deva Kasniz, Ravi Malhotra, Robert McRuer, Rod Michalko, David Mitchell, Angel Miles, Leroy Moore, Akemi Nishida, Corbett O'Toole, Beth Omanksy, Sara Palmer, Margaret Price, Leslie Roman, Carrie Sandahl, Susan Schweik, Tobin Siebers, Phil Smith, Sharon Snyder, Bethany Stevens, Tanya Titchkosky, Rosemarie Garland Thomson, and Linda Ware. You all formed a vibrant community for me, always pushing me to think harder, deeper, and even more dangerously about disability. In so many ways this book embodies so much of all your thinking. Thank you!

I am also very grateful to Samantha Briggs, Catherine Davies, Vikram Dravid, Lakshmi Goparaju, Pascal Herve, Rhoda Johnson, Ramu Kannan, Yolanda Manora, Priti Ramamurti, Dipinder Randhawa, Angelo Rivero-Santos, Aarti Saihjee, Ujwala Samant, Demetria Shabazz, Gowri Shankar, Ashwini Udgaonkar, Chandan Vaidya, and Demetria Shabazz. You nurtured me through the darkest moments of my life and kept me strong both by example and deed. The fact that I had the emotional strength to write this book is because of you. And to the large community of friends both in Tuscaloosa and in my virtual community on Facebook, you have been wonderful too in keeping me upbeat and happy with your caring words and much love.

To my graduate assistant Tasha Parrish, who has gone above and beyond the call of duty to help me finish this book, I am also grateful. Besides being brilliant, she is hardworking, and so generous with her time, I feel guilty I may have exploited her! Thank you Tasha.

To my family who has supported me in so many ways, you also have my sincere gratitude. Special thanks goes to Sunil and Ayse Erevelles, and Sushma and Ravikumar Joseph. Also my most special gratitude goes to my mother, who has always believed in me and worked really hard to support me and my work throughout my life but especially during Robert's illness and the months after his passing.

I am also grateful to my little six-year-old daughter, Maya, who over the last few months was willing to entertain herself while her mama struggled with the book. She has been patient, funny, adorable, helpful, and supportive not only through Robert's illness but throughout the process of writing this book.

And last but not least, I am grateful for knowing and loving my husband, Robert, for the past 15 years. We were intellectual and political allies. He, more than anyone else, nurtured my intellectual pursuits, earnestly reading drafts, giving me references, summarizing for me difficult arguments, many of which have now found themselves in this book. I had so wanted him to see this book published. But it was not to be. Being the primary caregiver made it really hard to do this work while he was alive, But all of what is in this book reflects our shared intellectual life together these past 15 years. And for that I am profoundly grateful.

INTRODUCTION: BODIES THAT DO NOT MATTER

If we must die, O let us nobly die...

Claude McKay (1919), *If We Must Die*

LIVING THEORY/WRITING LIFE

On September 15, 2006, my husband, Robert, was diagnosed with a Grade IV brain tumor—glioblastoma multiforme (GBM). That I can even spell the words now is a significant improvement because in the stunned minutes...hours...days following this pronouncement, I could barely even comprehend what was being said, let alone articulate the multiple syllables that would forever mark Robert's existence from that day on. I can only speak of my reaction during those early days because Robert was not allowed to grasp the significance of this life-transforming event completely, having been heavily drugged to prevent further seizures and pumped with steroids to reduce brain swelling in preparation for brain surgery a day later.

The neurosurgeon in this small southern college football town came highly recommended, his surgical skills indisputable. He must, however, have forgotten that section of his medical education (if there is one!) on how to talk to a patient and his or her family about a prognosis that promises a median survival rate of 14 months with only 4–5 percent of those diagnosed surviving beyond 5 years. As a result, when he first came to alert us to the seriousness of the situation, though he did not quote any of those ominous statistics, he did not inspire any hopefulness either, when in response to my repeated question, "What does this all mean?" he intoned in a deadpan voice, "Just enjoy your family." In retrospect, I would have preferred the stolid imperfection of statistical prediction that, ironically, seemed far more reassuring than listening to his oft-repeated incantation of intangible doom.

As an otherwise "healthy" 38-year-old, being told that one may quite conceivably have less than a year to live is not something one embraces wholeheartedly with the proverbial "skip in one's step and song in one's heart." We were both recently tenured in our respective colleges at the university. We were just beginning to make a name for ourselves in our respective fields of study. We had the most adorable two-year-old daughter any lovingly biased parents could ever hope to have, and were hoping to adopt a second child. And we were beginning to celebrate our impending liberation from the credit card debt that we had incurred as struggling graduate students. In addition, we were both political and intellectual allies—our work inspired and enriched by the other's insights. And so when words such as *cancer, radiation, MRI, chemo,* and *living will* stampeded uninvited into the seemingly enchanted perfection of our lives, we both allowed ourselves to wallow in the self-pitying lament of "Why me? Why us?"

In stressful moments, people often turn either inward or outward searching for a source of strength in religion, psychotherapy, meditation, exercise, or art. Academics like us turn desperately to our books hoping for some nugget of knowledge to sustain us. I did not have to look far for this sustenance, immersed as I already was in the field of disability studies that provided me with both the political and the theoretical tools to interpret the transformations that were bound to occur in our lives. I had been working in disability studies for over 15 years, since the time I was a graduate student in special education at Syracuse University, where I was introduced to the intriguing notion of reading disability outside the narrow confines of medicine, and recognizing it more usefully as a social and political category of difference. Challenged to think of disability beyond the restrictive normative notion of "the limit" (Titchkosky, 2005, p. 658), my intellectual work explores disability-as-possibility in the fields of education, social theory, and political activism. Immersed in disability studies scholarship, I had by this time acquired a valuable cache of tools that I knew would help me navigate the unpredictable terrain we were entering.

On the one hand, our interactions with the medical establishment as a daunting adversary yet a necessary ally was beginning to shape the daily contours of our lives. On the other hand, both Robert and I were introduced more intimately to the daily indignities that society, in general, directs at disabled people. I hasten to add here, however, that I do not mean to conflate the experiences of living with a disability and being sick. Sickness is usually perceived as a temporary condition, which when subjected to the benevolence of medicine brings the sick person back to a normal state. Disabled bodies on the other hand have proven to be more recalcitrant, reminding the medical and rehabilitation establishment of the limits of their authority in restoring the body to its "normal" state. As Mitchell and

Snyder (1997) observe, "[Because] [d]isability defies correction and tends to operate according to its own idiosyncratic rules...people with disabilities are said to be fated and unsalvageable...[and this] consequently situates the disabled person within the social space of difference that forever alienates the 'afflicted' from the normative conventions of everyday social and scientific interaction" (pp. 3–4). People living with chronic/terminal illnesses also pose similar challenges, and, as a result, also suffer from similar social effects of being designated as uncontrollably pathological. Perceived as the very embodiment of the irresolvable "case," and therefore a constant source of curiosity and experimentation, such bodies also find themselves "being on permanent display, of being visually conspicuous, while being politically and socially erased" (Garland-Thomson, 2002b, p. 56).

For someone as introverted and private as Robert, being catapulted into the public sphere unshielded from its unyielding gaze was very disconcerting. Dramatic as Robert's diagnosis was, it was eager fodder for public discussion, both sympathetic and sensational. And he found himself forced, unwittingly, to continue to prolong those 15 minutes of fame/infamy. Since one of the most intrusive side effects of having a brain tumor were grand mal seizures, we both thought it necessary to inform his students and colleagues about this possibility, so that they could respond appropriately in getting help, if the need arose. Further, since the onset of these seizures was unpredictable, Robert was no longer allowed to drive, nor was I comfortable about leaving him alone at home, forcing us, as a family, to travel en masse to every social event, be it a children's birthday party, a ballet class, or a doctor's appointment. Clearly, because Robert's diagnosis impacted almost all aspects of our family life, we often found ourselves making passing references to it in casual conversations, and this would immediately trigger an averted gaze, an uncomfortable change of topic, and a studious avoidance of any further conversation on the matter. On one occasion, a close friend, in a misguided show of admiring solidarity, emotionally burst out, "If I were you, I would have killed myself!"

The above narrative must strike a familiar chord with many in the disability community. Interestingly, for Robert, too, this was familiar terrain, albeit for different reasons and with a different twist. As an African American English professor teaching literary theory and the contemporary politics of race, Robert had already grappled both personally and intellectually with the now-familiar question that W. E. B. DuBois (1903) posed more than a century earlier: "How does it feel to be a problem?" Moreover, faced now with the triple jeopardy of race, gender, and disability, Robert was once again forced to re-engage with DuBois's notion of double-consciousness—"this sense of always looking at one's self through the eyes of others, of measuring one's soul by the tape of a world that looks on in amused contempt and pity."

For example, Robert's diagnosis brought to the forefront the ways in which disability can further complicate theorizations of the "different" body that is already marked by oppressive ideologies of race and gender. We felt lucky that most of the times Robert had a seizure, it happened in the privacy of our house. We were terrified that if this happened in a public space where no one knew him, then the consequences could be disastrous. The black male body, already a source of terror in white patriarchy (Davis, 1983; hooks, 1985), when transformed during a grand mal seizure—with rolled-back eyes, harsh grunting sounds, mouth drooling bloody foam, and the occasional loss of control of bodily function with its associated putrid smell—could become an even more terrifying spectacle as a result of the now-lethal triple combination of race, gender, and disability, the very embodiment of abjection (Kristeva, 1982). Our terror, I knew, was shared by other black men who, because their disabilities included involuntary physical movements (e.g., cerebral palsy) and/or real/apparent cognitive differences (e.g., mental retardation or autism), were often thought to be drug addicts or drunks, and therefore dangerous. To be perceived as a dangerous black man in the wrong place at the wrong time by a frightened person armed with a gun could result in death. Already having experienced being pulled over several times by the police for no apparent reason when driving through white neighborhoods (both in the northeast and in the south), Robert's fears were justified, despite the other privileges we had occasion to enjoy.

The fact that we did enjoy some privilege, notwithstanding our dire situation, was brought home to us when Robert started his cancer treatment. On the first day we showed up for radiation at the local hospital, it was easy to separate the novices from the veterans. Terrified and tense, the novices sat at the edge of their seats in solemn silence listening to the annoying cheery chatter of the veterans in the cramped waiting room. One of the veterans, a chatty 30-something blond male dressed scruffily in sweats, whom I will call Thomas, turned his attention to us and engaged Robert in conversation. Their conversation barely pierced my consciousness till I heard the man exclaim, "You are so lucky!" in response to something Robert said. Lucky? I tried to shake off the jarring incongruity of these words directed toward a person for whom the idea of "remission" was never even offered as a lifeline of hope. And then I heard him say, "The University! Wow! Don't they have great benefits! I would work in any job that they would offer me, just to get those benefits. You are so lucky!"

For several seconds, both Robert and I stared in dazed incomprehension at his tangible enthusiasm regarding our situation. Now, it was true that both of us were relieved of our teaching responsibilities that semester by concerned colleagues and a supportive administration, so we could concentrate on helping Robert get through the next few months. Since as faculty we do not get sick leave, our colleagues who were taking over our courses were doing so literally by the sweat off their backs, so that we could continue to get paid. The best doctors in the country doing research on brain tumors happened to be at the nationally known teaching and research hospital in the large city 40 minutes away, and were, therefore, part of the medical network covered by our insurance company. My 70-year-old mother was able to come all the way from India to stay with us and help out with our daughter and around the house so that I could focus completely on caring for Robert. And family and friends, both at home and elsewhere, rallied around us with food, gift checks, visits, and other help.

Our friend Thomas, on the other hand, diagnosed with lung cancer, worked in construction and was currently out of a job because of his treatment's side effects. He was meeting with a financial counselor over the next few days to figure out how his medical bills would get paid. He was single and living alone in a single, wide trailer with his dog, and could expect only occasional assistance (sometimes just the ride to and from the hospital) from a girlfriend who was unable to provide more care. He also developed some really bad reactions to his chemotherapy that necessitated a hospital stay and further added to his financial stress. His mother from Louisiana was expected to arrive in the next few days after resigning her blue-collar job to care for him, yet another fact that caused him even more guilt and financial worry. Listening to the nervous tension behind his cheerful friendliness impelled us to shift from our reactive stance of emotional solidarity to reconsider the political and theoretical implications behind what he was actually telling us.

Thomas's innocent observation brought to the forefront the significance of social class in disability studies scholarship. While social class does show up in disability studies' narratives, it is usually conceived of as a social/cultural experience (Davis, 2002), not as a critical analytical category. Moreover, there has been an increasing hostility, and often an almost-disdainful dismissal of class analyses in contemporary disability studies scholarship (Corker & Shakespeare, 2002; Davis, 2002; Paterson & and Hughes, 1999; Tremain, 2001). As a result, most disability studies scholars theorize disability through the medium of experience and textuality/discourse (Davis, 2002; Garland-Thomson, 1997; Linton, 1998; McRuer, 2006; Mitchell & Snyder, 1997; Siebers, 2008; Snyder, Brueggemann & Garland, 2002; Wendell, 1996). Even though I am very appreciative of the theoretical/literary brilliance of the rich pastiche of the disability experience represented in contemporary disability studies scholarship, in this book, I critically engage this extensive scholarship in order to make the case for the reintroduction of a class analysis in disability studies. Broadly speaking, then, the specific focus of this book is to advance the scholarship in disability studies by exploring the complex relationships that exist between disability and the other categories of difference (i.e., race, gender, and sexuality) and between the disabled and the nondisabled world when (re)constituted by transnational capitalism.

While authors such as Oliver (1990), Morris (1991), Charlton (1998), Russell (1998), and Thomas (1999) have produced persuasive analyses about the political economy of disability, their projects have focused specifically on the experiences of persons with disabilities. Though they have all hinted at possible connections between disability and the other constructs of difference, further exploration of these issues has been outside the scope of their respective projects. There has also been scholarship that has done much to advance the field of disability studies along the axes of difference. Harry and Kligner (2005), Ferri and Connor (2006), and Connor (2007) have noted that special education classrooms in US public schools are overpopulated by African American/Latino students, thereby acknowledging that race and disability coexist as uneasy bedfellows in educational contexts. Fine and Asch (1988), Morris (1991), Wendell (1996), Garland-Thomson (1997), Thomas (1999), and Smith and Hutchinson (2004) have discussed how issues of disability have exacerbated tensions within the feminist movement. McRuer (2006) has explored the relationship between queer theory and disability studies, and Quayson (2007) has examined the intersection of disability and postcolonialism within the context of literary studies. All this scholarship has done much to advance the field of disability studies. My project begins where their analyses have left off. In this book, I weave together each of these different strands of scholarship *to situate disability as the central analytic, or more importantly, the ideological linchpin utilized to (re) constitute social difference along the axes of race, gender, and sexuality in dialectical relationship to the economic/social relations produced within the historical context of transnational capitalism.*

My argument in this book begins with the body—the disabled body. Because contemporary feminist theories of the body have barely addressed disability, feminist disability studies scholars have attempted to redress this omission by demonstrating that the transgressive properties of disability can yield radical (re)conceptualizations of the body (Garland-Thomson, 1997; Wendell, 1996). However, they, too, have dismissed political economy, conceiving it as being hostile to body theory. I intend to remedy that misconception. Bodies do matter in political economy, and its analyses are not limited to the laboring body. Rather, I extend feminist poststructuralist Judith Butler's (1993) question: "Which bodies matter, and which bodies are yet to emerge as critical matters of concern?" (p. 4) by posing my own—Why do some bodies matter more than others? In raising this question "why," I intend to shift the tenor of the discussion from description to explanation.

To do this, I draw on the analytical framework of historical materialism, which Ebert (1996) describes as

> a mode of knowing that inquires into what is not said, into the silences and the suppressed or missing, in order to uncover the concealed operations of power and the socio-economic relations connecting the myriad details and representation of our lives... [Historical materialism]... disrupts "what is" to explain how social differences—specifically gender, race, sexuality, and class [and to which I add disability]—have been systematically produced and continue to operate within regimes of exploitation, so that we can change them. It is the means for producing transformative knowledges. (p. 7)

Using the analytical framework of historical materialism, the central focus of this book is to explore how the body, particularly the disabled body, is constituted within the social relations of production and consumption of transnational capitalism, and to foreground the implications these social/economic arrangements have for making bodies matter (or not). Thus, while asking why some bodies matter more than others, there are also other related questions that I explore: What are the possibilities and limits of different conceptual frameworks in attempting to explain how the (disabled) body matters? What historical conditions make some bodies matter more than others? Why does it not even matter to us that some bodies are actually invisible? What is the social/political/economic impact of this invisibility? Is it even possible for us to reimagine the historical conditions within which Other bodies can be made to matter?

The issues that I raise in this introduction and throughout the book are theoretical, political, and personal. Even though I use Robert's story in the introduction to this book, his story was neither the inspiration for this book, nor is it going to be its central focus. In fact, this book may have been completed by now, if Robert's diagnosis had not forced all other plans to the back burner for four tumultuous years. Unable to write during that time, I had, however, a lot of time to think, and it soon became apparent to me that I was actually living out the argument that I had been planning to write about. The diagnosis of the brain tumor brought to the fore the materiality of the body—marking its "dys-appearance" (Leder, 1990) in ways that demanded a passionate engagement with the matter of bodies, both theoretically and personally. Determined not to allow Robert to be reduced to his diagnosis (e.g., the GBM in room 7), aware of the social and political struggles that the disability community has faced over the years (segregation, economic violence, invisibility, even death), and imagining the possibilities if the social arrangements we lived in were different, I have come to realize that in writing this book I am simultaneously "living theory" while "theorizing life."

BODY MATTERS: EMBODYING THEORY

Contemporary social theory (and disability studies theory, in particular) has refocused its attention on the "...'lived body'...a body that simultaneously experiences and creates the world" (Paterson & and Hughes, 1999, p. 601). Having effectively critiqued the Cartesian separation of mind and body, the phenomenological argument—that the body is not just an objective, exterior institutionalized body or *Korper* (the body-in-itself), but is rather a living, animated, experiencing body or *Lieb* (the body-for-itself)—has been especially useful in the representation of the embodied experiences of people diagnosed with cancer (Grealy, 1993; Lorde, 2006). Phenomenological claims that both pain and suffering have epistemological value (Siebers, 2008)—meaning that they are more than just physical sensations to be interpreted within the biomedical model—have led to a conceptualization of pain and suffering as "a carnal property, culturally produced and producing" (Paterson & and Hughes, 1999, p. 602).

This carnal property of knowing offers a more intimate articulation of be-ing, what the phenomenologist Merleau-Ponty called "sense experience," with meaning emerging from "that heavy mass which is our body" (p. 139). Additionally, phenomenological understanding is intersubjective rather than individual, since "the meaning of the body resides between bodies, between those who live through them, in them, and those who bring them to mind" (Titchkosky, 2005, p. 664). Thus, on reflection, the preliminary description of our family's collective experience of brain cancer recorded as both a personal and a social narrative in the first few pages of this introduction could, in fact, serve as yet another intriguing attempt to write a "carnal" sociology.

Writing this carnal sociology provides not just aesthetic value, it is also therapeutic. In fact, over the past four years, when things were just not going well, both Robert and I often turned to "survivor stories" on the Internet for sustenance, especially drawn to those that provided corporeal details of their experiences with various treatments, diets, and lifestyles. More often than not, these intimate narratives of bodily transformation, even when negative, were nevertheless more reassuringly real than the impersonal medical reports that described bodies as objects with no relation to the actual embodied experience of living with terminal cancer.

For example, it was clearly evident that the terse medical jargon that once labeled Robert as a "Cushingoid male" could scarcely do justice to watching the actual embodied experience of his lean, muscled, 170-pound athletic frame transform into a 260 pound mass of wobbly flesh as a result of an insatiable appetite, triggered by the steroid dexamethasone, prescribed, ironically, to decrease brain swelling. Nothing in the medical definition of an "awake craniotomy" could portray the tumultuous cauldron of emotion Robert felt while he lay in the cold operating theater talking to his (thankfully) extremely gifted neurosurgeon and his team to ensure that they did not interfere with those parts of his frontal lobe associated with speech. The tense impersonality of the medical encounter had no place for the juvenile giggles that nearly bubbled out of us when the nurse co-coordinator of the clinical trial Robert was enrolled in, for whatever bizarre reasons, had difficulty finding the words to caution us to refrain from having sex for a few weeks after Robert would receive a cranial infusion of a tumor-fighting virus. And nowhere in the sterile notes that followed each medical encounter will there be a record of the comically poignant moment when the sonorous stomach growl that emerged from the new, eager-to-impress, neurosurgery resident disrupted the hushed tension in the room at the very moment when his mentor was gently breaking the unwelcome news to us that the tumor was unresponsive to the current treatment.

Clearly, the phenomenological version of a carnal sociology has the capacity to transform the somber cancer narrative into a sensuous exposition of the limits and possibilities of living with terminal illness. What phenomenological narratives do most effectively is to interpolate a corporeal complexity into the depiction of the life experiences of persons living with terminal cancer. And while such sensual accounts may enable both empathetic and empowering responses to what are otherwise desolate and discriminatory reactions to people living with terminal cancer, other theoretical perspectives have been quite wary of phenomenological narratives. In fact, alternative theories such as poststructuralism and marxism have critiqued those aspects of a carnal sociology that direct attention to individuals rather than the social and political arrangements that give meaning to specific embodied experiences (Corker & Shakespeare, 2002; Gleeson, 1999; Thomas, 1999; Tremain, 2006).

Poststructural theorists, in particular, have provided a relentless interrogation of that which masquerades for the real. Foregrounding language as the central medium through which experience is represented, poststructuralists argue that language itself, rather than being imbued with static meaning, is, instead, caught in the dynamic interplay of identity (what a thing is) and difference (what it isn't), such that meaning itself now becomes contingent, unstable, and, thereby, open to deconstruction (Corker & Shakespeare, 2002). For example, while one would be hard-pressed to offer a linguistically precise definition of what disability is, one could offer a series of imprecise circumlocutions to explain what it is not (being unable to walk...erect (?)...elegantly(?)...rapidly(?)...without a "special" shoe (...but then skates are not "special")...and so on and so forth). In another instance, Jacques Lacan replaced Freudian concepts of id, ego, and superego with alternative psychoanalytic concepts of the Imaginary, the Symbolic, and the Real, to explain how the mind is structured into a symbolic order of difference such that the Self is dependent on the Other for its existence, and yet, the unconscious represses difference (the Other) in its yearning for the imaginary stasis of sameness (the Self).

Moving from the intimate site of the psyche to the more impersonal space of the social, yet another French philosopher, Michel Foucault, explained how this repression is concealed and normalized through both ritualized and institutionalized techniques of power (biopower) that categorize, classify, distribute, manipulate, and, as a result, transform the human subject into a "docile" body that can be "subjected, used, transformed, and improved" (Foucault, 1977, p. 136). In other words, the Foucaultian social subject is shaped by the disciplining effects of knowledge and power that constitute identity, self, social norms, and institutions, and that masquerade as the normal and the real (Tremain, 2006).

While, on the one hand, Foucault theorized power as a repressive force, on the other hand, he also theorized power as productive in its ability to open up spaces for a resistant and transgressive agency. This dialectics of power/resistance is demonstrated in the poststructuralist feminist work of Judith Butler, who deconstructs the disciplinary violence of sex/gender norms as nothing other than a reiterative performance that opens up possibilities for transgressing gender boundaries (e.g., the drag queen); Donna Haraway's celebration of the (post)human subject as a cyborg that enacts an ironic transgression of the boundaries between the human being and the machine (e.g., the paraplegic wheelchair user); Julia Kristeva's theorizing of the abject (that which "disturbs identity, system, and order") as the means to embrace the repressed unconscious in an attempt to experience jouissance (violent and painful joy); and Giles Deleuze and Felix Guattari's conceptualization of the Body with/out Organs, the transgressive desiring machine rife with possibility.

In the stressful intimacy of the medical encounter, both Robert and I often found ourselves deconstructing our own contradictory relationship to modern medicine. According to the dominant discourses of modern medicine, the central task of the medical practitioner—the rational and objective scientist—is to return the body to normality and health using sophisticated heuristics, advanced technologies, and promising scientific breakthroughs (Price and Shildrick, 1996). Further, to draw maximum benefit from the time-restricted medical appointment, the patient is expected to yield up the most intimate secrets of the body as succinctly as possible and submit them for the physician's perusal so as to garner a coherent diagnosis from the corporeal complexity observed during the medical examination.

Thus, even though both Robert and myself were well schooled in the poststructuralist skepticism of scientific knowledge as irrefutable truth (he in literary theory, and me in disability studies), when we were literally brought face to face with a terminal illness, we held this skepticism at bay in the valiant hope that medical science would delay as long as possible the inevitability of impending death. Even though we were conscious of the fragility of the fractured subject, our almost instinctive reaction was our unconscious yearning for a previous state of fictional wholeness. Ill at ease with Robert's new unpredictable state of embodiment punctuated by seizures, headaches, nausea, bruises, infections, and edema, we were eagerly compliant and willing to submit to the authority of medical science in the hope that we could keep the fearful abject at bay. And this terror was very real for us because, in a social context where rationality is the precondition for the recognition of personhood, the progression of the brain tumor with its very real threat of diminished mental and rational capabilities, conjured up the image of the abject quite literally nipping at our heels.

And yet, notwithstanding the resolute faith we brought to the medical encounter, we were consistently confronted with the frustrating reality that medical science could not live up to its promise of objective certainty. First and foremost, notwithstanding the wealth of contemporary medical knowledge on the brain and its high-tech medical interventions (genetic coding, biomolecular medicine, gene and virus therapy, gamma-knife surgery, etc.), we were often reminded by Robert's neurosurgeon and neuro-oncologist about the humbling reality that there was much more that they did not know and that they could not even begin to predict. In fact, the most startling yet reassuring conversation we had was at our initial visit with the neuro-oncologist, who first recited the rather bleak statistics of survival for people diagnosed with brain cancer, and then summarily dismissed those statistics on the grounds that they could not account for the range of diverse bodies included in this study. Even though, medical discourse is granted an omnipresent authority over all bodily matters in mainstream discourse, both these medical practitioners/scientists very readily admitted (a) that they did not really know why and how Robert's tumor appeared in his frontal lobe; (b) that almost all the medical interventions they prescribed were very individualized; and (c) that their medical evaluations were nothing other than tentative and often imprecise interpretive readings of both corporeal text and scientific discourse.

On the hour-long ride home after one of our appointments, Robert and I speculated as to the disconnect between his doctors' commitment to the enlightenment project in scientific medicine, even as they were inadvertently undermining some of its sacrosanct tenets. We wondered if they were really aware that they were making epistemological claims, albeit intuitively, that conceived of truth as contextual (e.g., interpreting the statistics contextually), as inflected with multiple interpretations (e.g., the MRI as an imprecise reading of the brain), and as partial and unpredictable (e.g., unable to guarantee a cure let alone predict survival). Clearly, the imagined authority of medical discourse seemed powerless when confronted with the human body unwilling to yield its secrets by constantly transforming itself after every medical intervention, thereby confounding predictability and wresting itself from medical control.

Poststructuralism's deconstructive potential along with its limitless possibilities for (re)imagining the transgressive body makes for seductive scholarship—a point not lost on disability studies scholars who have done radical work in retheorizing disability outside the constricting limits of dominant discourse. Seduced by this ludic form of poststructuralism that reads the social as a matter of discourse/textuality and that posits desire/pleasure as the dynamic that can transform the social (Ebert, 1996), contemporary social theorists have dismissed other modes of theorizing as obsolete. To go against the grain and critically engage poststructuralism using historical materialism therefore runs the risk of being designated as an outmoded modernist. In spite of that risk, I cannot but ask: How does one theorize the disabled body as if it exists outside of the specific historical conditions that constitute its material reality?

The continued importance of that question, even in the face of poststructuralist deconstruction, was brought home to us in early December 2007. At that time we learned that even after two brain surgeries, six weeks of radiation, and three different chemotherapy regimens over the course of a year and a half, the tumor still persisted. Finding ourselves faced with the option of either turning to a new treatment regimen or watching and waiting helplessly while the tumor spread through Robert's brain, we were once again offered a possibility. According to several studies published in late 2007, two drugs, Avastin and CPT-11, which had previously been approved for colorectal cancer by the Food and Drug Administration (FDA) were proving to be effective for patients with recurring malignant gliomas by keeping them cancer-free or at least stable for a minimum of an additional six months. However, there was a problem. Since the drugs had not yet been approved by the FDA to treat brain tumors, our insurance company would not cover the drugs that, without the benefit of insurance discounts, would cost us about $30,000 for each bimonthly treatment.

For three terrifying weeks, we tried to imagine all our available options—selling our house, drawing on our retirement savings, borrowing from family, maximizing our credit cards—and realized that this would barely cover a mere three months of treatment. As a wife and mother, I found this to be a traumatic moment. Do you pour all your personal resources (modest as they were) into a medical treatment that may or may not work? Could you allow your partner (a husband, a father, and a scholar) to die without exploiting every possible option to sustain his life? For three harrowing weeks of the winter holidays, I wrestled with these demons, while our amazing neuro-oncologist and his exceptional nurse practitioners argued with our insurance company to cover the treatment. When the coverage was approved on January 2, 2008, it seemed as if Robert was given a new lease on life, our family another serving of hope. Sixteen months later, Robert's tumor had shrunk to a negligible mass that enabled him to finish writing a book on literary theory, teach four semesters at the university, and even apply for promotion to full professor. However, in November 2009 the tumor re-appeared more aggressively, and unable to receive any more treatment Robert passed away on January 31, 2010.

Now, a whole year after Robert's passing, I am sitting at my desk reflecting on this journey we went through together with our then five-year-old daughter, Maya. That Robert was able to survive for four productive years was only possible because of the economic and social advantages we enjoyed. Without the economic resources to sustain life, the very act of narrating and reconceptualizing one's body is an impossible task. This reflection echoes Marx and Engels's (1965) assertion in *The German Ideology:*

> [T]he first premise of all human existence and, therefore, of all history... [is] namely, that all men [*sic*] must be in a position to live in order to "make history"... [L]ife involves before everything else eating and drinking, a habitation, clothing, and many other things. The first historical act is thus the production of the means to satisfy those needs, the production of material life itself. And indeed this is an historical act, a fundamental condition of history, which today, as thousands of years ago, must daily and hourly be fulfilled merely in order to sustain human life. (p. 48)

There were others for whom the economics of health care had more devastating consequences—a reality painfully documented in Cohn's (2007) book, *SICK.* Cohn offers several poignant stories describing the real human costs of not having access to health care: how a woman having a heart attack died on account of overcrowded emergency rooms in Boston; how a retired security guard in LA lost his sight due to unaffordable diabetes treatments; how a mother of three in central New York did not survive breast cancer that went undetected because her husband's high-tech job did not provide health insurance. In all these stories, survival seemed contingent on economic rather than medical issues.

Unlike the people in Cohn's books, the brain cancer survivors on the Internet with their informative and hopeful blogs that we had come to depend upon for moral support represented a very different demographic.

They were people who were financially well-to-do; who could afford to travel cross-country in search of the best doctors and treatments; who had access to the intellectual resources to help them research their diagnoses; who were able to retire early and still have the resources to volunteer for both local and national fund-raising events; and who therefore became our heroes—those who refused to allow their impending deaths to diminish their capacity to serve.

The mainstream media has made much of these local heroes, paying homage to them in news reports, human interest stories, telethons, track events, silent auctions, cultural fairs, etc. One recent example was Randy Pausch, a professor of computer science at Carnegie Mellon, who lived with pancreatic cancer for two years before passing away in August 2008. Drawn rather reluctantly into the limelight on account of an inspiring "Last Lecture" he delivered at Carnegie Mellon, Pausch became an overnight celebrity because of his upbeat attitude that taught people about the "the importance of overcoming obstacles, of enabling the dreams of others, of seizing every moment" (because "time is all you have...and you may find one day that you have less than you think") (Amazon.com review).

While there is no denying that individuals such as Pausch have to be celebrated for showing the world that there is life after a cancer diagnosis (however brief it may be), both Robert and I were often frustrated that in media representations, the individual was often separated from the social and economic coordinates that framed his or her life. While Pausch was certainly remarkable in making sure his family lived life "fully" in order to make memories for his three very young children, and in bringing attention to others who were "not so fortunate," there was very little mention of the fact that none of this could have been possible without the considerable financial resources that sustained them as a family during and after his lifetime. In other words, I am emphasizing here that in celebrating the individual, we cannot ignore the social and economic conditions that make this celebration possible.

More importantly, these celebrations of the individual outside of social and economic considerations also obfuscate the historical conditions that produce the class antagonisms that are rampant in the context of health-care provision in the United States. Put simply, access to health care in the United States is predicated upon one's capacity to contribute to its profitability, such that medical decisions are made (sometimes unwillingly by doctors under pressure from insurance companies) based on an individual's capacity to pay for them (Cohn, 2007; Farmer, 2004). A brutal consequence of such a system is that the value of one's life is correlated to one's financial status, bringing into play a hierarchy of survival embedded in the social relations of production and consumption in advanced capitalism. In this context then, the central tenet of classical liberalism—the right to *life,* liberty, and the pursuit of happiness—is intimately tied to the economic conditions that sustain the unequal social relations of class. But these unjust economic arrangements are obscured by the deployment of discourses of morality that justify those who are denied this right by categorizing them as "the 'undeserving' poor: drug addicts, sex workers, illegal 'aliens,' welfare recipients, or the homeless, to name a few" (Farmer, 2005, p. 16). By partaking in this discourse of morality, it is easy to ignore that these rights' violations are not the outcomes of individual physical and moral weaknesses, but "are, rather, symptoms of deeper pathologies of power and are linked intimately to the social [and economic] conditions that so often determine who will suffer abuse and who will be shielded from that harm" (Farmer, 2005, p. 7).

The day the insurance company approved Robert's chemotherapy regimen, we were acutely conscious of our good fortune in having both our insurance company and our medical team concur that Robert was a worthy patient. Not all patients are that fortunate. During my late-night trawling through the Internet in search of treatments and stories, I have learned that the hope for a cure can be secured only for a chosen few. If you lost your job and went on disability, if you were a recipient of Medicare/Medicaid, and if for reasons that constituted you as an Other within the medical establishment (e.g., illegal "alien", lesbian/gay/bisexual/transgender (LGBT), racial minority, having mental illness and/or a cognitive disability, or seen as morally deficient), there were both written and unwritten rules that could disqualify you from accessing experimental treatments. I have also learned that while there are several private foundations that will provide resources for transportation, accommodation, and other financial aid needed for critical treatments, the application protocol itself is based on the presumption that the applicant has a certain level of social (race, ethnicity, sexuality, disability, and age), economic, and moral privilege to navigate this bureaucratic maze. As a result, lost in the clamor for a cure, in the depiction of health as a moral rather than a social issue, and in the telethons and fundraisers that support "conspicuous contribution" (Longmore, 2005), those citizens denied access to health care as a result of their social/political/economic conditions are rendered invisible because their lives are perceived as not worth living.

Grateful for having successfully "bought" Robert an extra two years of life, we often wondered what made Robert's life more valuable than millions of Others who do not seem to matter at all. When I raised this question with my doctoral students in a multicultural education course for nurse educators, one of my students argued that these distinctions of value were important because as she put it, "I would rather have Cadillac-like health care for my family than Volvo-like health care for everyone!" When pressed some more about how she would identify those who were deserving of this

"Cadillac-like" care and those who were not, she argued that superior care was the reward for all those who put forth a "good" fight? So did she mean then, that those who did not survive really did not want to live? Did they become our antiheroes because their lives enmeshed in the rather mundane struggle of paying bills, prioritizing which medicines to buy, shuffling in deferent obedience before dismissive medical professionals, and imagining the least painful way to get bankrupt, seemed to offer little to the public in terms of the heroics of living and dying?

This disregard for those without the material means to support them when faced with a terminal illness and/or disability is one of the by-products of "structural violence." According to Farmer, Nizeye, Stulac & Keshavjee (2006),

> Structural violence, a term coined by Johan Galtung and by liberation theologians during the 1960s, describes social structures—economic, political, legal, religious, and cultural—that stop individuals, groups, and societies from reaching their full potential...Because they seem so ordinary in our ways of understanding the world, they appear almost invisible. Disparate access to resources, political power, education, health care, and legal standing are just a few examples. The idea of structural violence is linked very closely to social injustice and the social machinery of oppression. (p. 1686)

In addition to foregrounding the concept of "structural violence" in their depiction of social inequality in the context of health care, Farmer and his colleagues, medical practitioners themselves, also make the case for interpreting disease and suffering within a historical materialist framework by calling on medical practitioners working in public health to link social analysis to everyday clinical practice:

> One reason for this gap [linking social analysis to clinical practice] is that the holy grail of modern medicine remains the search for the molecular basis of disease... [This] has contributed to the increasing "desocialization" of scientific inquiry: a tendency to ask only biological questions about what are in fact biosocial phenomena...Social analysis is heard in discussions about illnesses for which significant environmental components are believed to exist, such as asthma and lead poisoning...Can we speak of the "natural history" of any of these diseases without addressing social forces, including racism, pollution, poor housing, and poverty, that shape their course in both individuals and populations? Does our clinical practice acknowledge what we already know—namely, that social and environmental forces will limit the effectiveness of our treatments? Asking these questions needs to be the beginning of a conversation within medicine and public health, rather than the end of one. (Farmer et al., 2006, p. 1686)

This argument for a biosocial understanding of disease foregrounds the historical conditions that constitute the domain of possibility for the body. I have just made the argument that access to economic resources and, concomitantly, health care is necessary for the survival of the body. I am also arguing here that it is the lack of access to economic resources and, consequently, to health care that also contributes to the creation and proliferation of disability. This is a difficult argument to make in a context where disability is theorized as a possibility rather than a limit, because this begs the more controversial question: How is disability celebrated if its very existence is inextricably linked to the violence of social/economic conditions of capitalism?

When Robert's case was presented to a number of physicians at different times during his treatment, each of them found it difficult to explain why his tumor came to be. On learning that almost all the members of his mother's family who were deceased had cancer (breast, liver, pancreas, and brain), the doctors attributed Robert's cancer to genetics. But, if one were to apply Farmer's biosocial model to Robert's case, even genes, considered the fundamental building block of biology, could, in fact, be shaped by history. We know that genes mutate. We, however, do not know enough about the impact of social conditions on these mutations. Following up on this line of thinking, then, what are the implications of interpreting Robert's diagnosis in the context of his family history? Could genetic mutations influenced by a particular cast of historical conditions (poor housing, dangerous working conditions, or unhealthy nutrition) have an unfortunate impact on the great-grandson of former slaves, the grandson of sharecroppers, and the son of working-class parents, such that the tumor would appear in all its lethal malignancy in the frontal lobe of the only child of his mother's six children who never drank, never smoked, never inhaled, never cared for red meat, and never partied hard? Was it merely random chance or was it the deliberate march of history as written on the body?

The body hides its secrets zealously. Therefore, I agree with my colleagues in disability studies that critical scholarship on disability should engage the body. However, I disagree with them when they argue that political economy has little to say about the body. On the other hand, by locating Robert's experience with terminal cancer within the broader social/political/economic context that also includes Other bodies, I argue that a historical-materialist analysis can expose the structural violence embedded deep within the fleshy body, thereby impacting its transformative potential. A critical theoretical praxis that enables the conditions of possibility of the body, therefore, needs to engage theory at the level of explanation rather than description in order to realize this potential.

BODIES THAT DO MATTER: MAPPING OUT THE ARGUMENT

Class matters. And it most definitely matters to disabled people, even in the United States, one of the most powerful nations in the world. In the United States, one out of every four disabled people lives below the poverty line, and more than 75 percent have an individual income of less than $20,000. Class also matters in the context of health care. According to a 1995 survey, while only 4 percent of individuals with family incomes exceeding $50,000 reported fair or poor health, 21 percent of families with incomes below $15,000 reported fair or poor health (Mullahy, Robert & Wolfe, 2001). Moreover, disabled people rank among the uninsured at a rate slightly higher than the 14 percent national rate. This is because Medicare and Medicaid insure only about one-third of the disabled people, and private insurance often rejects those with disabilities and preexisting conditions (Shapiro, 1994). Issues of race and ethnicity further complicate this already dismal picture with 30.4 percent Hispanics, 9.9 percent whites, and 17 percent blacks being uninsured between January and March 2008 (Centers for Disease Control, 2008).

In the broader global context, the statistics regarding disability illustrate an even bleaker reality. According to a 2006 United Nations (UN) Report, there were an estimated 650 million disabled people living in areas where the services needed to assist them in "overcoming their limitations" were not available. In some third world countries, the disabled population is estimated to be as high as 20 percent of the general population, and when families and relatives are included, it is assumed that nearly 50 percent of the population could be adversely affected by disability. More importantly, the UN report identifies some of the social conditions that cause disability in these countries:

- Wars and the consequences of wars and other forms of violence and destruction, poverty, hunger, epidemics and major shifts in population;
- A high proportion of overburdened and impoverished families, and overcrowded and unhealthy housing and living conditions;
- Populations with a high proportion of illiteracy and little awareness of basic social services or of health and education measures;
- Inadequate programs of primary health care and services;
- Constraints, including a lack of resources, geographical distance, and physical and social barriers, that make it impossible for many people to take advantage of available services;
- Industrial, agricultural and transportation-related accidents;
- Natural disaster and earthquake;
- Pollution of the physical environment. (UN Enable, 2008)

The various reports just cited in the above paragraphs provide overwhelming evidence about how social and economic structures have a negative impact on the quality of life of disabled people across the globe, reiterating the fact that disability is clearly a social rather than a biological condition. Interestingly enough, at first glance, this argument repeats an already-established fact in disability studies—the distinction between the medical and the social models of disability. To readers unfamiliar with these models, the medical model of disability conceptualizes disability as deviance and lack located within the individual, and therefore all medical (and educational) interventions are geared toward bringing the individual as close to normalcy as possible (Corker & Shakespeare, 2002). The social model of disability, on the other hand, views disability as socially created such that disability oppression is linked to the material and ideological transformations of capitalism (Barnes, Mercer & Shakespeare, 1999).

However, more recently, disability studies scholars have critiqued the social model of disability for marking out a distinction between impairment and disability, which mirrors a similar debate in feminist theory regarding the relationship between sex and gender. In both debates, scholars working within the poststructuralist paradigm have critiqued the once-accepted dogma of impairment/sex being biological concepts, with disability/gender being their social manifestations. They have argued, on the other hand, that the distinction between the biological and the social is problematic because the very utterance of the biological almost instantaneously interpellates it into a linguistic order, and, in turn, also instantaneously brings into play the politics of the social (Butler, 1993; Tremain, 2001). Moreover, they claim that the social model is steeped in economic determinism, and that the distinction between impairment and disability break[s] the causal link between "our bodies" (impairment) and "our social situation" (disability) (Tremain, 2001). Throughout this book, I engage this critique by foregrounding the critical role political economy plays in the social construction of difference and explore its implications for the actual living conditions, and, concomitantly, the actual embodied existence of disabled people living within the social/political context of transnational capitalism.

By invoking transnational capitalism as the social/political context that frames this text, my analysis will necessarily have to have a global focus. While there have been a few books that have examined disability outside the United States, their discussions are restricted primarily to disability issues in the advanced industrialized countries (Gleeson, 1998; Oliver, 1990; Morris, 1991). When countries in Latin America, Africa, and Asia are included, they tend to be case studies whose analyses are generally restricted to the specific cultural contexts in which they are located (Ingstad &

Reynolds-Whyte,1995, 2007; Priestly, 2001). My project in this book is different. Moving away from the context of case studies, I will link the issue of disability to discussions of the economic and social transformations that have occurred in the global context as affected by colonialism, postcolonialism, and neoliberalism, and the impact of these transformations on disabled bodies located within the global.

My theorization of disability within the broader context of the global places me in critical contention once again with poststructuralist theorists in disability studies. More recently, in their rejection of political economy in theorizing disability, poststructuralist disability studies scholars have focused predominantly on disabled embodiment within the specific context of the local. Now, granted that even though poststructuralists who theorize language as the play of difference conceive of normativity as predicated on the existence of disability, they do little to explain how these relational categories of difference come into being in the first place. Moreover, notwithstanding these relationships of difference, poststructuralists conceive of social transformation as discursive, local, and individual (Corker & Shakespeare, 2002; Tremain, 2006).

On the other hand, throughout this book, I draw on a relational analysis that foregrounds the social relations that separate and connect subjects located within the broader context of transnational capitalism. Thus, for example, I examine the social construction of disability based on the experiences of both disabled and nondisabled people. More importantly, throughout the text I also explore the theoretical implications of disability when examined in relationship to the other categories of difference both in the First World and in the Third World. Broadly speaking then, this book will

1. explore the implications for theorizing disability at the intersections of race, class, gender, and sexuality within both the United States and global contexts;
2. describe the critical tensions and possible alliances that exist between third world feminist theory and disability studies;
3. describe the concrete ways in which globalization has impacted disabled people in both the "first" and "third" worlds; and
4. discuss the implications of retheorizing disability as a materialist construct in the context of radical democracy and global citizenship.

I have divided the book into six different chapters, with each chapter providing a different locus for the analysis of disability and organized loosely along a trajectory that progresses from the local to the global. Thus, for example, the first locus of analysis, which is the intimate and local site of the body, shifts to the site of intercorporeality via the relational analysis of different bodies, and then finally moves to the more complex locale of the global. Finally, in the last two chapters, I engage with the politics of including cognitive disability in disability studies scholarship (an aspect that is usually ignored in disability studies) and the politics/ethics of care, which I engage with at both the local and the global contexts of transnational capitalism, respectively.

In the first chapter of the book, I situate the body as the locus of analysis. To engage with materiality at the level of the body I utilize Hortense Spillers's (Spillers, 1987) evocative essay "Mama's Baby, Papa's Maybe: An American Grammar Book," to explore how the body becomes a commodity of exchange in a transnational economic context, and how this becoming proliferates a multiplicity of discourses of disability, race, class, gender, and sexuality. Using Spillers's conceptualization of a theory of the flesh, I will make the case for a historical materialist reading of disability. Demonstrating how discursive interventions may be inadequate for articulating a transformative theory of disability, I theorize how disability becomes a commodity that has both use value as well as exchange value—both of which are appropriated for profit in transnational markets. In this way, I begin to formulate what I term a "materialist disability studies" that draws on historical materialism to theorize how disability exists in dialectical relationship to race, gender, and sexuality.

In the second chapter of this book, I illustrate the applicability of this argument using a contemporary educational policy issue, sex education in the public school system in the United States. Though education is all about bodies and plays a critical role in the construction of "disabled" bodies, educational policy acts as if bodies do not exist. Challenging this trend, I will analyze the discourses of sex education using what Pillow (2003) has described as an "embodied policy analysis." An embodied policy analysis from the critical standpoint of a materialist disability studies foregrounds the absence of analyses regarding the actual materiality of bodies in educational contexts (student, teacher, and/or administrator) and how educational policies serve to control, shape, regulate, and reproduce them. Therefore, in this chapter, I will draw on the spatial metaphor of the postcolonial ghetto (La Paperson, 2010) to explore how the dominant discourses of sexuality actively produce the metropole and the ghetto. Then, drawing on a materialist disability studies, I will demonstrate how discourses of sexuality rely on the ideology of the "normate" to segregate, to exclude, and to dehumanize those sexual subjects who disregard the rules of normativity for social and economic purposes.

In Chapter 3, I extend the argument in previous chapters to engage in a discussion on intersectionality. In this chapter, which is co-authored with Andrea Minear, we draw on both theoretical and empirical arguments to demonstrate how the omission of disability as a critical category in discussions of intersectionality has disastrous and sometimes deadly consequences for disabled people of color caught at the violent interstices of multiple differences. Engaging specifically at the intersections of Critical Race Feminism and disability studies, we draw on two narratives located in the southern United States—a social context that is still coming to terms with its violent history of racial oppression in social institutions such as state mental hospitals and public schools. The first narrative offers a synopsis of a recent historical work entitled *Unspeakable: The Story of Junius Wilson* (Burch & Joyner, 2007), where an African American deaf man, Junius Wilson (1908–2001), was committed to a state mental hospital in North Carolina at age 17, following a false accusation of attempted rape from within his own community, imprisoned there for 76 years without ever having been tried or found guilty of a crime, and castrated because he was deemed criminally insane by court officials unable to communicate with him. The second contemporary narrative is based on interviews we conducted with a 13-year-old African American girl, Cassie (pseudonym), who is functionally illiterate, and her mother, Aliya Smith (pseudonym), both of whom are battling a violent and uncaring special education bureaucracy that is threatening to expel Cassie from her middle school. Deploying the theory of intersectionality from within Critical Race Theory (CRT) and disability studies scholarship, we describe how both individuals, located perilously at the interstices of race, class, gender, and disability, are constituted as noncitizens and (no)bodies by the very social institutions (legal, educational, and rehabilitational) that are designed to protect, nurture, and empower them.

In Chapter 4, I now shift to the broader context of the global. I have titled this chapter "Embodied Antinomies" because it exposes the contradictory and paradoxical relationship between the "normative" (first world) feminist theorization of the body and the third world disabled bodies—those bodies that are often the invisible member of the binary. Drawing on an often-ignored area of scholarship in both feminist disability studies and third world feminism—the impact of war and disability on the lives of third world women—I discuss how the violence of imperialism is instrumental not only in the creation of disability in third world contexts but also in rendering invisible the social and economic impact of disability in these contexts.

In Chapter 5, I engage with the critical issue of citizenship and its contentious relationship to disability. Within liberal discourses, the good citizen is one who is able to conform to exacting standards of both individual autonomy and practical/civic reason-ability. Within these stringent codes, disabled people, particularly those with severe cognitive disabilities, are radically excluded from discourses of citizenship. I will therefore draw on the argument of critical race theorists, who have foregrounded the limits of formal justice in the context of institutionalized racism (Crenshaw, Gotanda, Peller & Thomas, 1995; Delgado and Stefancic, 2000). Then, forging a linkage between CRT and a materialist disability studies, I advance my own argument that the disciplinary practices produced within the material conditions of late capitalism enact in complex and contradictory ways the "racialization of disability" and the "dis-abilization of race," and discuss the implications of this critique for an alternative theorization of citizenship and citizenship education that is not just inclusive of difference but is also transformative in its intent and practices.

Since third world women are also implicated in the actual paid and unpaid labor of caring for disabled people, in the final chapter in this book, I explore the critical tension that exists between nondisabled female caregivers and their disabled care recipients, when discussing the politics of caring work. Locating this discussion of caring within the historical contexts of colonialism, postcolonialism, and the current context of neoliberalism, I will show how the material conditions of caring actually support a conceptual linkage between disability, gender, race, and class, and explore the implications of this analysis for both feminist theory and disability studies.

This has been a difficult book to write because it has been an emotional writing. I began to think about this book just before Robert fell ill, and I have only been able to complete it a year after his passing. Behind the writing on every page are many other stories that could not be told—stories enmeshed in tears, in hope, in anger, and in love. Interwoven with my own pain were other stories of bodies who mattered most to those who cared for them, but who otherwise did not really seem to matter to anyone else. My purpose in this book was to foreground the material conditions that rendered them invisible notwithstanding their courageous struggles to survive. Thus, if some of them could not live long enough to tell their stories of struggle, it is fervently hoped that in some small way this book will ensure that their lives would not have been in vain.

CHAPTER 1

DISABILITY AS "BECOMING": NOTES ON THE POLITICAL ECONOMY OF THE FLESH

> We must concede at the very least, that sticks and stones *might* break our bones, but words will most certainly *kill* us.
>
> Hortense Spillers (1987), Mama's Baby, Papa's Maybe, p. 68

> So tell us:
> Where does the damp come from?
>
> Bertolt Brecht, A Workers Speech to the Doctor

IN HER EVOCATIVE ESSAY "MAMA'S BABY, PAPA'S MAYBE: AN American Grammar Book," African American literary critic Hortense Spillers (1987) writes, "...[B]efore the 'body' there is the 'flesh,' that zero degree of social conceptualization that does not escape concealment under the brush of discourse, or the reflexes of iconography" (p. 61). In this essay, Spillers startles her readers into recognition of the stark materiality of the body as constituted within the violent history of slavery. Spillers's conceptualization of the "flesh" as the "primary narrative" of embodiment proposes a visceral theorization that could arguably exceed equivalent contemporary theories of racialized, gendered, queer, and/or disabled bodies. Referring specifically to the Middle Passage, where black bodies jammed like animals into the holds of merchant ships were transported as (human) cargo to be sold as slaves in the New World, Spillers describes this terrible journey through the primary narrative of the flesh with "its seared, divided, ripped-apartness, riveted to the ship's hole, fallen, or 'escaped' overboard" (p. 67).

It is this primary narrative of "wounded" flesh that I turn to in order to conceptualize a historical-materialist theory of disability. But I do this with much trepidation, fully aware that I am invoking quite problematically a vision of tattered flesh, of bludgeoned body, of victimized subjectivity—images that fit uncomfortably with any radical aesthetic of disability. But I mean to be provocative, to trouble any easy conceptualization of disability, especially at the intersections of race, class, gender, and sexuality. Spillers's essay painfully unearths the violent history of slavery that gave rise to an American Grammar that continues to this day to propagate dehumanizing depictions of black bodies—both male and female. Spillers's analysis starts with the horrors of the Middle Passage, continues through the routine brutalities of slavery, and culminates in a present that remains grounded in the originating metaphors of captivity and mutilation. In this analysis what becomes exceedingly clear is that it is the materiality of racialized violence that becomes the originary space of difference. By materiality I mean the actual social and economic conditions that impact (disabled) people's lives, and that are concurrently mediated by the politics of race, ethnicity, gender, sexuality, and nation.

I propose here that Spillers's essay is as much about the materiality of racialized violence as it is about disability. While there is merit to the argument that disability is the most universal of human conditions (Garland-Thomson, 2002a; McRuer, 2006), there is an implicit assumption here that the acquisition of a disabled identity always occurs outside historical context. Spillers's argument reminds us otherwise. In the specific historical context of slavery, the attribution of disability to the female captive body, for instance, enabled this body to become a site where the flesh became the prime commodity of exchange in the violent conflation of both profit and pleasure. In this case, I situate disability not as the condition of being but of becoming, and this becoming is a historical event, and further, it is its material context that is critical in the theorizing of disabled bodies/subjectivities.

There is a danger in associating becoming disabled with a violent and oppressive history, because disability is already conceived of as "abject" (Kristeva, 1982). The "abject," according to Kristeva, is a place of radical exclusion where all meaning collapses and where the "deep well of memory...is [both] unapproachable and intimate" (p. 6). Tobin Siebers (2010) uses the term "an aesthetics of human disqualification" in relation to disability to describe "how individuals are disqualified...found lacking, inept, incompetent, inferior, in need, incapable, degenerate, uneducated, weak, ugly, underdeveloped, diseased, immature, unskilled, frail, uncivilized, defective, and so on" (p. 23). Fiona Kumari Campbell (2009) explains that this negative ontology is propagated via the structural practice of ableism, because the "presence of disability upsets the modernist craving for ontological security" (p. 13).

Conscious of the danger of invoking an ableist aesthetic, my project here is to echo Robert McRuer's (2006) provocative question, "What might it mean to welcome the disability to come, to desire it?" (p. 207). McRuer celebrates the transformative potential of disability and queerness to unsettle and radically rewrite abject identities. However, while I also echo McRuer's vision that another world is indeed possible—a world that welcomes and desires disability—I argue that to even re-imagine these discursive possibilities necessitates an engagement with the social conditions that constitute disability. Spillers's essay provides the historical context to begin this analysis, even though she never explicitly engages disability. Nevertheless, I argue that Spillers's essay, in its foregrounding of the brutal violence unleashed against the captive body, not just at the level of the skin (Ahmed, 1998) but in the very markings of "divided" flesh, has the potential to generate a historical-materialist analysis of disability that could enable transformative possibilities for all bodies located at the intersections of difference.

Historical-materialist analyses are not new to disability studies. Several British disability studies scholars have utilized this framework extensively (Barnes, Mercer & Shakespeare, 1999; Morris, 1991; Oliver, 1990; Thomas, 1999), especially in their formulation of the social model of disability. The social model of disability, with its emphasis on the social conditions that constitute disability, has been critiqued for its occlusion of the body in its problematic formulation of the dichotomy between disability and impairment (Campbell, 2009; Goodley & Roets, 2008; Shildrick, 2009; Tremain, 2001). Dismissing the "arid materialism of disability studies" (Paterson & Hughes, 1999, p. 599), contemporary disability theory has drawn on phenomenologists, such as Merleau-Ponty, as well as posthumanists, such as Foucault, Derrida, Butler, Haraway, Deleuze, Guattari, Agamben, Hardt, and Negri, to write a transgressive embodied subjectivity. In these theorizations, the disabled subject appears as the irregular and contingent effect of shifting signifiers producing disorganized collections of hybrid associations/ assemblages that morph into an unstable and transgressive Body-without-Organs (BwO) (Campbell, 2009; Goodley & Roets, 2008; Kuppers, 2009; Shildrick, 2009). No longer marked as abject, these transgressive theories of embodiment fiercely embrace a form of contra-aestheticism (Siebers, 2010) that mocks the normal, rejecting disability's limited role as prosthetic in identity politics, and engaging in the more transgressive political act of "coming out crip or crippin'" (McRuer, 2006, p. 71). Exciting and critically necessary as these theoretical interventions are for an outlaw ontology of disability, my project angles the analytical frame more purposefully to foreground the transnational historical context that enables be-coming disabled.

On one level, my project does not appear very different from either phenomenological or posthumanist disability studies scholars, who also conceptualize disability not as being but as "becoming-in-the-world" (Paterson & Hughes, 1999; Shildrick, 2009; Titchkosky, 2007). According to Shildrick (2009):

> [B]ecoming signifies a process that shifts and flows just as the body itself undergoes changes and modifications…as the irregular and contingent transformations and reversals that unsettle subjectivity—and identity—itself…How we come to know ourselves and others in the world is the matter of material engagement, often through the direct contact of flesh and blood encounters that do not simply *affect* us at the surface level but *effect* the very constitution of embodied being. (p. 25)

My difference with Shildrick (and other disability studies scholars who use posthumanist theories) becomes apparent in the critical significance I place on the transnational historical contexts in which these social relations/encounters between the self and others occur in the fluid and always incomplete process of becoming-in-the-world. While Shildrick admits that the inequalities produced within the historical context of globalization might disturb/distort the intercorporeal possibilities between diverse bodies, she, nevertheless, embraces what she calls an "ethics of encounter," which results in an "affective" response to difference, rather than a transformative one. In fact, a transformative politics is shunned because Deleuze's "'horizontal' rhizomatic proliferation of linkages" (p. 158) that Shildrick embraces rejects any "'vertical' and therefore hierarchical arborescence" (p. 158), as well as "any normative categories of inclusion and exclusion" (p. 159) in order to exceed "the fatal limitations of a morality based on the distinction between self and other" (p. 160).

The problem with "horizontal rhizomatic proliferation" is that it is rendered inadequate in the historical context of transnational capitalism, where bodies encounter each other often in violent collision such that captivity and mutilation are no longer metaphors, but instead inform a brutal materiality that foregrounds the hierarchical binary of Master/slave. Here, Deleuze and Guattari's (1983)"[d]esiring-machines" (p. 5) cannot support the seamless horizontal current of flow between intercorporeal entities, now interrupted by hierarchical social relationships where productive desire that is constitutive of some bodies is enabled through the consumption of the seared, divided, ripped-apart, mutilated flesh of other bodies. It is this violent moment of intercorporeal assemblages that produces disability, and its becoming-in-the-world foregrounds a dialectical tension between the historical and the contemporary, between production and consumption, between desire and need, between continuities and discontinuities, and between the conditions of possibility and the violence of its limits.

While I am aware that the dialectic is frowned upon by Deleuze and Guattari, I am unwilling to dissolve this dialectic in a discursive flourish, when confronted by the embodied materiality of this bloodied and broken flesh. To engage materiality at the level of the body in Spillers's essay requires that we recognize the processes by which the body becomes a commodity of exchange in a transnational economic context, and how this becoming proliferates a multiplicity of discourses of disability, race, class, gender, and sexuality. By conceptualizing disability as "becoming-in-the-world," while rejecting at the same time its ahistorical association with lack, I reframe McRuer's question to ask: Within what social conditions might we welcome the disability to come, to desire it? In raising this question, I situate "desiring disability" as a historical condition of possibility that does not reproduce economic exploitation on a global scale.

In the first sections of this chapter, I will broadly lay out the theoretical possibilities and pitfalls that shape disability theory. Then, using Spillers's (1987) conceptualization of a theory of the flesh, I will make the case for a historical-materialist reading of disability. Demonstrating how discursive interventions may be inadequate for articulating a transformative theory of disability, I theorize how disability becomes a commodity that has both use value as well as exchange value—both of which are appropriated for profit in transnational markets. The historical-materialist analysis I undertake calls for the rejection of further commodification of disability in transnational markets, and suggests ways to enable the "multitude" (Hardt & Negri, 2004) to organize transnationally to transform the social conditions so that the disability-to-come can always be desired.

DISABILITY THEORY: BETWEEN A ROCK AND HARD PLACE

The human body is one of the most fetishized commodities in late-capitalist societies. In fact, in an excessively consumerist capitalist culture, we are continuously bombarded with images of the body-as-commodity, images that detail what an ideal body should look like, how it should be packaged, the manner in which it should present itself, and the kinds of services it requires so as to maintain its profitability in the marketplace (Bordo, 2003; Featherstone, 1992; Hahn, 1987, 1988; Singer, 1989). As a result, the body has become "the most discussed, prescribed, and proscribed, disfigured, disguised, and disciplined surface in the physical world" (Fox, 1994, p. 25).

However, this preoccupation with the fetishized body, in particular, has been a relatively recent phenomenon in Western sociology. Pre-Enlightenment conceptions of the body, as prescribed in religious teachings of Christianity, viewed the body as weak and sinful and in need of strict control and regulation (Shilling, 1993; Turner, 1984). With the advent of Enlightenment beliefs in universal, inalienable, equal rights, a more secular humanist conceptualization of the body developed. Confronted with the contradictions of the prevailing inequalities of the time (on the grounds of race, class, and gender), and their own liberal allegiances to the universality of human rights, Enlightenment thinkers utilized the secular "objective" gaze of science and turned to scientific examinations of the physiological body in attempts to resolve these contradictions.

Setting up the European, bourgeois, heterosexual, healthy, male body as the normative standard against which to compare "other" bodies, science first began to flesh out differences between men's and women's bodies, marking the latter's biological differences as inferior characteristics. In this way then, bodies radically different from the constructed norm were construed as "deviant"; their deviance hierarchically organized via the constructions of race, class, gender, disability, and sexual difference; and the authenticity of their claims justified on the basis of observable biological "facts" that were verifiable by a secular science (Foucault, 1965, 1980; Gould, 1981; Mies, 1986; Paul, 1995; Shilling, 1993; Turner, 1984). Thus, it was only after the eighteenth century that the body subjected to the scientific gaze became institutionalized as the "natural" site of difference—a scientific belief that held sway in many circles till the second half of the twentieth century (Shilling, 1993).

Over the past few decades, several social theories of difference have sought to denaturalize and historicize the construction of the categories of race, class, gender, and sexual orientation as marked on the human body (Anzaldua, 1990; Butler, 1993; Callinicos, 1993; Gates, 1988; Gilman, 1986; Grosz, 1994; Haraway, 1989; hooks, 1985; Mies, 1986; Mohanty, 1991), and they have done so at the expense of the category of disability, which they often tend to reify. These theories have critiqued dominant ideologies that have habitually drawn upon biological and physiological arguments to justify the exploitation and exclusion of specific social groups in society. They have challenged the conservative argument that the exploitative and oppressive life situations of the unemployed, the homeless, poor women, people of color, lesbians, gays, bisexuals, transsexuals, intersex people, and third world people have been the result of their inferior/deviant/different physiological/psychological makeup. They have contested such allegations by active assertions of their own normality, and have instead placed the onus of their oppression on attitudes, language, and/or the historical, social, political, and economic conditions of social life. In other words, these groups have argued that these differences notwithstanding, they can still compete on equal footing with those subjects unmarked by biological difference.

This stance posits disability in an uneasy relationship with other social categories of difference. The historian Douglas Baynton (2001) has pointed out that even while disabled people can be constituted as an oppressed minority group, at the very same time the category of disability has functioned as an adequate justification of the oppression of other minority groups. Take, for example, the fraught relationship between race and disability. Baynton (2001) cites an 1851 article in the *New Orleans Medical and Surgical Journal* that sought to explain the "diseases and physical peculiarities of the negro race" (p. 37) by turning to physiological explanations buttressed by a burgeoning hegemonic science/medical industry:

> It is this defective hematosis, or atmospherization of the blood, conjoined with a deficiency of cerebral matter in the cranium and an excess of nervous matter distributed to the organs of sensation and assimilation that is the true cause of that debasement of mind which has rendered the people of Africa unable to take care of themselves. (p. 37)

Arguments such as the one above were used to justify the continued denigration of African Americans in US society, in both historical and contemporary contexts. Thus, for example, in 1994, when Charles Murray and Richard Hernstein claimed that there were racial differences pertaining to intelligence and ability because of a link between intelligence quotient (IQ) and genetics, their critics argued that race is a construct derived mainly from perceptions conditioned by events of recorded history, and that it has no basic biological reality. However, this rejection of the biological criteria is not in fact a rejection, but a reinscription, because the discourses of biology are still centered, only this time they are reinterpreted so as to satisfy the demands of "normality" made by the dominant ideologies—a demand that still reifies disability as the master trope of disqualification (Snyder & Mitchell, 2006). By revoking the alleged claims of biological difference to assert a biological wholeness, subjects marked by race, class, gender, and/or sexual orientation assume without question the basic premises of humanism and its associated attributes of liberal individualism (Garland-Thomson, 1997)—something that would be difficult for disabled people to do. By not challenging the very premises of humanism, such discourses, thereby, continue to maintain an ideological distance from disability.

In yet another example, the Marxist John Molyneux (1987) argues that it is the capacity of humans to think, to walk upright, to speak, and so on that makes them different from other species. In making such claims, Molyneux excludes from his revolutionary socialist vision all persons with both physical and/or mental handicaps. Similarly, posthumanist discourses, notwithstanding their discursive flexibility, have also written disability out of their theorizing of difference. The posthumanist body actually celebrates the transgressive and deviant body by inscribing it as "a site of *jouissance*, a native ground of pleasure, the scene of an excess that defines reason, that takes dominant culture and its rigid, power-laden vision of the body to task" (Davis, 1995, p. 25).

> [L]urking behind these images of transgression and deviance is a much more transgressive and deviant figure: the disabled body... The nightmare of [the transgressive] body is one that is deformed, maimed, mutilated, broken, diseased... Rather than face this ragged image, the [poststructuralist theorist] turns to fluids of sexuality, the gloss of lubrication, the glossary of the body as text, the heteroglossia of intertext, the glossolalia of the schizophrenic. But almost never the body of the differently abled. (p. 5)

Thus, even those who espouse radical discourses seem unable to reconceptualize an alternative world without being locked into the political constructions of what constitute the limits of humanness. Titchkosky (2007) illustrates this point by drawing on a newspaper article about a five-year-old Canadian girl, Courtney Popken, who was diagnosed with a nameless "exotic" disease that affects less than one in 100,000 people and which, the article explains, has left her "stiff as a board" to face the dismal future of a life worse than death. Such an argument, Titchkosky argues, relinquishes representational authority to the hegemony of medical discourse such that disability is now conceived of as simply a problem to be fixed, and if proven to be unfixable, then the disabled body cannot be conceived of as a viable mode of life. Titchkosky (2007) explains:

> [D]isability is made viable as a metaphor to express only that which is unwanted, and that which is devastatingly inept (p.5)... Directed at individuals with individualized body problems, the solution, any solution, including death, appears justifiable... Representing impairment as nothing but limit means that the medical paradigm masters the meaning of disability as nothing but loss in need of annihilation. Disability becomes a kind of limit without possibility, but this is, of course, impossible since limit is always potentiated by possibility. (p. 123)

This representation of disability as "deadly status" (Titchkosky, 2007, p.108) has caused disabled people to experience oppression in almost all aspects of their daily lives. In an attempt to describe this oppression, Biklen and Bogdan (1977) defined *handicapism* as a "theory and a set of practices that promote unequal and unjust treatment of people because of apparent and assumed physical and mental disabilities... [and which] manifests itself in relations between individuals, in social policy, and cultural norms and in the helping professions as well" (p. 206). While this dated term foregrounds disability, other disability studies scholars such as Campbell (2009) have used the term *ableism* to shift the focus from disabled bodies to, instead, emphasize "a network of beliefs, processes, and practices that produces a particular kind of self and body (the corporeal standard) that is projected as the perfect, species-typical and therefore essential and fully human" (p. 5).

Ableism is brought to bear on the body via the *normate* (Garland-Thomson, 1997, p. 8), the cultural Self whose boundaries are marked by its opposing twin—the disabled other, the very embodiment of corporeal difference. Ableism is effective because it purports to offer a *naturalized* understanding of what it means to be fully human based on "a fabrication that reaches into the very soul that sweeps us into life and as such is the outcome and instrument of a political constitution: a hostage of the body" (Campbell, 2009, p.6). The material effects of ableism result in the removal and/or erasure of disability even in social practices that purport to be inclusive. In fact, the precondition for inclusion of disabled people in mainstream society requires their assimilation (via special education, rehabilitation, and assistive technology) or their complete annihilation (euthanasia, abortion of disabled fetuses) (Campbell, 2009; Siebers, 2008; Snyder & Mitchell, 2006; Stiker, 1999; Titchkosky, 2007). It is in this context then that disability has come to represent "the boundary condition that resides just on the other side of hope...the condition one must escape rather than improve" (Ferguson, 1987, p. 63).

IMPAIRMENT AS EMBODIED POLITICS

Almost all subjects of difference who have posited an oppositional politics against normative traditions have begun these struggles from within the liberal humanist tradition. Humanist discourses have their historical roots in the Enlightenment, where the God-given, socially fixed, free subject of the feudal order was transformed by the secular capitalist state to become the free, rational, self-determining subject of modern political, legal, social, and aesthetic discourses (Sarup, 1989; Weedon, 1987). The general determining principles articulated through this philosophy are that human beings are the original sources of meanings, actions, and history; that the knowledges about themselves and their social world emerge from their experiences; and that these experiences are always preceded and interpreted by the mind, reason, or thought—an attribute that validates the subject's essential humanity (Eagleton, 1983; Rice & Waugh, 1992; Weedon, 1987). It is through the recognition of this essential humanity—a preexisting selfhood, a solid self-sufficient rational unit not defined by or in need of anything or anyone other than itself—that the individual has been guaranteed the universal rights of freedom, equality, fraternity—ideals that had emerged out of the historical context of the French and American Revolutions.

It has proven difficult for disability rights activists to claim a humanist subjectivity because, unlike feminists or antiracists or queer theorists, disabled people (especially persons with severe disabilities) cannot make unequivocal claims of meeting the prescribed criteria used to define and describe rationality and physical wholeness. Often, the difficulty to compensate for physiological difference also places the disability movement in an antagonistic relationship with other liberal social movements (Begum, 1992; Fine & Asch, 1988; Morris, 1991). As a result, some disability theorists, anxious to debunk the absolute nature of disability as rooted in biology, have argued that the deviance ascribed to these physiological differences are, in fact, social constructions of reality and not objective fact (Becker, 1964; Bogdan & Taylor, 1982; Edgerton, 1967; Finkelstein, 1980; Goffman, 1963; Scott, 1969).

Thus, for example, Blumer (1969) describes how the body as the material property of individuals plays an important role in the mediation of the individuals' self-identity and social identity, the meaning attributed to these identity constructions being produced amid the shared discourses arising out of social interactions (Shilling, 1993). In this context, social identity, like deviance, is not a property that is inherent in any individual, but is a property "conferred on" that individual through his/her interactions with the social world (Becker, 1964; Erickson, 1964; Garland-Thomson, 1997; Goffman, 1963).

Sociologists have applied this perspective in their efforts to study deviance, particularly deviance associated with disability (Bogdan & Taylor, 1982, 1987, 1992; Edgerton, 1967; Finkelstein, 1993; Goffman, 1963; Groce, 1985; Mercer, 1973; Scott, 1969). For example, Scott (1969) described how blindness is a learned social role, where the various attitudes and patterns of behavior that characterize people who are blind are not inherent to their condition, but are rather acquired through the ordinary processes of social learning as a result of encounters with sighted individuals as well as organizations and agencies for the blind. Hevey (1992) supports this claim when he talks about the social reaction to his condition of epilepsy:

> I realized that my disability was not in fact the epilepsy, but the toxic drugs with their denied side effects, the medical regime with its blaming the victim, the judgment through distance and the silence of bus stop crowds, bar rooms crowds and dinner table friends, the fear, and not least, the employment problems. All this was oppression, not the epileptic seizures, at which I was hardly present. (p. 2)

Thus, representations of disability often tend to reflect the preoccupations of nondisabled people, whose own fears of hostility and whose own political agendas have dominated these representations (Biklen & Bailey, 1981; Hevey, 1992; Morris, 1992; Oliver, 1990). In fact, much of the literature on disability in other disciplines has discussed these representations of disabled people as supercrips, freaks, monsters, criminals, fools, asexual, dangerous, as objects, and so on (Biklen & Bailey, 1981; Bourke, 1996; Davis, 1995; Garland-Thomson, 1996, 1997; Norden, 1994). Oliver (1990) has therefore argued that such imagery can only be rectified if

a social theory of disability...be located within the experience of disabled people themselves and their attempts not only to redefine disability, but also to construct a political movement amongst themselves and to develop services commensurate with their own self-defined needs. (p. 11)

Oliver's articulation of this social theory of disability (also called the social model of disability) has been critiqued in recent years because of the accusation that the social model of disability continues to treat the disabled body as an object that is acted upon by the world, rather than as a subject that has ontological significance. Drawing on the work of phenomenologist Merleau-Ponty, some scholars in disability studies (Paterson & Hughes, 1999; Shildrick, 2009; Titchkosky, 2007) have argued that the social model of disability makes a spurious distinction between disability (the social construction of difference) and impairment (the biological manifestation of difference). Claiming that the social model actually "concedes the body to medicine [and biology]," Hughes and Paterson (1997) argue that "the impaired body is part of the domain of history, culture, and meaning" (p. 326). Grounding social knowledge in the experiencing and experienced body, Merleau-Ponty explains:

All my knowledge of the world, even my scientific knowledge is gained from my particular point of view, or from some experience of the world without which the symbols of science would be meaningless...I am the absolute source, my existence does not stem from my antecedents, from my physical and social environment; instead it moves out towards them and sustains them, for I alone bring into being for myself (and therefore into being in the only sense that the word can have for me) the tradition which I elect to carry on, or the horizon whose distance from me would be abolished—since that distance is not one of its properties—if I were not there to scan it with my gaze. (pp. 135–136)

Merleau-Ponty suggests that the body is the first locus of intentionality, and following from this assumption, impairment has ontological significance for the disabled subject. In fact, it could be argued that impairment imbues the disabled subject with an intense embodied consciousness causing the disabled body to dys-appear (Leder, 1990). According to Leder, the body's "normal" tendency toward self-concealment allows for the possibility of its neglect and effacement. On the other hand, impairment enables the disabled body to experience an explicit self-awareness where the body becomes the focus of attention because of its dys-functional mode of operating within the norm, thereby enacting its own dys-appearance (not disappearance). In this context then, impairment is no longer merely a biological fact, but is, instead, a manner of becoming-in-the-world that reorganizes lived space and time as well as the social relations between the self and other bodies. As such, from a phenomenological perspective, impairment is simultaneously historical, social, and biological.

Further, Paterson and Hughes (1999) point out that the experience of impairment is not an intracorporeal phenomenon (within the body), but an intercorporeal one (between bodies), such that the social meaning of one's impairment is not static but is instead always incomplete and transitory, and always shaped and revealed "where the paths of...various experiences intersect and engage each other like gears" (Merleau-Ponty, p. 137). It is this relational notion of corporeality that Margrit Shildrick (2009) draws on to engage the intercorporeal possibilities of an embodied ontology. Talking specifically of the intimacy of intercorporeal experiences, Shildrick uses a phenomenological analysis to foreground how experiencing bodies are constantly crossing boundaries (through touch, through the stare), and as a result, all bodies are in a constant state of renewal and adjustment in changing physical and environmental contexts, making the body intensely aware, not just of its be-ing but also of its becoming-in-the-world. Impairment gets transformed, via Shildrick's analysis, as becoming "immersed in the flesh of the world where experiencing and being experienced by others is not a formal encounter between self and other but a matter of [a contingent, fluid, and messy] intercorporeality" (p. 37). Thus, disability as becoming-in-the-world produces what Paterson & Hughes (1999) have called the "carnal information" of the disabled subject that imbues even the experience of impairment (e.g., pain) as the source of social and cultural meaning.

This "carnal sociology" describes oppression of disabled people as embodied eruptions felt in the flesh and bones of disabled bodies (Paterson & Hughes, 1999). For example, Paterson and Hughes point out that success in the *lebenswelt* (or life world) for impaired bodies is structured around normative codes of movement and timing that are based primarily on the standards of nonimpaired bodies. As a result, liberal interventions such as integration in the community are not necessarily emancipatory, because the preconditions of inclusion are based on social codes that are formed without the carnal knowledge of impairment experienced by disabled bodies. As a result, Paterson and Hughes argue that the exclusion of disabled people is based on intercorporeal associations with nondisabled bodies that are all subjected to, what Iris Marion Young refers to as, the "meshes of microauthority."

Impairment, then, is not only embodied becoming, it also foregrounds "the textured life of [disabled]embodiment" (Titchkosky, 2007), where the "weight, substance, and sense of disability are woven into the readers' lives in a variety of ways" (p. 18). "...and where disability is made [intelligible] by...conceptual forms that we inherit as our ways of apprehending and orienting...to the matter of embodiment" (p.25). Titchkosky offers up as an example the textual representation of birth that includes pregnancy tests, prenatal classes, moms-to-be parking spaces, ultrasounds, baby showers, and birth announcements. In each of these textual representations of burgeoning embodiment, the textured life of disability is consistently represented as lack, as manifested in the oft-quoted exclamation: All I want is that my baby be healthy! Titchkosky's project, then, is to explore alternative possibilities that reject habitual readings of impairment as "nothing but limit," because as she claims, "limit is always potentiated by possibility" (p. 123). In this context then, a carnal sociology of impairment theorized as the process of becoming opens up a space for new and possible transgressive readings of disability that will disturb normative discourses of embodiment.

The liberal humanist perspective, therefore, offers a description of a knowable world, where the subject of difference (in this case the disabled body) is central to this world. It has done this by rejecting the universality and transcendence of objective truth so as to reaffirm and humanize the unique experience and unique perspective of the (disabled) body as itself uniquely "truth producing." The feminist scholar Iris Marion Young (2005), however, cautions that "the body as lived is always layered with social and historical meaning—and is not some primitive matter prior to an understanding of economic and political and cultural meanings" (p. 7). Therefore, I point to Young's famous essay, "Throwing Like a Girl: A Phenomenology of Feminine Body Comportment, Motility and Spatiality," where she describes feminine bodily comportment as having an "inhibited intentionality" as determined by the body's situation within "structures of constraint" (Folbre, 1994) that both enable and restrict its comportment, mobility, and spatial access within these same structures. Thus, to throw like a girl is neither a completely physiological activity, nor is it the free expression of a girl's unique gendered embodiment; rather, observing someone "throwing like a girl" enables us to understand becoming feminine as the multiple modes by which girls live out their lives while negotiating with these structures of constraint.

I draw on Iris Marion Young's argument to mark off some of the limits of humanist analyses in disability studies scholarship, even while I admit that this perspective offers a more nuanced theorization of disability and impairment as relational constructs. Humanism assumes a voluntarist subject that represents the bourgeois subject of late capitalism (the white, upper class, heterosexual, nondisabled male)—the subject who is "free to do what one wants, free to buy and sell, to accumulate wealth or to live in poverty, to work or not, to be healthy or to be sick" (Navarro as quoted in Doyal, 1981, p. 36). While both Shildrick and Titchkosky have carefully recognized the problems of uncritically engaging this humanist subject, their own work, while offering an indictment of heterosexual and nondisabled embodiment, continues to foreground (albeit unintentionally) the bourgeois nonracialized disabled subject with the "material" freedom to offer a more transgressive reading of disabled subjectivity. By doing so, what is left unquestioned are the historical and economic conditions that situate becoming disabled in a violent context of social and economic exploitation that may inhibit as well as complicate oppositional/transgressive theorizations of disabled subjectivity. It is to this fraught context, where be-coming disabled is produced within the actual material violence of transnational capitalism, that I turn to in the next section.

FLESH-ING OUT DISABILITY AND RACIAL EMBODIMENT

In Hortense Spillers's (1987) essay, "Mama's Baby, Papa's Maybe," the social context in which the embodied subject becomes-in-the-world is one suffused with an ineffaceable horror. Spillers, in this essay, locates the "origins" of African American subjectivity in the (trans)Atlantic slave trade, which starts with the unimaginable violence during the Middle Passage; continues through the dehumanization of slavery; and finally concludes by exposing dominant conceptualizations of the contemporary "Black Family" as a tangle of pathology. Her analysis pierces the body to expose "the hieroglyphics of the flesh" whose "undecipherable markings" become the cornerstone of an American Grammar that continues to this day to deny the African American his/her subjectivity, such that his/her body "becomes both the physical and biological expression of otherness... becoming both physically and generally powerless" (p. 67).

In this section, I argue that Spillers's essay is as much about disability as it is about race, even though the word "disability" is not mentioned even once in her essay. I find this startling because the "scene[s] of *actual* mutilation, dismemberment, and exile" (p. 67) that Spillers describes in her essay produce disabled bodies—black disabled bodies—who in an ironic turn are transformed into commodities that are exchanged in the market for profit. I call this ironic because the dominant paradigm has conceived of disabled bodies as having little economic value except in very limited contexts where their extra-ordinariness was made hypervisible, as for example, in the freak shows—another profitable venture (Adams, 2001; Bogdan, 1988). In Spillers's essay, on the other hand, it is in becoming disabled that the black body is at the height of its profitability, and it is the historical, social, and economic context of this becoming that I will now foreground in this section.

Before I undertake this analysis, however, I want to distinguish my position from other positions that have theorized the relationship between race and disability. For the most part, race for disability scholars and disability for race scholars are conceived of as "prosthetic metaphor[s]" (Barker & Murray, 2010, p. 219). In race studies scholarship, Ewart (2010) calls this practice "*dis*appropriation," where the language of disability is used "to affirm (an often-subordinate) voice to elucidate agency and figurative empathy for other oppressed and exploited populations" (p. 152). In disability studies scholarship, disability oppression/struggle is equated with racial oppression/struggle (James & Wu, 2006). In each of these cases, both *disability* and *race* are conceived of as tropes that can be used interchangeably to foreground the ubiquity of oppression, but that fail to explore the complex ways in which "the categories of race/ethnicity and disability are used to constitute one another or the ways that those social, political, and cultural practices have kept seemingly different groups of people in strikingly similar marginalized positions" (James & Wu, 2006, p. 4). Conscious of this critique, in this section, I will show how race and disability are imbricated in their collective formation of the black disabled body that now becomes a commodity that has economic, social, cultural, and linguistic implications for transnational subjectivities.

As mentioned earlier, Spillers's essay does not follow normative ways of engaging both disability and race because disability is never actually mentioned in her essay. Instead, Spillers focuses on the deliberate and violent process by which the black body is transformed into a commodity—without gender, without genitalia, without subjectivity—a commodity so abject that it exists even outside kinship relations (the most fundamental of social units), such that, in another ironic twist, its very aimlessness constitutes it as "an effective social and economic agent" (p. 74). I underscore both the historical and economic contexts here that are instrumental in the body becoming both racialized and disabled. I want to stress here that my argument is not that disability is like race or that race is like disability. Rather, I am arguing that within the specific transnational conditions of colonialism/neocolonialism, the becoming of black disabled bodies is indeed an intercorporeal phenomenon that foregrounds a violent hierarchical context that contemporary theorists of difference have been reluctant to address or even acknowledge.

Spillers's essay begins (and I use this verb very tentatively) in the fifteenth century, in the initial encounters between European adventurers and West Africans, as culled from the 1789 narrative of the Nigerian Olaudau Equiano or Gustavus Vassa and the Portuguese Gomes Eannes de Azurara's chronicle of the discovery and conquest of Guinea, 1441–1448. In both narratives, written from entirely different perspectives, the initial encounter between the Self and its Other produced the shocked recognition of radical difference. In these initial encounters, "white men with horrible looks, red faces, and long hair" (Equiano as quoted in Spillers, 1987, p. 67) came face to face with men and women "black as Ethiops, and so ugly, both in features and in body, as almost to appear (to those who saw them) the images of a lower hemisphere" (1: 28; De Azurara as quoted in Spillers, 1987, p. 70).

The sociocultural and psychic horror expressed by the Self when brought face to face with the *monstrous* Other mimics Julia Kristeva's (1982) argument that the abject inspires an irrational fear of engulfment and/or contamination. And, at face value, it would appear that both parties are guilty of this horror. However, as Spillers is quick to point out, this notion of simultaneous/mutual horror is a solipsism that conceals a more brutal reality—the intention of the One to subjugate the Other on the basis of difference perceived in skin color. To the ship crew of mostly European men, those bodies, "black as Ethiops and so ugly, both in features and in body," were nothing more than cargo to be transported to the New World by sea, and to be traded for unimaginable profit because of their obvious "physical" impairments." It is at this moment that the conceptualization of black subjectivity as impaired subjectivity is neither accidental nor should it be conceived of as merely metaphorical. Rather, it is precisely at the historical moment when one class of human beings was transformed into cargo to be transported to the New World that black bodies become disabled and disabled bodies become black. Further, it is also important to note that blackness itself does not stand in for skin color. After all, in his chronicle, de Azurara recognizes that "in the field of captives, some of the observed are 'white enough, fair to look upon, and well-proportioned' [while] Others are less 'white like mulattoes'" (Spillers, 1987, p. 70). In other words, *black* and *disabled* are not just linguistic tropes used to delineate difference, but are, instead, materialist constructs produced for the appropriation of profit in a historical context where black disabled bodies were subjected to the most brutal violence.

The other factor to recognize in these flesh-and-blood encounters of intercorporeality, which Shildrick celebrates in her own work, is that both blackness and disability are mutually constitutive on account of this social violence. Here, disability is again not just a linguistic trope, but the actual bloodied markings on the black body. Spillers cites William Goodell's account of North American slave codes that expose this brutal violation of black flesh:

> "The smack of the whip is all day long in the ears of those who are on the plantation, or in the vicinity; and it is used with such dexterity and severity as not only to lacerate the skin, but to tear out small portions of the flesh at almost every stake." The anatomical specifications of rupture, of altered human tissue, take on the objective description of laboratory prose—eyes beaten out, arms, backs, skulls branded, a left jaw, a right ankle, punctured; teeth missing, as the calculated work of iron, whips, chains, knives, the canine patrol, the bullet. (p. 67)

While Spillers describes these markings on the flesh as "the concentration of ethnicity" in a culture "whose state apparatus, including judges, attorneys, 'owners,' 'soul drivers,' 'overseers,' and 'men of God,' apparently colludes with a protocol of 'search and destroy'" (p. 67), I argue that these same markings on the flesh, quite simply, also produce impairment. Here, impairment is not just biological/natural, it is also produced in a historical, social, and economic context, where the very embodiment of blackness and disability "bears in person the marks of a cultural text whose inside has been turned outside" (p. 67). Here too, Rosemarie Garland-Thomson's (2002) depiction of disability as the set of practices that produce disabled/nondisabled bodies via a system of interpreting and disciplining bodily variation takes a brutally violent turn.

When the imbrication of blackness and disability produce violent markings on enslaved bodies, the assault on enslaved subjectivities is profound. Take, for example, one historical account cited by Spillers, which describes the detailed specifications provided as instruction to the crew of one of the most famous ships associated with the Middle Passage (*The Brookes*) on how to most profitably cram its human cargo on board:

> "Let it now be supposed... further, that every man slave is to be allowed six feet by one foot four inches for room, every woman five feet ten by one foot four, every boy five feet by one foot two, and every girl four feet six by one foot..." The owner of *The Brookes*, James Jones, had recommended that "five females be reckoned as four males, and three boys or girls as equal to two grown persons." (p. 72)

Instructed with much mathematical precision, bodily boundaries collapse and collide, stretch and shrink. The categorical permeability of boundaries has scant regard for the sovereign subject, because complex computations of equivalency are not bound by bodily limits. And yet, it is difficult to celebrate the fragility, malleability, and instability of these bodily boundaries borne out of so much violence as either transgressive or transformative. Rather, more profoundly, the intercorporeal permeability between these un-gendered, un-named, and un-remarkable bodies (except for their economic value as cargo) only serve to further erode any form of subjectivity that these bodies could claim for themselves.

Here, the historical conditions of a nascent colonialist transnational expansion of capitalism are responsible for the violent reconfiguration of the flesh, such that it becomes almost impossible to claim the sovereign subject, now mutually constituted via race, disability, and gender as a dehumanized commodity. And yet, even though the deconstruction of the sovereign subject is cause for celebration, how does one celebrate in the face of so much violated and wounded flesh?

DETERRITORIALIZING THE SOVEREIGN [ABLEIST] SUBJECT

Contemporary posthumanist theory has little use for the sovereign subject. Rather, subjectivity is now theorized as the "site of disunity and conflict" (Weedon, 1987, p. 21). More importantly, posthumanist thought has shifted away from theorizing the "body as flesh," to theorizing the "body as discourse," such that this posthumanist body appears as "volatile, liminal, slippery—a function of fragile and shifting discursive terrains" (Zita, 1996, p. 786); as a "mosaic of detachable pieces" (Braidotti, 1989, p. 152); as the "cyborg" (Haraway, 1990); and as the elusive BwO (Deleuze & Guattari, 1983). Therefore, given these radical possibilities, it would appear that the disabled body, inscribed indelibly by marked physical difference, assisted by prosthetics and communicative technology, and located within a discursive space that calls into question traditional notions of rationality and independence, would have much to gain from posthumanist theorizations.

From a posthumanist perspective, what then would we make of that tragic cargo of dismembered black bodies described in Spillers's essay? Because their bodies were broken down by the Master's whip, and their boundaries collapsed by the Master's calculations, these bodies become "a collage of segments and significations and propositions" (Bogard as quoted in Goodley, 2007, p. 149), such that they can now be read as the ultimate figures of disorganization that open up possibilities for "profound and complex linkages not only between diverse human beings, but between humans and animals, and human machines instead" (Shildrick, 2009, p. 157). As such then, these black dismembered bodies become *assemblages*, a construct that the philosophers Deleuze and Guatarri (1987) define as follows:

> On a first, horizontal axis, an assemblage comprises two segments, one of content, the other of expression. On the one hand it is a *machinic assemblage* of bodies, of actions, of passion, an intermingling of bodies reacting to one

another; on the other hand, it is a *collective assemblage of enunciations,* of acts and statements, of incorporated transformations attributed to bodies. Then on a vertical axis, the assemblage has both *territorial sides,* or reterritorialized sides, which stabilize it, and cutting *edges of deterritorialization,* which carry it away. (p. 88)

To read the enslaved dismembered bodies via the concept of the assemblage brings to the fore a disorderly conflation of intermingled bodies, the bodies themselves fragmented by frequent violent lashings (both real and metaphorical) into their molecular components. Here, these assemblages enunciate the violence written on their surfaces via their shifting morphologies—becoming first (human) cargo, then (human) property, and finally the very embodiment of dangerous deviance. In the specific context of colonialism and slavery, such enunciations permitted a further atomization that enabled a more thorough commodification, now becoming not just enslaved labor but also a laundry list of body parts that was distributed by medical institutions for purposes of medical education and medical research, as described in this advertisement from the *Charleston Mercury* on October 12, 1838:

> To planters and others—Wanted, fifty Negroes, any person, having sick Negroes, considered incurable by their respective physicians, and wishing to dispose of them, Dr. S. will pay cash for Negroes affected with scrofula, or king's evil, confirmed hypochondriasm, apoplexy, diseases of the liver, kidneys, spleen, stomach and intestines, bladder and its appendages, diarrhea, dysentery, etc. The highest *cash* price will be paid, on application as above, at No. 110 Church Street, Charleston. (Goodell as quoted in Spillers, 1987, p. 68)

According to Deleuze and Guattari, becoming-other is committed to unravelings, contingencies, fluidities, and contradictions. In the example above, the constitutive effects of race, disability, and the market coalesce in complex ways to effectively unravel the boundaries between bodies/subjects and destabilize their internal organizations so as to further enable their becoming-other. One of the outcomes of this becoming was that this captive flesh was now reconfigured into its atomized constituents, and in the process, enacted an objectification so complete that the "entire captive community becomes a living laboratory" (Spillers, 1987, p. 68). Moreover, in an ironic contradiction, iterative inscriptions of disability as "abject," "useless eater," and "undue burden" are transformed such that now (black) disabled fragmented bodies become highly valued commodities to be exchanged in the market by their Masters for "the highest *cash* price."

Enslaved black disabled bodies were also stripped of all other social markers (e.g., gender), because those invested in transporting those bodies seemed "not [at all] curious about this cargo that bled, packed like so many live sardines among the immovable objects" (Spillers, 1987, p. 70). When enslaved black women were stripped off their gender, they were simultaneously placed outside the narrow confines of white bourgeois femininity, reduced to the "bare life" (Agamben, 1998) as beasts of burden, and thereby once again subject to violence that reconstituted the intimate contours of their bodies. In Spillers's essay, she describes scenes where "[a] female body strung from a tree limb, or bleeding from the breast on any given day of field work because the 'overseer,' standing the length of a whip, has popped her flesh open, adds a lexical and living dimension to the narratives of women in culture and society" (p. 68).

The erasure of gender from black (female) subjectivity enabled the violent inscriptions on black (female) flesh, and, as a result, the now-impaired black (female) body is reconfigured. This brutal violence of history marks another irony. Stripped of her gender, the black impaired (female) body (in contrast to her white bourgeois sisters), experiences a form of deterritorialization that enables her to find a line of flight outside the strictures of patriarchal femininity. Exiting the organism that signifies a limiting totality, the enslaved black disabled (female) body, now un-gendered, her flesh fissured, and organs in disarray, exists in an uneasy tension with another posthumanist analytic—the BwO. In *A Thousand Plateaus* Deleuze and Guattari (1987) define the BwO as follows:

> [T]he body without organs has replaced the organism and experimentation has replaced all instrumentation, for which it no longer has any use. Flows of intensity [of which pain is one], their fluids, their fibers, their continuums and conjunctions of affects, the wind, fine segmentation, microperceptions, have replaced the world of the subject. Becomings, becomings-animal, becomings-molecular have replaced history, individual or general. (p. 162)

The transgressive possibilities generated via the BwO shifts the disabled body outside the restricted strictures of the sovereign subject. Opposed to the overdetermined totality of the organism, the disabled body, in a "vibrational move that oscillates and dances" (Kuppers, 2009, p. 249), morphs into a nomadic collective of assemblages, creatively extending its rhizomatic roots to venture into a space characterized by "continuums of intensities, becomings, and smooth spaces" (Markula, 2006, p. 14). As such the disabled body as the BwO is "a medium of becomings as it produces the intensities needed to create the abstract lines of flight of deterritorialization... [a medium] full of gaiety, ecstasy, and dance and populated by intensities" (Markula, 2006, p. 14).

Disability studies scholars Margrit Shildrick (2009), Dan Goodley (2007), and Petra Kuppers (2009) have all drawn on this notion of BwO to inscribe disability as the embodiment of possibility rather than as lack. Echoing Deleuze and Guatari's rejection of binaries and hierarchies, these scholars celebrate the linguistic possibilities for disabled bodies inscribed via very diverse modes of coding that include the biological, political, economic, and cultural realms, among others, and at the same time, allow for radical recodings that can bring into play an alternative "regime of signs... [as well as] states of things of different status" (Kuppers, 2009, p. 224). Each of these scholars inadvertently presumes an autonomous, white, bourgeois, and voluntarist subject as the precondition for such radical possibilities.

Kuppers, however, gestures toward the intersections of race, class, gender, and disability when she extensively quotes from a poem by Lynn Manning, an African American poet, playwright, and actor, who became blind at 23 years of age as a result of a gunfight in a bar in the impoverished neighborhood in which he lived. In the poem, "The Magic Wand," Manning foregrounds identity as partial/temporal/incomplete when living within the intersecting frameworks of race, class, gender, and disability. Manning writes: "I whip out my folded cane / and change from black man to blind man / with a flick of my wrist" (as quoted in Kuppers, 2009, p. 229). Thus, Manning's identity shifts between "a welfare-rich pimp / to disability-rich gimp / And from 'white man's burden' / to every man's burden" (as quoted in Kuppers, 2009, p. 229). Kuppers celebrates the rhizomatic potentialities in Manning's poem, where "identities are neither essentialized nor compounded, [but are] instead...in tactile relation with each other" (p. 229). Here, blackness, disability, and poverty are not additive forms of discrimination, but rather are mutually constitutive of each other. She is especially enamored by Manning's depiction of his unstable/temporal/multiple/contradictory subjectivities, now (re)territorialized into fragmented events via the intercorporeal interactions between himself and his audience at different moments in his performance. By doing so, Manning, inadvertently conjures up the vision of the BwO that becomes the medium through which the intensities of violence/pain/possibility/discrimination pass in order to deterritorialize the sovereign subject.

However, Kuppers's exclusive focus on the multiple modes of becoming in Manning's poem glosses over one salient fact that Manning points to—his agency or the lack thereof. When Manning writes, "My final form is never of my choosing; / I only wield the wand / You are the magicians" (p. 229), he recognizes the power/privilege that Others wield in order to inscribe his body with barely concealed discriminatory stereotypes in the specific social and historical contexts in which these inscriptions occur. When Manning remarks that his metamorphosis into a series of transitory becomings is clearly not of his own choosing, he does not necessarily contradict Deleuze and Guattari's own claim that there cannot be any naïve resurrection of the autonomous humanist subject. And yet, Deleuze and Guattari allow for a certain degree of agency—the possibility to act on the desire to become something other than what was ordained when transforming into the BwO. In a chapter entitled, "How Do You Make Yourself a Body without Organs," in *A Thousand Plateaus*, they write:

> You have to keep enough of the organism for it to reform each dawn; and you have to keep small supplies of significance and subjection, if only to turn them against their own systems when the circumstances demand it, when things, persons, even situations, force you to; and you have to keep small rations of subjectivity in sufficient quantity to enable you to respond to the dominant reality. Mimic the strata. You don't reach the BwO, and its plane of consistency, by wildly destratifying. (p. 160)

In proffering the above advice, Deleuze and Guattari, in the tradition of Marx and Engels, Althusser, Foucault, and Butler among others, are merely foregrounding the possibilities of the subject being both produced and productive. In fact, it is the capacity to deterritorialize the totality of the organism that is the most appealing aspect of this perspective. And it is in appealing to the not-yet-fully-determined corporeal possibilities for disabled bodies that Kuppers (2009) writes:

> The rhizomatic model of disability produces an abundance of meanings that do not juxtapose pain and pleasure or pride and shame, but allow for an immanent transformation, a coming into being of a state of life in this world, one that is constantly shifting and productive of new subject/individual positions.... It cannot have truth status, for it is empty of specific meaning. It is a movement rather than a definition.... [I]t is radically singular, flexing its membranes to touch words (*disabled, pain*), experiences (pain, joy) and other concrete objects in the world (stairs, pills, people, the ground, a table around which we are sharing our libations). (p. 226)

In the above quote, Kuppers celebrates the radical possibilities for disabled bodies and disability poetry. Here, disability poetry becomes "a minor literature" that draws community into "a rhizomatic relation... [that] is quite tectonic, tactile, sonorous, harmonic, touching things to one another rather than creating an arboreal structure of connection, root and branch and twig" (p. 239). Transgressive as these possibilities are, I join Kuppers in a rather cautious celebration. Unlike Kuppers, I interpret Manning as parting ways with Deleuze and Guattari in their will to flatten out the landscape upon which such becomings occur. This is because the context in which Manning's body becomes the rhizomatic BwO is ripe with violence emerging out of hierarchical social relations that constitute race, class, disability, and gender for social and economic exploitation. Though Kuppers admits that "[s]omething is given up in this way of writing, some clarities are lost, but other clarities might be gained" (p. 239), I argue that to lose clarity about social context would actually enact another more profound violence. As I have pointed out in earlier sections of this chapter, all these becomings—becoming black, becoming disabled, becoming enslaved, becoming poor, becoming un-gendered—become because of the deliberate intercorporeal violence produced out of hierarchical social and economic formations (arboreal structures), rather than arise out of the arbitrary/indeterminate horizontal flows of intensities (rhizome). Thus, to follow Deleuze and Guattari's directive to set aside a historical-materialist critique, because "arborescence promotes grand narratives which function as strata, where everyday intensities (thoughts, feeling and actions) are grasped and individuals' lives are territorialized by these narratives" (Goodley, 2007, p. 148), would mean that we actually set aside and thereby avoid confronting the actual violence that breaks bodies up into commodities that are exchanged in the marketplace for profit.

Setting aside a historical-materialist critique would also mean that we would set aside any confrontation with the "necropolitics" of slavery (Mbembe, 2003). In the context of slavery, Mbembe writes:

> As an instrument of labor, the slave has a price. As a property, he or she has a value. His or her labor is needed and used. The slave is therefore kept alive but in a *state of injury*, in a phantomlike world of horrors and intense cruelty and profanity. The violent tenor of the slave's life is manifested through the overseer's disposition to behave in a cruel and intemperate manner and in the spectacle of pain inflicted on the slave's body. Violence, here, becomes an element in manners like whipping or taking of the slave's life itself: an act of caprice and pure destruction aimed at instilling terror. Slave life, in many ways, is a form of death-in-life. (p. 21)

Mbembe's depiction of slave life as death-making is part of his larger argument about necropolitics, which he describes as the everyday practices that uphold contemporary forms of subjugation of life to the power of death. There are two aspects of this terror. The first aspect addresses the actual physical violence that marks the flesh and inscribes the body as impaired. The second aspect lies in the spectacle and/or performance of terror that oscillates between a random capriciousness and a focused resoluteness. As a result, according to Jasbir Puar (2007), "[T]he body informs the torture, but the torture also forms the body. That is the performative form of torture not only produces an object, but also proliferates that which names it. This sutures the double entrenchment of perversion into the temporal circuitry of always-becoming" (p. 87).

Both Mbembe and Puar focus on the discursive violence of this terror that not only (re)constitutes the body, but also serves as a spectacle of becoming, the sign of (not-so-good) things to come. In doing so, however, it is notable that both Mbembe and Puar neglect to discuss disability at any length in their respective arguments, despite the fact that in social contexts with so much gratuitous violence, disabled bodies proliferate. I, therefore, propose that a third aspect of terror be added to this discussion—the historical conditions that enable the actual material violence that produces disability. Here, my analytical deployment of necropolitics is not to associate disability with necrosis (actually I will be doing just the opposite), and so my focus is not on *what becomes* and *how becomings occur* but rather on *why becomings occur.*

Mbembe's accounts of the "morbid spectacle of severing" during the Rwandan genocide, where "bodily integrity has been replaced by pieces, fragments, folds, even immense wounds that are difficult to close," echo the vivid depictions of fissured flesh that Spillers describes in the context of slavery (p. 36). Neither of these events are arbitrary; they can however be linked together, notwithstanding their different geographical and temporal locations via the painfully common heritage of colonialism. Here, rather than posing a simple causal effect (namely that colonialism produces disability), I argue, on the other hand, that both disability/impairment and race are neither merely biological nor wholly discursive, but rather are historical-materialist constructs constitutive of the historical conditions of transnational capitalism.

Posthumanist politics of reading materiality as a matter of textuality, desire, and ironic invention does not take into account the actual conditions of people's lives. By rejecting all moves to analyze social conditions in their totality, posthumanists argue, instead, for local, fragmented, and partial analyses that fail to foreground the global structures that produce differential effects on different populations. By locating their emancipatory practices within the space of the social imaginary, as opposed to the actual materiality of economic conditions, posthumanists continue to uphold an idealist vision of emancipation that may never be achieved because it exists within the realm of fantasy.

THE DISCURSIVE POLITICS OF *SEVERELY DISABLED DESIRING MACHINES*

My analysis up to this point moves me into the very dangerous and uneasy territory of possibly subscribing to the dominant view of disability as "deadly status"(Titchkosky, 2007, p. 108). I could be accused of theorizing the disabled body as "a mere symptom of…capitalism [or slavery, for that matter]"

(Titchkosky, 2007, p. 131); as a master trope of disqualification (Mitchell & Snyder, 1997); as a subject of lack (Shildrick, 2009); or as a form of aesthetic nervousness (Quayson, 2007). But that is neither my intent nor my project. Rather, as noted in the introduction to this chapter, I mean to be provocative and push the unacknowledged boundaries that limit a clearer and more critical discussion of disability.

In order to show my hand more clearly, I foreground once again a question first raised by Robert McRuer (2006), which I had casually posed at the beginning of this chapter: "What might it mean to welcome the disability to come, to desire it?" In raising this question, McRuer poses a challenge to dominant notions of disability that conceive of disability as undesirable in the context of "compulsory able-bodiedness"—the body of practices, beliefs, concepts, and disciplines that uphold the "natural" order of things. Disabled bodies, by contrast, being the "unorthodox made flesh . . . [by] refusing to be normalized, neutralized, or homogenized" (Garland-Thomson, 1997, p. 24) mount a spirited challenge against one-dimensional notions of the "natural," and instead make available more transgressive becomings that often infiltrate the boundaries between human/animal/machine. However, rather than being radically celebrated for their transgressive potentiality, disabled bodies have historically been ejected from the social—conceived of as objects of lack rather than as subjects of desire.

Recognizing this problem, Margrit Shildrick (2005, 2007, 2009) proposes a radical (re)conceptualization of the disabled subject as sexual subject. Taking on a psychoanalytic approach to this question, Shildrick challenges normative conceptualizations of disabled sexuality as "improper" or even perverted (2005). Part of the problem, Shildrick (2007) argues, is that, because the consummation of sex, by its very nature, portends (dangerous) encroachments from Other bodies, attempts to safeguard humanism's sovereign subject from such encroachments demands a careful vigilance. Thus, according to Shildrick, "Insofar as the other in its alterity is always a possible threat to the integrity of the self, the radically different other who fails to observe the same boundaries is doubly so" (p. 226). Additionally, because sexuality invokes a certain form of vulnerability in the context of sexual intimacy with a possible stranger, Shildrick (2005) points out that disabled bodies, because of their habitual association with abnormality, are often counted as terrifying (sexual) strangers. As a result, the disabled body is often presented as a site of tragic loss/psychic anxiety, which disenables any possibility of articulating more positive crip sexuality. Therefore, Shildrick argues that there is a need to urgently foreground the aesthetic and intellectual value of disability.

Other disability studies scholars have also sought to counter such exclusions. McRuer (2006), drawing from epistemologies at the intersections of queer theory and crip politics, proposes the transgressive politics of a *critically queer/severely disabled* identity. McRuer draws on queer feminist theorist Judith Butler's argument to point out that a mere critique of the norm does not necessarily lead to its subversion. Since almost all attempts to replicate heteronormative norms are always partial, incomplete, and unsuccessful, at some point, almost all subjects (especially those who claim heteronormativity) can be conceived of as *virtually queer*. As a result, in a context where virtually queer identities inadvertently become prevalent, Butler proposes a more politically deliberate *critically queer* counterperspective—one that would demand collective action "to work the weaknesses in the norm" (McRuer, 2006, p. 30) in the quest for more transgressive subjectivities.

Transposing this argument to disability, McRuer puts forward a *severely disabled position* that "[resists] the demands of able-bodiedness and... [has] demanded access to a newly imagined and newly configured public sphere where full participation is not contingent on an able body" (p. 30). More significantly, according to McRuer, this *severely disabled perspective* would refuse "mere" toleration, and call out the inadequacies of compulsory ablebodiedness. McRuer's articulation of the severely disabled perspective in all its "fabulous" queer history of "fierce" and "defiant" critique replicates in many ways Deleuze and Guattari's articulation of the "desiring machine." According to Elizabeth Grosz (1994):

> A "desiring machine" opposes the notion of unity or oneness: the elements or discontinuities that compose it do not belong to either an original totality that has been lost or one that finalizes or completes it, a telos.... Desire does not create permanent multiplicities; it experiments, producing ever-new alignments, linkages, and connections, making things. It is fundamentally nomadic not teleological, meandering, creative, nonrepetitive, proliferative, unpredictable. (p. 168)

To retheorize disability via the "desiring machine" opens up an exciting world of possibility that distances the disabled body from its repressive associations with lack. Conceived of as the very antithesis of totality, a severely disabled position destabilizes the regulatory strictures of able-bodiedness and enables the proliferation of contingent, experimental, and, most importantly, productive modes of becoming. As a result, if (severely) disabled bodies epitomize the very essence of lack, then Deleuze and Guattari's formulation of desire as a productive force offers fresh new opportunities for disabled bodies as "desiring machines" to constitute a more transgressive real. According to Deleuze and Guattari (1983):

> If desire produces, its product is real. If desire is productive, it can be productive only in the real world and can produce only reality. Desire is a set of

passive syntheses that engineer partial objects, flows, and bodies, and that function as units of production.... Desire does not lack anything. It does not lack its object. *It is, rather the subject that is missing in desire, or desire that lacks a fixed subject: there is no fixed subject unless there is repression.* (p. 260) (my emphasis)

Conceptualizing disabled bodies as desiring machines also foregrounds the productive possibilities of desire to forge transgressive connectivities with other bodies/animals/machines. Barbara Gibson (2006) delineates three such connectivities that pay scant attention to the boundaries of organisms/machines: man-dog (blind man and his seeing eye dog); man-machine (ventilator user and his ventilator); and woman-woman-man (two disabled persons and one personal care attendant). Each of these connectivities opens up very productive possibilities for disability that rethink the binaries of independent/dependent and self/other—binaries that have historically always conceived of disability as simply lack. While I have addressed the first two connectivities (man-dog, man-machine) in some fashion in the previous section of this essay, where I discuss subjectivity via the BwO, it is the third connectivity (woman-woman-man) that I, now, foreground in this section.

In the example Gibson provides in her essay, she describes a situation where a personal attendant is assisting a disabled employer having sex with her lover (who may or may not have a disability) in a presumably heterosexual relationship. Normative notions of expressing desire within a context that traditionally requires the privacy of two consenting autonomous adults is now supplanted by a more defiant "un-natural" sexual relationship—a ménage à trois—where not all parties consummate this relationship in exactly the same fashion, with some aspects of the relationship experiencing more (passionate) intimacy than others. Even though the attendant's role is merely as facilitator of this "coupling," Gibson argues that "she [the attendant] experiences a leaking of her identity, a mingling of her own sexuality with theirs; their coupling is also hers (a *ménage*).... [in what] is perhaps easily imagined as a type of boundary transgression" (p. 192). This is because, Gibson reminds us, the attendant cannot actually remain absolutely neutral, given that she is already involved in participating in the intimacies of feeding, bathing, and cleaning her employer—actions that highlight their interdependencies for personal assistance and employment. Gibson goes on to explain this profound connection as follows:

> The sexual experience of the attendant is an erotic expression of this interdependence, extending it onto other planes. Without a sexual *act*, the two (the three) intermingle on multiple strata, becoming one—(an)other. The attendant is pulled in and pulls back as the others are involved in their own

oscillations between *me* and *us*. All these becomings intermingle. Subjectivity is never completely abandoned; it remains a charged point of departure and return but it leaks and flows, closes and opens. (p. 192)

By foregrounding the transgressive possibilities that emerge via the expression of *severely disabled* desire, Gibson not only conceives of *severely disabled bodies* as *(severely)* erotic desiring machines, she also radically rewrites the terrain of (normative) sexual desire in an associated queering of sexual norms, sexual behaviors, and sexual subjectivities. But these transgressive possibilities do much more than that. This is because, as Shildrick (2005) points out, the conception of disabled subject as desiring machine foregrounds transgressive possibilities "not just [in] sexual performance, as such but [also] of the performativity of self through gender identification, the naturalization of sexual preference, and ultimately the truth of the self" (p. 332), and in doing so actually rewrites the very "parameters of [radical] personhood" (p. 333).

THE MATERIALITY OF DESIRE WITHIN RACIAL/QUEER/CRIP POLITICS

On one level, the discussion in the previous section could be offered as a tentative response to McRuer's (2006) provocative question: "[W]hat might it mean to welcome the disability to come, to desire it?" (p. 207). The promise lies in the transgressive possibilities of intercorporeal intimacies shared between/with *severely disabled* desiring machines. Upholding Deleuze and Guattari's claim that desire is what propels life, conceptualizing disability via desire "sets up a series of practices...that assembles things out of singularities and breaks things, assemblages down into their singularities" (Grosz, 1994, p. 165), and it is this breaking apart and putting together in more enabling ways that (re)constitutes disabled subjects as more erotic (sexual) subjects of desire (a discussion I will expand on in Chapter 2). In theoretical terms, then, conceptualizing disability via desire not only deconstructs the sovereign subject but also sets up what Gibson (2006) calls "an ethic of openness"

[that] acknowledges the vulnerability of the subject at the moment of ethical engagement with the unmarked other...Connectivity is a potential to uncover new and varied ways of becoming and considering how things could be otherwise...to explore connections and appreciate differences: becoming other(s) in multiple ways, a multiplicity of flowing connections made, released and reformed. These multiple becomings point towards a freedom. Not freedom from interference but freedom to experiment, explore, peek outside of the limits, journey there and back again. Refuse and re-fuse. (p. 95)

However, even though this "ethic of openness" is brimming with transgressive and affective possibilities, I, once again, express a rather cautious optimism for this theoretical approach that rejects hierarchies, binaries, and histories. This cautious optimism is not shared by many disability studies scholars for whom the possibility of theorizing disability as productive desire rather than as repressive lack represents a major breakthrough in imagining and embracing a more hopeful future for disabled subjects (Gibson, 2006; Goodley, 2009; Kuppers, 2009; Shildrick, 2009). While I do understand that theorizing the disabled subject outside the stultifying discourses of lack/abjection is indeed a breakthrough, I am not so sure that engaging in theorizing outside historical, hierarchical, and binary social arrangements is an enabling politic. Thus, my project runs counter to Deleuze and Guattari's (1987) argument for multiplicities, lines of flight, assemblages, desiring machines, and strata, in their embrace of the rhizomatic rather than the arboreal. After all "[n]ature doesn't work in this way. In nature, roots are taproots with a more multiple, lateral, and circular system of ramification, rather than a dichotomous one. Thought lags behind nature" (Deleuze & Guattari, 1987, p. 5).

I find Deleuze and Guattari's appeal to "nature," perhaps, the most problematic aspect of their argument in reference to disability, because disability studies scholars have worked hard to foreground the "natural" as intensely political, and as a result, often intensely oppressive as well. Thus, when Shildrick (2009) asks, "What is it about the variant morphology of intra-human difference that is so disturbing as to invoke in the self-defined mainstream not simply a reluctance to enter into full relationship, but a positive turning away and silencing of the unaccepted other?" (p. 1), the answer lies not in "nature," but in the complex hierarchies of social relationships within specific historical conditions that determine "the issue of who is to count as a sexual subject" (p. 81).

To answer Shilrick's question, I turn to the theoretical perspective of historical materialism—the perspective that has been categorically dismissed by contemporary social theorists as too deterministic, disembodied, and narrow in its theorization of difference. Acutely conscious that this may be an intellectually unpopular move, I, nevertheless, propose a materialist reading of desire as part of my continuing attempt to theorize "becoming-as-(disabled) other" as a historical event. In his critical reading of Spillers's essay, Marxist literary theorist Robert Young (2009) argues that, when Spillers suggests that the dominant symbolic activity of the ruling episteme regarding race and gender, in particular, is grounded in the economics of slavery, "the logical extension of her argument would put Spillers' project on a firm materialist ground because she articulates the political economy of the symbolic" (p. 119). Young laments that Spillers, unfortunately, retracts from engaging this political economy to, instead, "[deconstruct] the grammar of dominant epistemologies... [to end up] in a very surprising and yet familiar space; a reclamation of the [voluntarist] subject" (p. 119).

Echoing Young's critique, and expanding it to include theories that engage the discursive conceptualization of disability via desire, I argue here that even desire, far from being a "natural" experience, is, in fact, a historical event. Young defines materialism as "an historical understanding of social relations ensuing from exploitative labor practices, which informs a revolutionary praxis aimed at transformation" (p. 1). Thus returning to Spillers one last time, I join with Young in arguing that to theorize desire as an intimate web of social relations "ensuing from exploitative labor practices" will actually enable us to respond to McRuer's provocative question that promises a world of transformative possibilities for disabled subjects.

Posthumanist theories have shifted the analytical lens away from foregrounding the modes of production, productive forces, and relations of production, to focus predominantly on the "regimes of signs, flows of libidinal energy, coding" (Lecercle, 2005, p. 42). This is because, according to Deleuze and Guattari (1983), desire is both autonomous and productive. They write:

> The truth of the matter is that *social production is purely and simply desiring production itself under determinate conditions* (emphasis in text). We maintain that the social field is immediately invested by desire, that it is historically determined product of desire, and that libido has no need of any mediation or sublimation, any psychic operation, any transformation, in order to invade and invest the productive forces and relations of production. *There is only desire and the social, and nothing else.* (p.29)

However, in Spillers's essay, Deleuze and Guattari's argument falters in the face of the historical conditions of slavery. In earlier sections of this chapter, I had already indicated how the deconstruction of the sovereign subject occurred in a context of brutal violence, which seemed a far cry from an emancipatory, transgressive subjectivity that posthumanist discourses were hoping for. Further, the transformation of these bruised and brutalized bodies into (un)desire(able) subjects also occurred in a similar context of brutal violence. According to Spillers, the actual theft of the body produced a contradictory discourse, where the enslaved body became simultaneously "the source of irresistible, destructive sensuality," while "being reduced to a thing, becoming *being for* the captor" (p. 67).

This contradiction was enabled through the determined efforts of the Master to intervene in the most intimate social relationships between his slaves—their kinship ties—by transforming even these intimate relationships into an economic asset for profit. With the abolition of maritime slave trade, the plantation economies in the Americas needed an alternative source of slave labor. As a result, in another ironic twist, previously un-gendered (female) enslaved bodies used for production were now perceived as gendered commodities vital to the (re)production of the slave population. Because it was necessary that the children born to the slave mother would not belong to her but to the Master who owned her, the Master forbade the formation of kinship ties between slaves, often enacting complicated social arrangements to ensure that the slaves were unable to sustain these ties. In this context, patrimony, in particular, was also frowned upon, because the father figure (whether he was the slave owner or the male slave) could not/would not claim his children as it would enable the possibility of inheritance (both economic and social), and add an unwanted complication to the economic enterprise of slavery. Thus, Spillers (1987) explains that

> the offspring of the enslaved, "being unrelated both to their begetters and to their owners...find themselves in the situation of being orphans"...I would call this enforced state of breach another instance of vestibular cultural formation where "kinship" loses meaning, since it can be invaded at any given and arbitrary moment by the property relations. (p. 74)

Clearly, property relations played a crucial role in the destruction of kinship ties between enslaved populations. Further, the release from normative (heterosexual, patriarchal, and nuclear) kinships ties did not necessarily signify a release from their oppressive constraints, nor did it enable enslaved bodies to form alternative antipatriarchal, queer relationships unconnected by bloodlines via rhizomatic extensions. That would be the posthumanist dream, one that Kuppers foregrounds in her rhizomatic analysis of disabled subjectivity. Because the rhizome is antigenealogy (Deleuze & Guattari, 1987, p. 23), Kuppers (2009) celebrates the fact that since

> [t]here is no necessary family resemblance for disabled people, we mostly have to make our families ourselves, choose our community. Often, there is no patrilinear descent, no matriarch, no heteronormative narrative that duplicates itself into the future. To call for a ritual of non-essential, strategic *disability* community is a rhizomatic act: to put out feelers. (p. 233)

Celebratory as Kuppers's observation is, I cannot but foreground the historical and economic context in which such rhizomatic relationships are enabled to flourish. In a slave economy, the very meaning of kinship, both normative and oppositional, was intimately tied to property relations, and enslaved bodies were just that—property. Here, clearly, the breakdown of kinship ties occurs in a hierarchical context, where the slave master trades his dehumanized cargo for profit because "slavery creates an economic and social agent whose virtue lies in being outside the kinship system" (Spillers, 1987, p. 175). Located outside the normative kinship system, enslaved bodies, nevertheless, forged other connections that could loosely be termed "community" in an attempt to survive the brutalities of the slaver. However, Spillers (1987) is quick to point out:

> We might choose to call this connectedness "family" or "support structure," but that is a rather different case from the moves of a dominant symbolic order, pledged to maintain the supremacy of race. It is that order that forces "family" to modify itself when it does not mean family of the "master," or dominant enclave. It is this rhetorical and symbolic move that declares primacy over any other human and social claim, and in that political order of things, "kin," just as gender formation, has no decisive legal or social efficacy. (p. 75)

There is no flattening out of the social relationships here, only a hierarchy that is undeniable. Moreover, these relationships are not "natural," but are, in fact, forged in an intensely political context where economic practices take precedence over affective connections between subjects—an observation that causes Spillers (1987) to admit that "the feeling of kinship is not inevitable..., [rather] it describes a relationship that appears "natural," but must be "cultivated" under actual material conditions" (p. 76).

Additionally, the justification for the exclusion of enslaved bodies from kinship relations was based on the imbrication of race and disability as inscribed on the enslaved body. This exclusion was justified because of the dominant belief that Africans were of a lower social and intellectual order than their European masters on account of their "natural" inability to forge kinship relationships that allowed

> the vertical transfer of a bloodline, of a patronymic, of titles and entitlements, of real estate and the prerogatives of "cold cash," from fathers to sons and in the supposedly free exchange of affectional ties between a male and a female of his choice... the mythically revered privilege of a free and freed community. (Spillers, 1987, p. 74)

The materialist implications of such exclusions were significant. Africans were transformed into impaired, un-gendered, racialized bodies because they were presumed unfit to uphold the economic transactions that kinship relations demand. Concomitantly, they were transformed into a commodity precisely because their exclusion from "natural" kinship ties also denied their claims to sovereign subjectivity, free to forge relationships that were recognized in a slave society. But it is not just the exclusion from legally recognized kinship ties that impacted enslaved bodies. The imbrication of race and disability also located desire firmly within the social relations of production and consumption such that both male and female slaves were mere commodities in the sexual transactions that ensued in the quest for both profit and pleasure.

It is no secret that enslaved women were used both for the Master's pleasure and for the master's profit. Conceived merely as objects of desire, slave women were utilized not only to meet the Master's sexual needs, but also in a very concrete way to reproduce the labor force in the slave economy. Drawing from Frederick Douglas's autobiography, Spillers, therefore observes that, as a result, "genetic reproduction becomes, then, not an elaboration of the life-principle in its cultural overlap, but an extension of the boundaries of proliferating properties.... through the institutional apparatus: war and market" (p. 75).

Within this violent context, is it even possible to imagine that the enslaved female and/or her sexual oppressor could derive pleasure from these intimate couplings? The answer to this question foregrounds the critical importance of articulating a political economy of desire even in the face of posthumanist critiques to the contrary. Posthumanist thought would argue that desire is not constrained by the social, because even in the most repressive social organization of slavery held to rigid codes of race, gender, class, and sexuality, erotic desire seemed determined to transgress every boundary. Here an outlaw erotics flourished, taunting the laws of miscegenation and class antagonisms. Nowhere is this better illustrated than in *Incidents in the Life of a Slave Girl*, an autobiography by Linda Brent/Harriet Jacobs that Spillers uses in the essay.

Located in a context where rape by the Master was a normative experience for black female slaves, Brent describes a fraught relationship between herself and Mrs. Flint, the wife of a doctor who owned Brent. Suspecting that her husband, the doctor, was having sexual relations with his slave, Mrs. Flint, consumed with jealousy, would visit Brent at night time, assuming the role of a ghost and attempting to "ride" the victim "in order to exact confession, expiation, and anything else that the immaterial power might want" (Spillers, 1987, p. 76). Here is Brent's account of these visitations:

> Sometimes I woke up, and found her bending over me. At other times she whispered in my ear, as though it were her husband who was speaking to me, and listened to hear what I would answer. If she startled me, on such occasion, she would glide stealthily away; and the next morning she would tell me I had been talking in my sleep, and ask who I was talking to. At last, I began to be fearful for my life. (Brent as quoted in Spillers, 1987, p. 77)

Brent's narrative, clearly a psychodrama, provided yet another discourse of disability that Spillers alludes to, but fails to foreground. In Spillers's reading of Brent's narrative, she alludes to a discourse of madness associated with each of the three protagonists: (a) the "madness" of the master that "arises in the ecstasy of his unchecked power"; (b) the "madness" of his wife who, through impersonating the sexual power of her husband, "attempts to inculcate his or her will into the vulnerable, supine body" of his slave; and (c) the attempts by Mrs. Flint to convince Brent that these nightly visitations were the hallucinations of an immoral "mad" woman. Here, another becoming is foregrounded—one that is now grounded in the articulation of desire within a violent, abusive, and hierarchical context. Here, even though these intercorporeal intimacies traverse with impunity the boundaries of race, gender, and sexuality in a complex queering of outlaw desire, the only subject who can enjoy the "freedom to experiment, explore, peek outside of the limits, journey there and back again" (Gibson, 2006, p. 95) is the master, Dr. Flint. Thus, Spillers rightly observes that "[u]nder these arrangements, the customary lexis of sexuality, including 'reproduction,' 'motherhood,' 'pleasure,' and desire' are thrown into unrelieved crisis" (p. 76).

Additionally, Spillers insightfully foregrounds a seemingly improbable alliance that could have been forged between mistress and slave because both were subject to "the same fabric of dread and humiliation" (p. 77). Spillers goes on to explain:

> Neither could claim her body and its various productions—for quite different reasons, albeit—as her own, and in the case of the doctor's wife, she appears not to have wanted her body at all, but to desire to enter someone else's, specifically, Linda Brent's, in an apparently classic instance of sexual "jealousy" and appropriation. In fact, from one point of view, we cannot unravel one female's narrative from the other's, cannot decipher one without tripping over the other. (p. 77)

Here, as per Spillers's observation, the violent intimate expressions of desire could have been productive in enabling transgressive queer connectivities that had the potential to destabilize the impermeable social boundaries in the slave economy. But I used the verb "could have," because this clearly did not happen in this context. In fact, the only possibility for this alliance to flourish would have been if both protagonists were collectively invested in dismantling the social relations of production and consumption that had produced yet another violent instance of the "bare" life.

And finally, this analysis yields yet another discourse of disability that is intimately imbricated with race, gender, and sexuality in a context that foregrounds the continuities between the historical social relations of a slave society and the contemporary social relations supported by neoliberal capitalism. In an earlier section of this chapter, I had already discussed the social and economic conditions within which impaired black (female) enslaved bodies were un-gendered to enable a more effective appropriation of their (re)productive labor for profit. Additionally, with the impaired black (female) body becoming un-gendered, this becoming also situates becoming queer in a materialist context, such that, as in Linda Brent's autobiographical narrative, the female enslaved body "in an amazing stroke of pansexual potential.... [can] be invaded/raided by another woman or man" (Spillers, 1987, p. 77). From a materialist perspective, the queering of this enslaved body occurs in a specific historical context where femininity loses its sacredness at the precise moment when the flesh becomes the primary commodity of exchange. In fact, the very indeterminacy of gender identity occurs at the very moment of captive birth, for the only reason that reproductive labor can be appropriated by the Master for profit.

While it is true that much of my discussion in this chapter emerges from a historical period that has substantially been transformed, I argue, however, that the implications of these unsettling practices have transcended several historical periods and continue to have relevance even today. In fact, the impetus for Spillers's essay came from the 1965 Moynihan Report on the Negro family, which attempted to explain away the continued lack of social and economic progress of African Americans in the United States. Rather than implicating white supremacist capitalist patriarchy, Moynihan laid blame at the door of black female-headed households, such that he implicated the perceived matriarchal culture propagated by (un-gendered) black women for emasculating African American men in a culture that is normatively patriarchal. Moynihan wrote:

> Ours is a society which presumes male leadership in private and public affairs...A sub-culture, such as that of the Negro American, in which this is not the pattern, is placed at a distinct disadvantage.... It is clearly a disadvantage for a minority group to be operating under one principle, while the great majority of the population...is operating on another. (as quoted in Spillers, 1987, p. 65)

To avoid mapping the historical continuities evident in this practice of conceiving black bodies as socially pathological would be a costly mistake. In fact, it is through the analysis of these historical continuities that it is possible to foreground the complex ways in which the discourses of race, gender, and sexuality are implicated in African American subjects becoming disabled. The argument continues to play out in contemporary contexts, especially in education, where the "underachievement" of African American males in the lower classes still continues to be blamed on the overachieving matriarchal African American women and the missing patriarchal figures of African American males in the African American female-headed household. Unwilling to read the real material violence against black subjectivities, it seems a little too easy to read disability as embodied otherness (notwithstanding its "inherent" potential for resistance), rather than situate becoming disabled in an economic context "too obviously [committed] to administer to the [masters] own lusts, and make a gratification of their wicked desires profitable as well as pleasurable" (Spillers, 1987, p. 76).

MAKING [DISABLED] BODIES MATTER

So then, we are back again to McRuer's question: "[W]hat might it mean to welcome the disability to come, to desire it?" (p. 207). In response to McRuer's question, I have argued that the social meanings of disability, race, gender, and sexuality are constituted within the historical conditions of transnational capitalism. I have also pointed out that it is the economic context (e.g., colonialism) that has blunted the capacity for the *severely disabled desiring machine* to realize its transgressive potential. That the potential for transgression is there is evident in the multiple ways in which the impaired black un-gendered enslaved body is nonchalantly tossed across many social boundaries, and, as a result, inadvertently (re)writes the social texts that were diligently being monitored by the disciplinary discourses of biopower. Unfortunately, however, in the specific context of slavery, these (re)writings came at the cost of the complete erasure of agency of the enslaved body— now transformed into a commodity that was forced to transgress social boundaries purely for the benefit of profit. Here, I define human agency in the context of Marx's famous quote in the *Eighteenth Brumaire of Louis Bonaparte*:

> Men [*sic*] make their own history, but they do not make it just as they please; they do not make it under circumstances chosen by themselves, but under circumstances directly found, given and transmitted from the past. (Marx, Engels & Tucker, 1978, p. 595)

Marx's argument that transforms agency from an autonomous act to a historical event can also be applied to the concept of desire. Contrary to Deleuze and Guattari's claim that productive desire is autonomous from the social, I join with Rosemary Hennessy (2000) to argue that this conceptualization of productive desire conceives of consumption practices as if they occur outside of the exploitative social relations of production, and as a result, the BwO, now becomes "the undifferentiated subject of self enjoyment" (p. 71). But, as I have shown through Spillers's essay, desire is mediated via the social relations of production and consumption, such that the Master's ability to consume is dependent on the slave's capacity to produce. Moreover, the very articulation of the Master's desire is dependent on the appropriation of the un-gendered (female) slave body for his pleasure. In contemporary contexts, both Hennessy as well as McRuer, in their separate texts, draw on the work of John D'Emilio to foreground a materialist analysis of desire in their materialist conceptualization of queer identity in capitalism. According to D'Emilio, the locus of production shifting from the household into the market, and the new demand for women to participate in the workforce and in consumer culture, enabled the "gradual unhinging of sexuality from its pro-creative function as regulated by the family's patriarchal gender system" (Hennessy, 2000, p. 103), and this shift enabled the proliferation of "public" queer identities. In making this argument, Hennessy is careful to point out that this does not necessarily mean that "class trumps sexual identity," but rather that "the consolidation of new sexual identities that pursues the logic of commodification limits the development of collective agency" (p. 106), or, in other words, the "multitude" (Hardt & Negri, 2004).

So what does disability have to do with all of this? To answer that question, I take another detour to briefly discuss Robert Young's (2009) theorization of race as a commodity fetish, and explore its implications for a materialist disability studies. Within the context of literary studies, Young is critical of the contemporary trend in cultural theory, where posthumanist scholars eschew metanarratives and humanist scholars extol the experiential, because, he argues that, these trends displace a historical understanding of class relations within contemporary transnational capitalism. As a result, race theory offers an "idealist notion of race as an expressive causality and an empiricist notion of race as a positivity" (p. 4), and in doing so blocks a materialist understanding of race.

To make the argument for a materialist theory of race, Young turns to the Marx's labor theory of value as it manifests itself in capitalist production. According to Marx, the very basis for participation in labor is to provide for specific needs that are essential for human survival—food, clothing, and shelter. Marx identified this labor as having a use value (i.e., being of use to someone). At the same time, within the context of capitalism, which is predominantly an economy of exchange, labor itself becomes a commodity, which does not merely have a use value, but is instead assigned an exchange value in the marketplace—the value of that labor being compensated by a wage. According to Marx's theory of surplus value, labor power—the capacity for work that an employer buys from a worker—produces more value than it is compensated for, thereby producing surplus value in the form of profits that are appropriated by the capitalist. As a result, it is productive labor—labor that actually produces surplus value—that has more economic value in capitalist economies. In this way, Marx also demonstrated that notions of efficiency and productivity are both historical constructs associated with the modes of production by which the capitalist can extract surplus value from the commodity labor power.

It is in this context, then, that Young proposes theorizing race as a commodity fetish, where he foregrounds the use value of race as a commodity. Humanist/posthumanist arguments focus on the use value of race outside of economics. In other words, these theories essentially argue that race is useful to deny sameness, and mark difference within the social. Young, on the other hand, argues that race has to be understood such that its use value always operates in relation to its exchange value, within the exploitative context of commodity production. Examining race in this context, Young argues that what links racism to capitalism is not just the creation of racial divisions within the working classes, but rather that "it is the very commodity structure where race is useful precisely because it can be exchanged for less" (p. 8). Young then continues: "[I]f race signifies 'less than' at the point of (re)production, then it is ideologically (and morally) legitimate for the asymmetrical distribution of resources and thus, this race difference contributes toward increasing surplus value, thereby reinforcing the fundamental logic of capitalism: accumulation" (p. 9).

Then, in an interesting twist to his argument, Young goes on to claim that race is not just a commodity, it is a commodity fetish. In *Capital, Volume 1*, Marx explains:

> The commodity is a mysterious thing, simply because in it the social character of men's labor appears to them as an objective character stamped upon the product of that labor; because the relationship of the producers to the sum total of their own labor is presented to them as a social relation, existing not between themselves, but between the products of their labor... There is a definite social relation between men, that assumes in their eyes, the fantastic form of a relation between things... This is what I call the Fetishism which attaches itself to the products of labor, so soon as they are produced as commodities, and which is therefore inseparable from the production of commodities. (Marx et al., 1978, p. 320–321)

Taking up this concept, Young argues that the use value of race fetishizes our conception of the social, and as a result, this occludes a critical understanding of the historicity of social relations where race is deployed in the calculus of surplus extraction (its exchange value). While this notion of race as a commodity fetish is well documented in Spillers's essay, what is not documented is how disability relates to this argument. In this chapter, I have argued that becoming disabled is also a historical event where disability also has a use value that is deployed simultaneously with race to justify the creation of the enslaved un-gendered body. Moreover, I argue that it is the actual act of impairment that is used both to create and at the same time to justify this construction. However, by reading disability as "natural," rather than as a historical event, what is obscured are the social relationships that produce disability as lack. And so, like Young, I, too, argue that the use value of disability lies in its deployment as a commodity fetish in transnational capitalism.

It could be argued that in reclaiming political economy, I have once again constructed a disembodied disabled subject. In response to that critique, I argue that my project, on the other hand, seeks to situate embodiment in a historical context in order to foreground the materiality of the flesh. Moreover, in opposition to normative constructions of disability as lack, I answer McRuer's question by simply reframing it: Within what social conditions might we welcome the disability to come, to desire it? In this chapter, I have attempted to answer this question by situating "desiring disability" as a historical condition of possibility that does not reproduce economic exploitation on a global scale. In doing so, I offer a critique of posthumanist discourses that see possibility as reinvesting signs with more transgressive meaning. On the other hand, I echo Robert Young, when he argues, "Change will not come by emancipating signs from totalities but by displacing the relations of production. For although the relations of production do not evade, they nevertheless always exceed the fate of the sign" (p. 7).

CHAPTER 2

OF GHOSTS AND GHETTO POLITICS: EMBODYING EDUCATIONAL POLICY AS IF DISABILITY MATTERED

> I see her shape and his hand in the vast networking of our society and in the evils and oversights that plague our lives and laws. The control he had over her body. The force he was in her life, in the shape of my life today. The power he exercised in the choice to breed her or not. The choice to breed slaves in his image, to choose her mate and be that mate. In his attempt to own what no man can own, *the habit of his power and the absence of her choice* (my emphasis).
>
> I look for her shape and his hand.
> Patricia Williams (1991), *The Alchemy of Race and Rights*, p. 19.

IN THE ABOVE EPIGRAPH, CRITICAL RACE FEMINIST PATRICIA WILLIAMS (1991) describes the impossibility of ever transcending the violence of historical time to escape the haunting power of the slave owner Austin Miller, an eminent Tennessee lawyer and jurist who was the master and bed-mate of her great-great-grandmother, and hence one of Williams's forebears. Delving determinedly into these "ghostly matters" (Gordon, 1997) of colonial oppression and erasure, Williams (1991) writes:

> I track meticulously the dimensions of meaning in my great-great-grandmother as chattel: the meaning of money, the power of consumerist world view, the death of those we label the unassertive and the inefficient. I try to imagine where and who she would be today. I am engaged in the long-term project of... finding the shape described by her absence in all of this. (p. 19)

In this chapter, I argue that "her shape and his hand" (Patricia J. Williams, 1991, p. 19) still continue to cast a shadow on the "vast networking of our society…our lives and laws" (p. 19), or, as in this particular context, educational policy. Continuing the discussion in Chapter 1, I demonstrate once again how historical continuities and discontinuities continue to haunt the present in very material ways. Specifically, I will explore how educational policy as an embodied social phenomenon is similarly rooted in a contradictory history that demands the simultaneous submissive visibility and ruthless erasure of the bodies of colonized others—a demand that is enacted with a casual acceptance of "the habit of his power and the absence of her choice" (p. 19). Thus, more than 50 years after *Brown v. Board of Education*, the "savage inequalities" (Kozol, 1992) manifested in the distribution of educational resources, and the widening achievement gap between elite students and those marked oppressively by race, class, gender, sexuality, and disability, are met with a complacency that accepts these enactments of power and erasure as natural and normative.

Education policy makers would, however, loudly proclaim their commitment to the daunting task of ensuring equity and excellence for all students notwithstanding their differences. They would argue that the reforms they have put in place demand "accountability" from administrators, teachers, and other educational personnel to uphold the democratic goals of US public education as documented by copious pages of assessment data. But nowhere from among the mountains of data they have amassed is there a recognition that behind the numbers are bodies—restless, unpredictable, passionate, and not always docile.

In this chapter, I argue for a different kind of policy analysis from the vantage point of transgressive embodiment, what Wanda Pillow (2003) has described as an embodied policy analysis. An embodied analysis foregrounds the erasure of material bodies in educational contexts (student, teacher, and/or administrator), and describes how educational policies serve to control, shape, regulate, and reproduce them. Such a position stands counter to traditional policy analysis that is committed to a technical rationalist framework with claims to scientific and ideologically free ("the view from nowhere") methodologies (Marshall, 1997; Pillow, 2003). Thus, even though educational contexts teem with diverse bodies, traditional policy analysis prefers to focus on outcomes and standards, rather than having to deal with unruly, messy, unpredictable, and taboo bodies—bodies that are shaped by, and, in turn, shape the social, political, and economic contexts they inhabit (Michalko, 2002; Pillow, 2003).

Placing the body as central to an analysis of "accountability" shifts the focus from test scores and normative standards to those bodies who take these tests and to those who interpret these test scores, to those bodies who attempt to meet these normative standards, and to those who administer them, and especially to those bodies who reject/resist these same disciplinary measures. In other words, an embodied policy analysis will ask the following questions: To whom is public education accountable? Through whose authority are these standards/goals/outcomes deployed? How do these practices of power constitute normative and deviant subjectivities? And what processes are in play to neutralize and/or erase oppositional subjectivities? Such an analysis of "accountability" would run counter to normative educational policy analyses that are animated by the haunting of "her shape and his hand."

Additionally, this analysis of "*finding her shape described by her absence* (emphasis in text) captures perfectly the paradox of traveling through time and across all those forces...being there and not there, past and present, force and shape" (Gordon, 1997, p. 6). Working through this same paradox of traveling through time, I foreground the political economy of desire at the intersections of race, gender, and disability in the historical context of a colonial slave economy (as discussed in Chapter 1) to serve as the backdrop against which to analyze the contemporary context of US public education. In this analysis, I pay close attention to the disciplinary discourses that are animated in the (re)organization of educational space into the affluent metropolis and the desperate ghetto, while haunted by the historical (dis)continuities of colonial/neocolonial education. Here, I draw on La Paperson's (2010) conceptualization of the ghetto—not as "a fixed sociological space...[but rather as] a dislocating procedure" (p. 10)—that draws on the "apparatus of empire" (p. 21) to exclude, contain, and control the proliferation of excessive bodies in special education, alternative schooling, and the school-to-prison pipeline. As such, this embodied policy analysis emphasizes"[g]hostly matters [that] looks for a language and [a praxis] for identifying hauntings and writings with the ghosts any haunting inevitably throws up" (Gordon, 1997, p. 7).

Sexuality is one such context where the mere expression of desire is haunted by ghosts. In fact, the epigraph that I begin this chapter with foregrounds how *the habit of his power* subsumed *her* desire into *his* own. Expanding the discussion in Chapter 1, I continue to foreground desire, this time, however, in the more contemporary context of US public education. In this context, the loci of analyses are the spatial configurations of inclusion/exclusion that manifest themselves specifically through the sex curriculum in public education. The topic of sexuality sits uncomfortably in discussions on educational policy and accountability standards. A recognition of sexuality in educational contexts enables unruly decadent leaky bodies to challenge the rigid authority of evaluative standards and disciplinary practices because of their unpredictability, their impulsiveness, and their intensities.

As a result, the terror of dangerous (sexual) bodies (her shape) has persistently haunted the sex curriculum.

Because my predilection is to engage ghostly hauntings in order to expose the violence that is obscured, I engage how sexuality continues its historical mandate in the production of normative and abnormal subjectivities. Heteronormative in its ideological content, discourses of sexuality, being both restricted and restrictive, play a critical role in defining the "normal" child, while at the same time intervening in the most personal/private space of intimacy. The pregnant teen, the lesbian, gay, bi-sexual, trans-sexual, questioning, and intersex (LGBTQI) young adult, and the disabled student are some examples of students for whom the mere expression of their sexuality casts them as abnormal. Therefore, in this chapter, I draw on the spatial metaphor of the postcolonial ghetto La Paperson, 2010) to explore how the dominant discourses of sexuality (his hand) actively produce the metropole and the ghetto. Then, drawing on a materialist disability studies as articulated in Chapter 1, I demonstrate how discourses of sexuality rely on the ideology of the "normate" to segregate, to exclude, and to dehumanize those sexual subjects who disregard the rules of normativity for social and economic purposes. Finally, in the last section of this chapter, I foreground the material conditions that make present *her shape* in the transgressive/unruly act of "coming out crip."

QUARANTINED IN THE POSTCOLONIAL GHETTO

In the "dirty politics of schooling" (La Paperson, 2010), certain words attain particular significance. Take quarantine: a condition of enforced isolation. When Foucault wrote that being quarantined is almost synonymous with inclusion, he implied that it is a synonym for the dirty job of pathologizing control. To quarantine requires space, preferably secluded, but also one that can easily be patrolled to protect the outside from those on the inside... "of being there and not there" at the same time. An example of another haunting. And Other ghosts.

In the moral geography of schooling, one such quarantined space is the alternative school, which students who are deemed at risk for school failure are forced to attend (Lehr, Tan & Ysseldyke, 2009). It is a little terrifying to note that according to the 2001–2002 data, the numbers of students isolated in these quarantined spaces exceeded more than 613,000. Students are banished from regular classrooms because they are perceived to be at a higher risk of substance abuse, suicide, sexual activity, and teen pregnancy. Nearly 12 percent of the students who attend alternative school are identified with emotional and behavioral disabilities and have individualized educational plans (IEPs). However, just like other quarantined spaces (think

Guantanamo Bay), some of these alternative schools privilege the punitive over the therapeutic, becoming the dumping ground of at-risk students who are deemed a threat to the "normal" practices of school and whom teachers are too terrified to teach. Without the requisite best practices—positive behavioral and social support, based on functional assessments,—students often "relapse" after short returns to the classroom, and when cure cannot be realized, they often drop out. Of those who did not complete school, 36 percent were identified with learning disabilities and 59 percent with emotional and behavioral disorders (Lehr & Lange, 2003).

More troubling, however, is the fact that it is predominantly black and brown bodies that are pathologized in this way. For example, at Jena High School, (the school that inspired the march to free the Jena 6), Boyd (2009) reported that, in the 2006–2007 school year, 22.1 percent of all students were subject to in-school suspension (ISS). However, of the 90 black students in the school, 41.1 percent got ISS, while only 18.2 percent white students received a similar punishment. These statistics reflect larger societal trends, where minority youth comprise more than 60 percent of the number of children detained by juvenile justice systems. Moreover, it was not just that African American and Latino students were punished more than white students, but that they were punished for less serious and more subjective reasons (Skiba, Homer, Chung, Rausch, May & Tobin, 2011; Skiba & Knesting, 2001). Further, students of color with special needs were two times more likely to be suspended than children without special needs, and those labeled with emotional or behavioral disabilities were 11 times more likely to be suspended from school (Brown, 2007). Additionally, while whites report the same amount of gang membership and behavior as blacks and Latinos, perception among law enforcement officers has been that it is mostly youth of color who participate in gang-related crimes.

If the social behaviors of young men of color are overwhelmingly pathologized, then, almost in tandem, the sexual behaviors of young women of color are subject to a similar fate. Thus, even though the highest percentages of teenage mothers are white women, it is mostly African American and Latina teen mothers who are overwhelmingly pathologized (Roxas, 2008). However, this is not to say that the statistics for teen mothers of color are not high. Over 25 percent of teen births occur to African American women, and over 28 percent occur to Latina women even though they represent only 15 percent of the total school population. More troubling, however, is that traditional schools provide little or no support to these students, and many of them are usually sent to self-contained classrooms and alternative settings without any academic resources even though many of them had academic problems earlier. And this quarantining is often unquestioned, even though Title IX of the Educational Amendments Act of 1972 charges schools with the responsibility of providing equal educational opportunity to pregnant and mothering teens. In fact, there are explicit directions barring expulsion from schools, exclusion from course-work and extracurricular activities, and discrimination.

The bodies of the LGBTQI youth, who are made deliberately invisible because their very existence is taboo in public schools, are also quarantined both metaphorically and materially. There are few, if any, policies to protect them from the daily violence meted out in a homophobic school climate that is defended with a pseudomoral zeal (Nichols, 1999, Holmes & Cahill, 2004. According to a National School Climate Survey, 85 percent of LGBTQI youth reported hearing homophobic remarks, 80 percent reported verbal harassment, one in five reported physical assaults because of orientation, and 10 percent reported being assaulted because of their identity or nonconformity. Seventy percent just felt unsafe in schools. In communities and schools of color, these youth were confronted with the dual violence of racism and homophobia even within their own communities (Homes & Cahill, 2003). For example, in a 1991 National American Indian Adolescent Health Survey, 28 percent of gay Native Americans as compared to 17 percent of heterosexual peers had run away from home. Amid the implicit and explicit support of homophobic violence in public schools, the fact that 39 percent of LGBTQI students had committed suicide and that 52 percent has tried more than once to do so, did not set off any warning bells to put better policy in place. Even in more progressive schools, the attempt has been to pathologize the individual, labeling these students as "at risk" and offering programs that regard sexuality as an individual problem and a private issue, rather than to challenge homophobia and the heteronormative practices of schooling (Quinlivan, 2006).

The failure of educational policies to normalize these youth affects the actual dislocation of these youth into the postcolonial ghetto. The term "ghetto" in the context of the quarantining of pathologized bodies in public schools needs some elaboration as does the term "postcolonial." Echoing La Paperson's (2010) caution that if the term "post," meaning "after the fact," signals that the era of colonialism is long since passed, I utilize, on the other hand, La Paperson's reconstruction of the unintended meanings of the term "postcolonial":

> The verb form of *post* (emphasis in text) as in "keep someone posted" refers to keeping someone informed of the latest development or news. Post + colonial studies then announce the latest development on colonialism. Or the noun *post* is a place where an activity or duty is carried out. Post+colonial then refers to the place, people, or cultural arena where colonial activity or duties are carried out... [P]ost + anything in academic jargon signifies that things

are much more complicated than previously thought. At the very least, post + colonial refers to our complicity in empire, in our own colonization, and in that of others. It refers to how the categories colonizer and colonized are no longer distinct. (p. 8)

To describe segregated spaces in school as the postcolonial ghetto requires a discussion of how ghetto colonialism connects to other forms of colonization within the larger project of empire. La Paperson considers the ghetto "a specialization of the colonial cartography" (p. 21), where dislocation is its primary function. Unlike the overseas colony that served as 'imperialism's outpost," the ghetto according to La Paperson serves "as imperialism's outcast: the alley and the underground of imperial outlaw" (p. 21). Thus, while "imperial education is training for inclusion into the metropole (e.g., college-going culture, speaking standard English, embracing ableist ideologies), colonial/ghetto schooling on the other hand "is a form of management of populations in the ghetto" (p. 24). Thus, for example, "ghettoized zones in schools are those in which the rights of students are suspended and state agents are allowed free reign to implement any set of neocolonial educational and disciplinary tactics…violence that would never be permitted in their privileged counterparts" (p. 18).

The shift to the ghetto is not an "accident of discrimination" (La Paperson, 2010, p. 8), but rather a deliberate act of dislocation by the school system. The ghetto itself is constituted by three critical elements: (i) *walls* that serve to contain bodies; (ii) legal and civil *divestment* that ensures educational, social, and economic deprivation of those contained; and (iii) *racial marking*, where minority status is assigned to those bodies that are contained (p. 10). To this, I would also add as the fourth element, the *signifying practice of disability as lack* that is used to justify these dis-locations

I argue here that colonial/ghetto schooling is haunted by the ghost of disability. In making this argument, I am aware that I may be associating disability once again with a "deadly" status. However, the ghosts I am talking about are not dead or missing people. Rather, they represent the absent presence of *her shape* that is rendered invisible by *his hand.* My allusion draws from Avery Gordon's (1997) work on the sociology of "ghostly matters," when she writes:

If haunting describes how that which appears to be not there is often a seething presence, acting on and often meddling with taken-for-granted realities, the ghost is just a sign, or the empirical evidence if you like, that tells you a haunting is taking place… [A]nd haunting is a very particular way of knowing what has happened or is happening. Being haunted draws us affectively, sometimes against our will and always a bit magically, into the structure of feeling of a reality we come to experience, not as cold knowledge, but as a transformative recognition. (p. 7)

Gordon's description of a "haunting" is what I deploy in this chapter to explain the imbrication of disability with race, gender, and sexuality located in the postcolonial ghetto actively patrolled and administered via oppressive educational policy (in this case, the sex curriculum). Here, though disability is conspicuously absent in all discussions of the sex curriculum, the threat of "becoming disabled" haunts both the discourses of the ghetto and sexuality. Our disdain for the ghetto and its outlaw sexualities is premised on an unspoken threat of an association with disability—the one human condition that has historically justified dis-location on the grounds of a pathological biology. In fact, it is these very same pathological effects historically associated with disability that continue to haunt contemporary representations of the ghetto.

Thus, similar to how we conceive of disability as pathology, there is a sense of hopelessness that is assigned to ghetto spaces. Liberal discourses play up the pathology of a culture of poverty caused, they argue, by racial and economic isolation. This is contrasted with the place of "universal rights" that exists outside the ghetto—a space where rational and normal enlightened subjects exist. In this colonial imaginary, there exists a "pure white space" (or in this case, a "pure normative space"), somewhere outside the limits of the ghetto that now embodies all "that which is left over, the matter out of place" (p. 13). The ghetto is also imagined as a "zone of violence," with a refusal to recognize that violence occurs not because of what 'happens" in the ghetto, but rather because of what "is done" to the ghetto and its inhabitants. Such representations ignore the ways in which institutional violence is created in the ghetto in the first place. Because of its feared pathology, there is also always the move to destroy the ghetto, to always shift its inhabitants someplace else—such that it becomes a space that is always open for continuous dispersal . . . of going "nowhere for good" (p. 21).

It is not a difficult stretch to see the "alternative spaces" in public schools as serving as postcolonial ghettoes that use definitions of disability as intransigent pathology in order to allow forms of racial, class, gendered, and sexual segregation under the guise of special education and rehabilitation. In this way, disability serves as an "outlaw ontology" used to justify the exclusion of individuals on the basis of race, class, gender, and sexuality in the postcolonial ghettoes of public schooling. Claiming and/or passing as normal while maintaining a dis-stance from the "real" aberrancy of disability is amply rewarded in educational contexts. Put simply, "we" therefore, try really hard not to be like "them." For example, in the context of sex education, the discourses of morality are instrumental in assigning the following populations to the category "them": pregnant teens, LGBTQI youth, transgendered youth, disabled youth, and youth living with HIV/AIDS. These students who express themselves outside of the prescribed norms experience social and educational isolation—experiences that have devastating consequences on these students' future lives as citizens (Pillow, 2003; Thomas, 1999). Oppressively marked thus by race, class, gender, sexuality, and disability, many of these students struggle in their later years in low-paid service jobs, dependent on social welfare, and often incarcerated in the nations' prisons. It is in this context, then, that the material violence waged against those who reject the cult of normativity is apparent.

SEX CURRICULUM AS COLONIZING DISCOURSE

That the control of sexual desire was central to colonialism has been well documented by Spillers, whose work I have discussed in Chapter 1. The terrible power of this control is also evident in the epigraph by Patricia Williams at the beginning of this chapter. So absolute was the habit of his power on the (sexual) lives of his slaves that it appeared as if it was the mandate of the master to "breed her or not... [t]he choice to breed slaves in his image, to choose her mate and be that mate." It is this same habit of *his* power over sexual desire that continues to haunt contemporary discourses of sexuality in society. And nowhere is this more evident than in the sex curriculum in public education. If, as I argued in Chapter 1, (sexual) desire is a materialist construct exchanged as a commodity for profit, then the regulation of (sexual) desire, I argue, is also motivated by social, political, and economic concerns. It should therefore come as no surprise then that the task of defining, disciplining, and policing sexuality has been appropriated by one of society's most significant state apparatuses—the public school.

Sexuality in school is, therefore, a taboo subject, even though discourses of sexuality proliferate there. What can be said about sex, who can say it, and what age group is appropriate to receive this education is subject to the control of several competing ideologies as well as to the close surveillance by competing political groups such as parents/caregivers, teachers, the school management, educational policy makers, civil liberties organizations, and conservative and liberal ideologues (Allen, 2008). If and when sex is talked about in US public schools, the only pedagogical conversation that is usually legally permitted is one where the terror of desire is propagated via the proliferation of fear. Thus, the "official knowledge" of the sex curriculum is restricted to health education classes, where students learn about the biology, the methodology, and the epidemiology (sexual diseases) of intimate sexual activity (Allen, 2008; Ashcraft, 2006; Farrelly, O'Brien & Prain, 2007; Fine & McClelland, 2006; Janssen, 2009; Lamb, 2010).

Expanding the colonizing mission of differentiating between the spaces of purity and contamination according to the dictates of *his* hand, the sex education curriculum produces an "official" knowledge base committed to its project of ghetto schooling, where the surveillance and management of unruly bodies is its main function. As a result, it comes as no surprise that in her 1988 article in the *Harvard Educational Review*, Michelle Fine identified the three most pervasive discourses in the sex education curriculum that are guaranteed to generate fear, terror, and blame, and exercise the most complete control: *sexuality as violence*; *sexuality as victimization*; and *sexuality as individual morality*. More than 20 years later, little has changed. In fact, in the last few years, the predominance of abstinence-only programs to the exclusion of any other competing paradigm has reduced the sex curriculum to exhorting students to simply not do "it" (Fine & McClelland, 2006).

But sexuality is so much more than just "doing it." For example, the French philosopher Michel Foucault has asked:

> How is it that in a society like ours, sexuality is not simply a means of reproducing the species, the family, and the individual? Not simply a means to obtain pleasure and enjoyment? How has sexuality come to be considered the privileged place where our deepest "truth" is read and expressed? For that is the essential fact: since Christianity, the western world has never ceased saying: To know who you are, know what your sexuality is. (as quoted in Shildrick, 2005, p. 332)

The sex curriculum as currently taught in US public schools, however, refuses to recognize the centrality of sexuality in young people's lives, except as something they have to be taught to fear. In doing so, this sex curriculum does little to explore the social meanings of sexuality, and the implications these meanings have for the construction of student subjectivities (Fine, 1988; Fine & McClelland, 2006; Pillow, 2004). And yet, this reticence to discuss sexuality in the classroom is ironic given that sexuality is central to the everyday practices of schooling, especially those aspects of sexuality that can be easily transformed into commodities for profit. For example, important events such as the school prom, activities such as beauty walks and homecoming parades, teams such as cheerleading and the dance line, and even athletics, abound with (normative) sexual imagery, (normative) sexual expectations, and (normative) sexual behaviors that, in turn, mediate the social relationships between students. Thus, in public education, the hidden (sex) curriculum serves as both a disciplinary tool and a normative social practice that orients students to "a way of being in the world" (Fisher, 2009, p. 64)—one that ensures "the habit of his power and the absence of her choice."

Caught in the normative mantra of emphasizing the presence of sexual risk, while ensuring the absence of sexual desire (Fine & McClelland, 2006), the key elements of sex education as articulated via Public Law 104–193 teach that

- abstinence from sexual activity outside of marriage is the expected standard for all school-age children;
- sexual activity outside the context of marriage is likely to have harmful psychological and physical effects; and
- a mutually faithful monogamous relationship in the context of marriage is the expected standard of human sexual activity (Wiley & Terlosky, 2000, p. 79).

The oft-repeated directive in the above law permits sexual activity to occur only within the narrow purview of heterosexual marriage—a life choice that is assumed will sustain the social, emotional, and moral (sexual) health of all students. Such a directive is not based on scientific/psychological/medical facts. Rather, the basis of these directives lies in nonscientific anecdotal research (Wiley & Terlosky, 2000) mired in ideologies of sexuality and morality that reflect the perceptions of adults' needs and interests rather than those of students (Allen, 2008). Moreover these directives have their historical roots in the discussion in Chapter 1 in the reproduction of oppressive social relations mediated by race, class, gender, and disability. In stark contrast, research conducted by several scholars on students' perceptions of the sex curriculum demonstrated that students often positioned themselves as sexual subjects who are legitimately sexual, instead of preferably nonsexual (Allen, 2008; Ashcraft, 2006; Fine, 1988; Fine & McClelland, 2006; Fisher, 2009; Pillow, 2004; Trimble, 2009). Here, once again, notwithstanding *his heavy hand*, it is possible to discern the faint outlines of *her shape* claiming a determined presence in resistance to the habit of his power.

Fine and McClelland (2006), Fisher (2009), and Pillow (2004) demonstrate in their research how school policies on student sexual activity overwhelmingly discriminate against poor, working-class, female, disabled, black, Latino, and LGBTQI youth, where a form of "sexual vigilantism" is unleashed that defines their sexuality as corrupt and labels them as students who are unsalvageable, reminiscent of another haunting. Additionally, gender stereotypes abound within the sex curriculum, where young women are referred to as victims, even while placing complete responsibility on them for birth control, and where young men are forced to bow to the pressure of acting uncontrollably sexual (Fine, 1988; Fine & McClelland, 2006). It is here then that the practices of colonial/ghetto schooling become painfully evident.

But, perhaps, most dangerous is the "active silence" that is present in the sex curriculum—the hush that occurs when the very persons charged with protecting youth "not only violate but also coerce" their desires into silence (Fisher, 2009, p. 62). Thus, in order to expose the violence of "active silence" in public education, I advocate a political "outing" of several coercive discourses of normalization within the sex curriculum. "Outing" these normative discourses of sexuality is critical, because these discourses not only structure the way we think, but also constitute our subjectivities (Allen, 2008). Additionally, "outing" the spurious commitment of educational discourses to a language of effectiveness exposes how such measures effectively cloak important power dynamics and naturalize strategies for approaching teen sexuality that often perpetuate unjust social conditions (Ashcraft, 2006, p. 2149). In the sex curriculum, in particular, the "active silence" around "agency, initiation, and subjectivity" (Fine & McClelland, 2006, p. 86), I argue, represents the desperate attempt to carefully patrol the borders in a shameful pretence of keeping those circumscribed within those borders safe.

Outings abound in educational contexts where the most threatening outings revolve around sexual subjectivities. While an "outing" may culminate in one's absolute exclusion from the educational context (a teacher being fired from her job for being lesbian), another less extreme, but nevertheless damaging, outcome may cause one to be labeled, pathologized, and/or even more painfully rehabilitated. And much of this often takes place (despite the rhetoric of inclusion) in public education under the guise of efficiently managing difference. I, therefore, turn the tables on public education in order to "out" the practices and ideologies within the sex curriculum that label, pathologize, rehabilitate, and ultimately exclude those subjectivities that resist the dominant discourses of heteronormativity. More specifically, this "outing" of exclusion in the sex curriculum necessitates the foregrounding of that which is invisible and un-sayable. This implies that we ask questions of the sex curriculum that go beyond the narrow focus on effectiveness (meaning how effective sex education is to prevent teen pregnancy), to address how the cultural directives embedded in official policies position teachers and students within schools, and how the valuing of certain subjectivities rather than others might impact students' social and academic well-being in schools and in society at large (Fine & McClelland, 2006; Trimble, 2009; Wiley & Terlosky, 2000).

It is through "outing" these "active silences" that it is also possible to "out" the exclusion that occurs under the aegis of the sex curriculum. For example, in her 1988 article aptly subtitled "The Missing Discourse of Desire," Michelle Fine identified "the authorized suppression of a discourse of female desire" in the sex curriculum (p.30). Fine insists, however, that this "official" suppression is ineffective in closing down "all" sexual expression. Instead, Fine describes how young female students articulate through an "erotic" discourse their opposition to the "active silence" that allows only the narrative of female victimization to prevail. This narrative of female victimization supports heteronormativity, which laughably recognizes only adult married women as capable of consent, and in doing so, constitutes all other females as potential victims who are denied sexual subjectivity. Fine (1988) explains:

> The ambivalence facing female heterosexuality places the victim and subject in opposition and derogates all women who represent female sexual subjectivities outside of marriage—prostitutes, lesbians, single mothers, women involved with multiple partners, and particularly Black single mothers... "Protected" from this derogation, the typical adolescent woman, as represented in the sex education curricula, is without any sexual subjectivity. The discourse of victimization not only obscures the derogation, it also transforms socially distributed anxieties about female sexuality into acceptable, and even protective talk. (p. 42)

At the same time, while attempting to suppress the discourse of (black) female desire, one of the most blatant contradictions in the abstinence-only sex curriculum is that, while, on the one hand, young women are pathologized for refusing to maintain a stoic silence around sex, the actual abstinence-only curriculum is engaged in "explicit talk about sex, sexual immorality, and lewdness" (Pillow, 2004, p. 175). Pillow, using a Foucaultian analysis, names this practice "a continued incitement to discourse" (p. 175). Put simply, "incitement to discourse" can be described as the secret that one is endlessly urged to speak of in order that the state can better regulate and contain it. In the specific context of teen pregnancy, Pillow's (2004) book *Unfit Subjects: Educational Policy and the Teen Mother* describes in great detail the proliferation of discourses of alarm (sex is dangerous/dirty); discourses of heteronormativity (reassertion of traditional gender roles in heterosexual marriage); and discourses of control (Norplant implants) that surround teen sexuality and teen pregnancy. Thus, this incitement to discourse constructs teen mothers as "bad" girls through a variety of "stigma stories" that make both the sexually active teen girl as well as the teen mother hypervisible to the public eye. Moreover, the process of pathologizing these young women rests on overtly sexualized images of pregnant girls that inspire both visual consumption and moral condemnation, as well as rely on the trope of disability. To illustrate this argument, Pillow uses feminist scholar Nancy Lesko's description of a 1985 *Time* magazine cover story of teen pregnancy:

> The image of a young girl with swollen belly dominates the discourse of teen pregnancy... She stands sideways, to accentuate her fully pregnant, fully sexual body. Her ripe body is juxtaposed with her child's face, which

communicates sadness, pessimism, and confusion. Her face forecasts uncertainty—the apparent consequences of irresponsible sexuality. This image signals "disorder" or "alarm": a child having a child, a young woman too soon sexual, a spectacle, a grotesqueness. (as quoted in Pillow, 2004, p. 175)

In a similar fashion, Lamb (2010), too, describes the proliferation of discourses of LGBTQI youth that represent them as socially and sexually maladjusted to mainstream life. With the insistence on the normativity of heterosexual relationships culminating in heterosexual marriage in the abstinence-only curriculum, LGBTQI youth are often excluded from the curriculum, except to describe them as lacking "high personal standards and strong character" because they are portrayed as expressing their desires in ways for which their bodies "were not designed" (p. 63). By insisting that sex should occur only within marriage, the only options available to these youth are either to remain celibate or to participate in heterosexual marriage, both of which are incompatible to their desires (p. 64). Even the more liberal discourses of sexuality portray LGBTQI youth as a social category of risk—at risk of suicide, discrimination, low self-esteem, and HIV/AIDS (Fisher, 2009, p. 65), even though being labeled "at-risk" is clearly an outcome of the discourses of containment that abound in the sex curriculum. Adding to all this is a further incitement to discourse regarding HIV/AIDS in the curriculum, which reflects societal fears about homosexuality, disease, and governmental intrusion into one's private life (Vander Schee & Baez, 2009).

Similarly, in the context of pregnant teens, Pillow (2004) reports that educational policy, in its pathetic attempts to offer support services to low-income pregnant teens of color, draws on the problematic discourse of "pregnancy as disability" (p. 103) to justify these special services. Pillow (2004) and Fine and McClelland (2006) report that school districts operating under this disability model overwhelmingly remove African American and Latina teen mothers as well as low-income white teen mothers to separate special school facilities. In this context then, the sex curriculum excludes pathologized subjectivities not only via the ideological dictates of heteronormativity, but also via the actual spatial dis-location of these Other students from the normative mainstream.

Broadly speaking then, the sex curriculum with its commitments to heteronormativity locates several bodies outside the realm of acceptable sexual subjectivities. Moreover, even when discourses of overt sexuality are readily deployed in educational contexts (e.g., school prom, the beauty walk, cheerleading, dance line, etc.), heteronormative discourses regulate which students can participate in the celebration of their sexual subjectivities. Those bodies that buck the normative sexual aesthetic (black/brown bodies, gay/

lesbian/transsexual/intersex bodies, disabled bodies, poor bodies, etc.) are quite simply segregated even in presumably inclusive settings. Thus, I argue here that the "outing" of the heteronormative discourses of desire in the sex curriculum, in turn, "out" practices of dis-location in the educational ghetto.

Perhaps most dangerous is how the sex curriculum exploits societal fears about "pandemic" diseases such as HIV/AIDS to legitimize state intrusion into the intimate lives of students. For example, Vander Schee and Baez (2009) describe how liberal and neoliberal policies utilize the sex curriculum to discipline students into embracing heteronormative sexual subjectivities through HIV/AIDS education. Using the New York City Department of Education HIV/AIDS curriculum that was implemented in December, 2005, Vander Schee and Baez describe how this curriculum utilized medical discourses such as "risk-factor epidemiology and psychosocial models of behavioral change" (p. 36) to support neoliberal economic and sociopolitical rationalities that urge responsible individuals to control their health for not only their own sake but also for the socioeconomic good of the nation. Vander Schee and Baez explain how medical language that carries the authority of professional expertise and appears to exist outside of politics is particularly productive for enacting state practices, because by constructing "science" and "chastity" as "unquestionable points of truth," sexual health becomes a value essential to determining the boundaries between "good" and "bad" as well as "normal" and "abnormal" health-related behaviors (p. 41). They, therefore, argue that the (sex) curriculum—by marrying medical knowledge and moral values—places constructs such as "normal," "risk," "science," and "health" beyond political critique and accountability, and in doing so is effective in normalizing the (school) population and making them more amenable to social administration (p. 43).

Because HIV/AIDS education uses language that is burdened by heavy moral baggage, HIV/AIDS is, therefore, predisposed to be the disease of "otherness" and "immorality" (Erevelles, 2006). Already mired in discourses of stigma because of its historical association with male homosexuals and intravenous drug users, who are also disproportionately African American and Hispanic, the discourse on HIV/AIDS separates the in-groups from out-groups. Those whose infection has resulted from "deviant" behaviors are contrasted with those whose infection has resulted from circumstances beyond their control (e.g., infants, hemophiliacs, and those who have received blood transfusions), thereby setting up a moral hierarchy of the deserving and "non-deserving victims" of this condition (Erevelles, 2006). McRuer (2002) quotes Paula Treichler when he argues that people living with HIV/AIDS face not only "an epidemic of transmissible disease," but also an "epidemic of signification" (p. 221). Here, preexisting racist, homophobic, sexist, and ableist fantasies are reinvigorated in and through the AIDS crises, especially by those who imagine themselves as "immune" from the epidemic.

Vander Schee and Baez also point out that the sheer brilliance of neoliberal curriculum lies in the strategic maneuvering by which subjects are controlled through their freedom—a masterful move of postcolonial politics. Using Michel Foucault's definition of the verb "to govern," meaning "to structure the possible field of action of others" (as quoted in Vander Schee & Baez, 2009, p. 35), they describe how "modern forms of government individualize in such a way that subjects understand their actions as based in autonomous choice and freedom to act" (p. 35). Because the school was deemed a crucial site for propagating governmental rationalities associated with sexuality, generally, and HIV/AIDS, specifically, the sex curriculum has a dual mission. On the one hand it supports the liberal mantra of the autonomy of individual choice, while on the other hand it privileges an authoritarianism that molds the autonomous subject according to predetermined developmental norms and educational needs. Broadly speaking then, the sex curriculum interpellates students into the politics of "intimate citizenship" (Allen cited in Trimble, 2009, p. 57), where students are exhorted to exhibit control over one's body, feelings, relationships, and intimacies, etc., and make socially grounded choices about their sexual identities. Thus, the sex curriculum serves as "a principle and a tool of normalization" (Janssen, 2009, p. 2), where the act of exclusion is portrayed as an inclusive practice that is freely chosen by responsible sexual citizens who seem to patrol on their own volition "the parameters of personhood" (Shildrick, 2005, p. 333).

IMPERIALISM'S OUTCASTS: (NON)CONVERSATIONS ABOUT DISABILITY AND SEXUALITY

If the sex curriculum serves as "a principle and a tool of normalization," then students with significant physical and cognitive disabilities are quite "naturally" excluded from its authoritative heteronormative domain. The grounds to justify this exclusion are really quite simple. So committed are the ideologies of "proper" sexuality to stringent standards of normativity that those bodies who are deemed unable to meet these standards are also perceived as not having any sexuality at all (Kafer, 2003; Shakespeare, 1999; Shildrick, 2005; Tepper, 2000). In fact, students with physical and/or cognitive disabilities are actively excluded from even participating in the sex curriculum in inclusive settings, where paternalistic professionals draw on the rhetoric of protection to deny these students choice and control in their sexual lives (Erevelles & Mutua, 2005; Tepper, 2000). Moreover, the sex curriculum is already enmeshed in the discourses of "moralism, law, stigma, shame, violence, and isolation" (Sherry, 2004, p. 775)—discourses that are so easily applied to disabled people such that any expression of their sexuality is regarded as "inherently kinky, bizarre and exotic" (Kafer, 2003, p. 85). Thus, steeped in the ideologies of normalization, perversion, victimization, and protection, the sexuality of disabled people "is denied loudly and repeatedly, not silently" (Kafer, 2003, p. 85) in the sex curriculum.

These ableist assumptions about sexuality mirror similar myths applied to queer subjects, where discourses of contagion, infection, contamination, unnaturalness, and perversion abound (Sherry, 2004; Thompson, 2007). Such assumptions contradict the other overwhelming assumption of asexuality that is applied especially to people with cognitive disabilities. Thus, while on the one hand, the mere articulation of their sexuality is associated with sexual deviance, excess, and aberration, on the other hand, people with cognitive disabilities are "taken as being asexual, or a third gender" (Shakespeare, 1999, p. 55), where notions of asexuality are wedded to immutable child-like innocence at best or outright incompetence and incapability to "really" understand what sexuality means at worst (Thompson, 2007). Thus, caught between a rock and a hard place, the "official" discourse regarding the sexuality of young adults with cognitive disabilities, in particular, rejects all notions of complexity regarding their gender and sexual identities.

Erevelles and Mutua (2005) illustrate one such example of how the "official" discourse of inclusive settings casts many disabled adolescents/young adults into gender/sexual passive positions as recipients of assistance and consumers of help. In a case study of Sue Ellen, a 19–year-old woman with Down syndrome, we describe how adolescence propels disabled young people into a temporal space where physiological transformations (e.g., breasts, menstrual periods, erections, etc.) can no longer sustain dominant constructions of the disabled adult as an asexual perpetual child. Sue Ellen's calm but insistent acknowledgement of her sexual desires, and her assertion that she intends to realize these desires in a sexual relationship with her boyfriend, is initially disconcerting to her mother, Martha, who tries to play off the relationship as purely platonic. Sue Ellen on the other hand is hell-bent on making known to her mother her (sexual) desire to kiss Billie Joe, and later on to marry and have children with him. Her disclosures regarding her sexual future, notwithstanding the traditional heteronormative narrative, forces her mother, Martha, to rethink her own assumptions regarding her daughter as a sexual being—not a girl any longer but a woman in her own right.

Rejecting the "official" discourse, Sue Ellen's articulation of the "erotic" discourse is smothered under an "active silence" because of the real fear that parents with disabled girls have regarding sexuality in a violent and sometimes misogynist world. For young women with developmental disabilities, sexuality is viewed more as a problem rather than as an affirming part of human life (Sweeney, 2007). Thus, while school personnel, parents, and other caregivers may recognize the importance of relationships and sexual roles of young adults with cognitive disabilities, the primary focus of the sex curriculum (if even offered to these students) is to prevent sexual abuse (Addlakha, 2007; Aunos & Feldman, 2002; Dukes & McGuire; 2009), much of which hinges on the critical question of what constitutes valid consent to have sex. Because valid consent to have sex depends on an access to knowledge and an understanding of both sexuality-related decisions and the different aspects of sexual expression, many caregivers worry that cognitive disabilities of young disabled adults may interfere with their ability to make responsible decisions regarding their sexuality (Dukes & McGuire, 2009). In the case of Sue Ellen, the traditional special education program she graduated from did not offer her any knowledge to make these critical decisions. And thus, just like the sex curriculum offered to nondisabled students, the nonconversation regarding sexual desire, sexual knowledge, and sexual relationships become another dangerous exclusion in the school curriculum.

According to Michael Tepper (2005), students with disabilities learn that they are disabled even before they learn to see themselves as sexual people. He argues that sex educators need to be aware of the medical aspects of disability, the range of abilities within individuals, and their psychosocial development. In another study located in Turkey, Isler et al. (2009) argue that disabled adolescents are socially isolated, and therefore have fewer opportunities to interact and learn from their peers. They also note that many of these adolescents lacked basic biological information about their bodies. Sullivan and Caterino (2008) also report that in the case of adolescents labeled as having autism spectrum disorders, those who were denied access to sex education were more likely to masturbate under inappropriate circumstances, while those who had access to some form of sex education were likely to engage in more person-oriented sexual behaviors in appropriate contexts. Thus, it would appear that school systems seem hell-bent on producing a sex curriculum that excludes the central issues that would promote healthy sexual behaviors. Moreover, since educational structures neither view disabled students as sexual nor support their sexual activity, the exclusion of disability issues in the sex curriculum actively contributes to the problem that some disability scholars have dubbed "lack of sex access" (Shuttleworth & Mona, 2002).

This "lack of sex access" is often justified under the guise of protecting girls and women with disabilities from sexual abuse, rape, and other forms of sexual violence. In a study by Hassouneh-Phillips and McNeff (2003), it was noted that 72 percent of women with physical disabilities have been abused by an intimate partner, family member, caregiver, health care provider, or other service provider. Low sexual esteem (one's sense of self as a sexual being) was seen as one of the major factors contributing to the vulnerability of disabled women to sexual abuse. This is because female sexuality in medical rehabilitation is limited to discussions on menstruation and the ability to conceive and give birth. Steeped in heteronormativity, these discourses assume that women are passive subjects, that there is a "usual" position for heterosexual intercourse, and that the ability to participate in sexual activities is measured by the ability to perform and not by the ability to feel. Tepper et al. (2001) observed that, as a result, many disabled women were mistrusting of their own bodies' ability to give pleasure to others and to themselves. They, therefore, often faced "cognitive genital disassociation"— the act of shutting down and shutting out sexuality by assuming that sexual pleasure is no longer possible.

Further, because the (hetero)sexuality of disabled people is always already deviant, any proclivity of disabled people for queer practices and desires only magnifies that deviance (Kafer, 2003). Since dominant ideologies deem disabled women as incapable of finding male partners, it is assumed that their turn to lesbianism is often as a last resort. Moreover, Kafer points out that just like with the nondisabled population, children and adults with disabilities, who live with their families, may be prevented from even discussing their (same) sex desires with their parents and siblings. Even for those disabled adults living out in the community, the fear of coming out is still present because they are afraid that their personal assistants may quit on them. Here again, the "active silence," propagated by heteronormative discourses of sexuality, seeks to make even the smallest possibility of queer crip desire laughable. For example, Lofgren-Martenson (2009) reports the response of one caregiver in a short-term home for young adults with cognitive disabilities:

> There are no people here with the usual sexuality...That means that there can't be any homosexuals, right? (Laughter). In any case not in the sense of "sex". Maybe a guy will be really really close friends with a boy rather than a girl...that is possible...no, I have a real hard time imagining two fags here at the day center. (p. 23)

PROSTHETIC (EDUCATIONAL) POLICIES AND THE POLITICS OF DIS-LOCATION

The techno-rationality of educational policies would appear very much at odds with my illusory ruminations about hauntings. This is because, firmly rooted in the here and now of the present, these techno-rationalist discourses embrace the reassuring certainty of standardized tests, the impersonal surveillance of docile bodies, and the placid anticipation of predetermined outcomes. But, there are certain problems with this façade of ahistorical objectivity. A certain capriciousness that haunts its stolid demeanor. Haunting these policy discourses is the existence of an absent presence. There are no bodies recognized here. Just test statistics. Research-based outcomes. A cornucopia of lifeless data. In the stolid precision of statistical measurement and evidence-based research, the introduction of bodies to the discussion is a dangerous and messy act. Bodies have a history. Bodies transform in context. Bodies are mobile. Bodies are unpredictable. Bodies are not always compliant.

In the essay, "Bodies Are Dangerous," Wanda Pillow (2003) marries French philosopher Foucault's work on genealogy with feminist critical policy analysis to interrupt the rationalist methodologies of educational policy analysis so as to (i) focus on how discourses of power influence how bodies (e.g., teen mothers-to-be) are named, defined, and experienced within the politics of schooling; (ii) analyze the unconscious rules of the discourses of power; and (iii) foreground the historical conditions within which these discourses of power are embodied in social practices. Pillow's analysis of teen pregnancy enables the "asking [of] what has not been questioned;... [the] telling of what is unspoken and unspeakable, creating spaces for multiple subjectivities, theories and practices to operate" (p. 155). In short, Pillow's analysis foregrounds how educational policy research is haunted by the "ghosts" of its exclusionary practices—"the habit of his power" as represented in the naturalized violence meted out against bodies considered "deviant"/ "different"/"dangerous," and segregated in "special educational programs" that separate these bodies from the general population. Such policy practices are not unique to pregnant teens, but are, in fact, routinely experienced by those bodies already oppressively marked by race, class, gender, ability, and sexuality (e.g., African American males attending inner-city schools, students with severe disabilities, students with cognitive disabilities, and LGBTQI youth) who are also reproduced, represented, regulated, and restrained in similar ways (Dunbar, 2001; Noguera, 1995; Watts & Erevelles, 2004).

At the same time, Pillow's analysis is limited by its poststructural/ Foucaultian emphasis on local/specific contexts, and in doing so fails to map the historical continuities and discontinuities that exist between seemingly different/unconnected educational policies that produce similar effects on disenfranchised/marginalized groups in school contexts. It is for these reasons that I have utilized a materialist disability studies perspective to deconstruct the normative constructs supported by most educational policies, and to map the interconnections that separate and yet, at the same time, interconnect these different marginalized student bodies to each other.

A materialist disability studies perspective describes how disability, both as an ideological and materialist construct, is mutually constitutive of race, gender, and sexual orientation within the exploitative conditions of transnational capitalism (Erevelles, 2000).

During her research on teen pregnancy, Wanda Pillow (2003) recollects a school administrator's comment that "bodies are dangerous" (p. 145). According to Pillow, paying attention to bodies in educational contexts seems taboo, because bodies "remain uncontrollable in many ways, receptive to and disruptive of power" (p. 146). This reality is contrary to traditional assumptions of the body being "a fixed system of muscle, bone, nerves, and organs...amenable to scientific examination...a site of established fact" (Kirk qtd in McWilliam & Taylor 1996, p. 17). Such logic supports the distinction between the biological (nature) and the social (nurture) bases of difference, based on the assumption that those differences associated with the biological body are, in fact, inalienable and therefore inviolable. In educational contexts, this translates into seeing as educationally salvageable only those dis-abled students whose differences are socially based. Education for all other bodies whose dis-ability is seen to be biological is considered a futile venture.

Michel Foucault (1977), in his book *Discipline and Punish*, has drawn analogies between the birth of the prison and the social organization of schooling in the eighteenth century. According to Foucault, institutions such as schools regarded the student body as both "an object and target of power," and utilized various technologies of discipline and punishment so as to make the body completely docile. Those whose bodies challenged the rigidity of this discipline and proved to be "unruly bodies" (Erevelles, 2000) were subjected to the "ceremony of punishment"—"an act of terror" (Foucault, 1977, p. 54) that was utilized to make everyone aware of the unrestrained presence of disciplinary power in the school. In this way, schools, just like the prison/asylum, became very effective in their attempts to regiment, control, and discipline those who came to be known as "social outcasts of education" (Noguera, 1995, p. 194). In the context of accountability, "the social outcasts" are clearly those students whose biology marks them as unsalvageable.

Student populations who are designated as social outcasts of education are not just disabled students, but also include nondisabled students of color, who are labeled "at-risk"; pregnant teens, especially those who are girls of color from low-income neighborhoods; students who exhibit low English proficiency, who are also seen to skew performance scores, and are often excluded from these evaluations; and some LGBTQI students, who are deemed emotionally unstable and socially isolated. Unfortunately, however, theorists of race, class, gender, and sexual orientation, rather than seeing some commonality with disability, have, instead, actively sought to distance themselves from disability, fearing that associating with disability will imply that their difference would equate with a biological deficit—an association they assume will be dangerous. As a result, disabled students are often left out in the cold.

However, disability is an intimate part of contemporary educational discourses. This is because educational discourses shore up their adherence to normativity by constructing disability as the very antithesis of "regular" educational practice, and therefore a condition that must be either rejected, avoided, and (if need be) excluded. However, because difference (on the basis of race, class, gender, sexual orientation, and disability) is also an integral part of public education in a democratic society, educational practices support difference if and only if difference can be controlled, disguised, and/or rendered invisible—in other words if difference is "prostheticized."

Mitchell & Snyder (2000) describe the prosthesis as a device that accomplishes the illusion of enabling an individual to fit in, and de-emphasizes his or her differences so that she or he can return to a state of imagined normativity. In other words, in most educational contexts, students are required to deploy "prosthetic practices" that enable them to "pass" by hiding their dis-ability. Failure to do so results in punishment, segregation, and/or expulsion. As a result, disability becomes the organizing logic utilized by the educational bureaucracy as the "master trope of disqualification" (Mitchell & Snyder, 2000, p. 3) to legitimate exclusionary and oppressive practices meted out against students marked by race, class, gender, ethnicity, and sexual difference.

Mitchell and Snyder (2000) describe comparable practices within the literary domain as "narrative prosthesis"—a concept that they argue "situates the experience and representational life of disability upon the ironic grounding on an unsteady rhetorical stance [i.e. the prosthesis]" (p. 6). Shifting from the literary domain to the educational, I argue that "prosthetic educational policies" foreground the pervasiveness of disability as the central device in the organization of social difference in narratives of public education that are also mired in a similar uncertain ambiguity.

By its very nature, a prosthesis is specific to an individual, and therefore demands individual intervention. Similarly, the primary focus of educational policy is the individual student rather than society, and those who fail to conform to these normalizing imperatives face exclusion and the use of force. Linda Graham (2007), however, foregrounds a slight modification to this practice of exclusion. Citing Foucault, she explains that "it is not [really] exclusion but quarantine. It is not a question of driving out individuals but rather establishing and fixing them, of giving them their own place, of assigning places and of defining presences... Not rejection but inclusion"

(p. 201). Thus, rather than cutting loose the bodies that resist normalization, educational policy seeks to "capture, sort, spatialize and rehabilitate individual school children (Graham, 2007, p. 203) in alternative school programs that resemble the clinic, the prison, and/or the ghetto. Graham (2007) explains:

> Whilst the exclusions appear as a quest for greater inclusion, this results in an illusory interiority; an ever more strange inclusion where the maintenance of notions relating to normal and mainstream ensure that certain children exist as the *included* Other. This results in an uncontested naturalized domain at center, offering up particular individuals to the full force of the gaze whilst leaving others in the relative but contingent safety of the shade. (pp. 210–211)

Notwithstanding the rather dismal landscape shaped by *the habit of his power* and *the absence of her shape*, disabled scholars/activists have actively challenged heteronormative discourses of sexuality in the transgressive political act of "coming out crip." In doing so, they have celebrated their sexuality, while at the same time they have rejected the rigid requirements of heteronormativity. However, the hegemony of heteronormative discourses of sexuality has made this task especially difficult, because the stringent standards of what is conceived as sexually desirable are presented as predetermined, naturalized truth forms. As a result, in the rigid hierarchy of sexual desirability, people who do not fit the marketed profile such as those who are older, larger, darker, gayer, and mentally or physically disabled are constituted as sexually undesirable (Tepper, 2000). Recognizing this dismal context, disabled scholar Tom Shakespeare has written that "the challenge for disabled people is not HOW to do it but WHO to do it with" (as quoted in Sherry, 2004, p. 773).

In its casual acceptance of the sexual undesirability of disabled people as indisputable fact, public education supports a sex curriculum (if it has one at all) that starts with the assumption that disabled students have low sexual self-esteem, which makes them vulnerable to sexual abuse and teen pregnancy. In this normative context, sexual desirability is conceived of as an individual problem even by disabled people and not as a political construct, such that it is only very recently that sexual access has become a critical-agenda item in disability activism. Thus, for example, disabled sex scholar Barbara Waxman-Fiduccia asks:

> Why hasn't our movement politicized our sexual oppression as we do transportation and attendant services?... [B]ecause we are afraid that we are ultimately to blame for not getting laid; that it is somehow a personal inferiority. And in the majority culture this secret is a source of personal embarrassment

rather than a source of communal rage against the sexual culture itself. (as quoted in Tepper, 2000, p. 284)

However, the new generation of disabled scholars and activists has refused the heteronormative sexual narrative of self-blame to write an alternative script that foregrounds the politics of crip sexuality. They have pointed out that the dominant sexual narrative is one of exclusion that denies sexual access to disabled people in one of the most intimate and critical aspects of their lives (Stevens, February, 2010). Moreover, they have argued that the mere articulation of one's sexuality is an intensely political act that links up with other oppressive practices. Thus, for example, cripsex scholar/activist Bethany Stevens, in her blog "Crip Confessions," writes:

> Bodiosexual justice is a neologism...that is meant to convey how our trans and disabled bodies are similarly stigmatized, how this stigma impacts our sexual health, and how our oppressions stem from similar sources thus encouraging us to work together to further embodied justice...[H]ow queer bodies—those deemed "Others" through the social construction of the imagined normate, including aging, poor, fat, raced, trans bodies, and disabled bodies etc.—are often denigrated through interlocking systems of structural and conceptual oppressions. (Stevens, February 2010)

By locating the issue of sexuality squarely within the context of oppressive practices and structures, Stevens's argument forces a more political narrative of sexuality rife with pity and paternalism. For disabled young adults and disabled girls and women, in particular, the central focus of the sex curriculum in inclusive education continues to propagate fear—the fear of sexual abuse, the fear of sexual violence, and most terrifyingly, the fear of reproduction. In fact, the sex curriculum's almost singular focus on preventing disabled bodies from reproducing themselves echoes in many ways the eugenic-like policies of the earlier century. This imperative to control the reproductive capacity of disabled people is so rampant that it occurs not in dark and dangerous laboratories, but in the casual medical advice gynecologists offer their disabled patients. This is well illustrated in a poem "At the Gynecologist" by Petra Kuppers and Neil Marcus (2008), in their book *Cripple Poetics: A Love Story:*

> You might not want children because
> issues in his family
> gene dances
> he said, our chirpy gynecologist,
> looking straight at me, slant at my lover
> instruments out

Love him, but not children like him?
White coat atoms settle into their dance:
dream plane, wish bone, Galton's galvanized knowledge
eugenic technology that flies off our bodies' awkward edges
erasure of the spastic tender
touch, deliberate, the vaginal membrane. (pp. 100–101)

Here, Kuppers and Marcus, both disabled artists, capture in exquisite lyr-
icism how the violence of eugenics interwoven in the light-hearted medical advice of their gynecologist produces much more potent damage than
merely advising against pregnancy. Kuppers and Marcus, instead, show us
that such warnings not only cast disabled people as undesirable, both sexually and otherwise (*Love him, but not children like him?*), but also attempt to
force disabled people to accept the very impossibility of sexual desire (*erasure
of the spastic tender touch, deliberate*).

There have been several counterdiscourses to this all-pervasive narrative
that refuses the erasure of her shape. I found one such narrative (among
many) on the webzine *Bent: A Journal of Crip Gay Voices,* where one of the
authors, Julio Moreno, writes:

> I want to demolish the belief system that insists crips are sexless, that our dif-
> ferently-shaped or oddly functioning bodies are repulsive. I reject the notion
> that we are powerless, ugly, needy, dependent... I also want to talk about how
> our bodies can become vehicles for sexual satisfaction. I want to talk about
> how my stump, or your spinal injury, or someone else's muscle spasms can
> become tools for pleasure, loci of intense delight. I want to explore how the
> very texture of difference can be exciting. Visualize your hand or your tongue
> exploring a crip body, its unexpected curves, unusual shapes, the absence of an
> arm or a leg offering intensities a conventional body cannot provide, the lack
> of sight or hearing transforming the remaining senses. (2002, November)

Like Kuppers and Marcus, Moreno rewrites a script that depicts disability
not only as sexually desirable but also as one that expands normative notions
of sexual pleasure and sexual eroticism—both of which have rarely been
associated with disabled bodies. It is for this reason that Shakespeare (1999)
points out, "Non-disabled men have things to learn from disabled men, and
could profitably share insights into gender relations, sexuality, and particularly issues of physicality and the body" (p.63). In fact, the complexities of
the disabled body allow for the freedom to reinvent sexuality in innovative
and pleasurable ways. This sentiment was also echoed by a disabled lesbian
interviewee in an article by O'Toole (2000):

> Aw yeah but what about things like masturbation, self satisfaction, finding
> out about different sexual options with women? Doing things that please

oneself without following the rules. That is, don't we REALLY in some ways get a better deal than so many straight, narrow and sheltered women married to men? (p. 218)

However, even when the disability community loudly celebrates disability as desire, dominant discourses, even in inclusive settings, continue to paint this as deviant. This is especially true for young girls and women with cognitive disabilities, who, as I described earlier, are perceived as perpetually childlike or as nymphomaniacs perpetually hungry for sex. These were the exact traits attributed to the young woman with cognitive disabilities who was raped in Glen Ridge in New Jersey in 1993 by a group of male athletes. The young men took her to a nearby house, told her to undress, and performed various sexual acts on her that included the insertion of a fungo bat, a broom handle, and a stick into her vagina (Block, 2000). Block (2000) writes that in the criminal trial, the defense attempted to prove that the young woman "craved sex," and was "aggressive in her attitude and approach toward boys" (as quoted in Block, 2000, p. 248). And even the prosecutor participated in her dehumanization in the trial by using stereotypes of people with cognitive disabilities as being unable to say "no," and as being inadequately protected from sex. The real danger is that positions such as these cloud the discourse on sexuality in inclusive education, such that rather than exploring and enabling young adults with cognitive disabilities to negotiate their sexual relationships in meaningful and satisfying ways, the only discourse allowed to remain unquestioned is one of sexual denial under the guise of protection.

However, notwithstanding these dominant narratives, disability scholars and activists continue to do the hard but exciting work of "coming out [as sexy] crip." Even in the midst of denial, stereotypes, silencing, and sterilization, there are loud whispers of what Stevens (forthcoming) calls "a Cripsex Revolution." One such example, Stevens describes, is the performance art collective *Sins Invalid*, which provides "an unashamed claim to beauty in the face of invisibility." It would be a shame if public education ignored these radical voices. Put quite simply, a "severely disabled" position in public education would pay close attention to the voices of disabled young adults in the articulation of their sexuality. As disability studies scholar, Alison Kafer (2003) writes:

> It is in imagining the stories disabled queers might tell each other about intimacy, touch, desire, and identity that... provides inspiration, guidance, and ground for thinking. What are the possibilities—for intimacy, for relationships, for politics—privileges, to tell our stories? Possibilities that cannot be known in advance, that cannot be restricted to particular bodily norms, that cannot be limited to certain desires. (p. 85).

It is in the quiet insistence of this Cripsex Revolution that possibilities are opened up for "finding the shape described by her absence in all of this" (Williams, 1991, p. 19).

HER SHAPE/HIS HAND: TOWARD A
MATERIALITY OF (CRIP) SEX/DESIRE

Thus, notwithstanding the "the habit of his power," "her shape" persists as a ghostly presence that refuses to materialize into nothingness. It is her persistence that is to be celebrated here—a persistence honed by historical struggles that have desperately resisted complete erasure. But there is no romance in this resistance. As I have shown in both historical (slavery) and contemporary (sex curriculum) contexts, the resistance to erasure comes at a great cost. Moreover, these acts of resistance are not grand acts of heroic struggle but can be fleetingly glimpsed in the mundane routines of every-day life. As La Paperson (2010) reminds us, "Daily lives preoccupied with subsistence are radical. They contain forms of solidarity, of space and time fragmentation, and of strategic resource acquisition that persist somewhat autonomously from the workings of power" (p 8). Focussing therefore on the radicality of "[d]aily lives preoccupied with subsistence," I argue that a transformative politic that seeks to find her shape amidst all this absence, necessitates that we move from the compelling focus on ideological and disciplinary discourses of sexuality to foreground the material conditions that enable transgressive sexual politics. In other words, what material conditions would enable the presence of her shape in the sex curriculum that would celebrate different/transgressive sexual subjectivities?

To do so, I return to Fine and McClelland's (2006) essay where they draw on a concept they "call thick desire. By thick desire, they mean that "people are entitled to a broad range of desires for meaningful intellectual, political, and social engagement, and the possibility of financial independence, sexual and reproductive freedom, protection from racialized and sexualized vio-lence; and a way to imagine living in a future tense" (p. 300). In the specific context of this chapter, the realization of thick desire provides students (espe-cially teen women) with "a set of publicly funded options that give... [them] a) the opportunity to develop intellectually, emotionally, and culturally; b) imagine themselves as sexual beings capable of pleasure and without the danger of carrying the undue burden of social, medical, and repro-ductive consequence; c) have access to information and health care resources; d) be protected from structural and intimate violence and abuse; and e) rely on a public safety net of resources" (p. 301).

Additionally, Fine and McClelland argue that the lack of access to these material conditions, especially in low-income, low-performing schools, have further adverse effects on students, especially poor students of color. For example, high-stakes testing and the unequal placement of young women of color in juvenile detention facilities create the conditions that place young Black, Latina, Native, poor, and working-class women in very dangerous sexual situations. Further, the absence of educational, health, sexual, and reproductive resources in these facilities may cause many of these young women to return infected with an STD or a baby with a disability, who may be placed in foster care. In making this argument, Fine and McClelland remind us that intimate choices are never wholly private, but are often profoundly economic, political, and social. Therefore, I would argue that a materialist disability studies position would theorize youth sexuality as the *thick desire* for "opportunity, community, pleasure and protection from coercion and danger" (p. 326).

However, it is sobering to remember that the realization of thick desire requires a radical transformation of the colonizing nexus of power relations. This will be a more difficult task. Part of the reason is that the sex curriculum and its associated educational policies of dis-location, segregation, incarceration, and "unvisibility of the hypervisible" (Gordon, 1997; p. 16), create the conditions where those conceived of as sexually deviant and resistant to *the habit of his power* are made to vanish from the official record (La Paperson, 2010). The violence here is potent because

> [i]nvisible bodies, no doubt by definition can be done away with much more easily than visible ones. Since...ghosts...and the like take up no physical space in our empirical word, the liquidification of them involves no bloodletting, leaves no corpses, and calls for no official inquiry. (William LaFleur qtd in Gordon 91997, p. 142).

Thus, the sex curriculum becomes a context that "produces a new region of displacement...mapping those cartographies of nowhere onto [sexual] bodies" (La Paperson, 2010; p. 10) and creating an army of ghosts. However, it is in the "cartographies of nowhere"—the alternative school, the self-contained classroom, the "ghetto" school—that the issue of haunting translates into transgressive praxis. It is these hauntings that foreground once again "the paradox of travelling through time and across all those forces...being there and not there, past and present, force and shape" (Gordon, 1997, p. 6). It is this paradoxical time travel that foregrounds both the historical continuities and discontinuities of social (class) relations mediated by race, gender, disability, and sexuality as per the dictates of transnational capitalism. Thus, it is this paradox of time travel that forces us to confront the trauma of the Middle passage, confronting what reaches down deep beneath waters or beneath the symbolics of emanicipation, free labour, and free citizen. This trauma links the origins of Slavery with a capital S to the origin of modern American freedom, to the paradigmatic and value-laden operations of the capitalist market. This is the market whose exchange relations continue to transform the living into the dead, a system of social relations that fundamentally objectifies and dominates a putatively free society. (Gordon, 1997; p. 168)

Thus, in a conceptual time travel between Chapters 1 and 2, I return to the argument that students marked oppressively by race, class, gender, and sexuality, are dis-located into the postcolonial ghettoes of alternative schooling on account of a variety of labels. There is rarely a "biological" basis for these labels. It is also generally understood that the assignment of these labels is arbitrary—I would say historical—rooted in the very American Grammar book that Spillers discusses with such poignant passion in her essay, "Mama's Baby, Papa's Maybe: An American Grammar Book." The material consequences of these assignments are horribly damaging—students move from segregated classrooms to alternative schools to becoming school dropouts to becoming completely alienated from the labor market and the wider social world, and eventually many of them find themselves in prison—a humiliating passage along the school-to-prison pipeline. This dis-location thereby portends the actuality of colonialism—no longer merely a metaphor but an actual material practice. More specifically, this dis-location reproduces what I call the modern (maybe postmodern) version of the Middle Passage that continues the historical tradition of transforming children of color (and other students who resist *his* power) into "diseased, damaged, and disabled Negroes deemed incurable and otherwise worthless" (Goodell as quoted in Spillers, 1987, p. 68), commodities used to feed the prison industrial complex, and served up again for consumption via the media (shows such as COPS, OZ, or the news) in another brutal conflation of pleasure and profit. We have now the production of another social pathology blamed on the violent historical construction of the broken black family living in the postcolonial ghettos still bearing the wounds of broken flesh marked by the violent lashes of history. And so we have come full circle. Still feeling his power. Still noting her absence. After all these years.

CHAPTER 3

"UNSPEAKABLE" OFFENSES: DISABILITY STUDIES AT THE INTERSECTIONS OF MULTIPLE DIFFERENCES

WITH ANDREA MINEAR[1]

On October 29, 1984, Eleanor Bumpurs, a 270 pound, arthritic, 67-year-old woman was shot to death while resisting eviction from her apartment in the Bronx. She was $98.85, or one month, behind in her rent. New York City mayor Ed Koch and police commissioner Benjamin Ward described the struggle preceding her demise as involving two officers with plastic shields, one officer with a restraining hook, another officer with a shotgun, and at least one supervising officer. All the officers also carried service revolvers. According to Commissioner Ward, during the course of the attempted eviction, Eleanor Bumpurs escaped from the restraining hook twice, and wielded a knife that Commissioner Ward said was "bent" on one of the plastic shields. At some point, Officer Stephen Sullivan, the officer positioned furthest away from her, aimed and fired his shotgun. It is alleged that the blast removed half of her hand so that, according to the Bronx district attorney's office, "it was anatomically impossible for her to hold the knife." The officer pumped his gun and shot again, making his mark completely the second time around

Williams, P. J. 1997, p. 234.

IN HER ESSAY "SPIRIT MURDERING THE MESSENGER," CRITICAL RACE Feminist (CRF) Patricia Williams (1997) describes the brutal murder of a poor, elderly, overweight, disabled, black woman by several heavily armed police officers. Trapped at the intersections of multiple oppressive contexts, Eleanor Bumpurs's tattered body was quite literally torn apart by her multiple selves—being raced, classed, gendered, "and" disabled. In the essay, Williams reads this murder as an unambiguous example of "racism [experienced] as... an offense so painful and assaultive as to constitute... 'spirit murder'"(Williams, 1997, p. 230). While we agree that racism was one of the potent triggers of this murder, there is no way to clearly determine how racism as it interacted with the deadly combination of class, gender, and disability oppression cohered to produce "the animus that inspired such fear, and such impatient contempt in a police officer" (Williams, 1997, p. 234).

Toward the end of the essay, Williams (1997) struggles to fathom why the officer who fired the fatal shots saw such an "'immediate threat and endangerment to life'... [that he] could not allay his need to kill a sick old lady fighting off hallucinations with a knife" (p. 234). In this quote, Williams recognizes Eleanor Bumpurs's disability when invoking her arthritis and possible mental illness. However, Williams deploys disability merely as a descriptor—a difference that is a matter of "magnitude" or context—what another CRF scholar Angela Harris (1997) has described as "nuance theory" (p. 14). In explanation, Harris points out that even though feminist scholars such as Catherine MacKinnon recognize that different women have different experiences, they, nevertheless, continue to center white women as the norm, while relegating other oppressive forces such as racism to the footnotes so as to "nuance" the general analysis. Such analyses, Harris writes, only mark the claim that "[if] things are bad for everybody (meaning white women) then they are even worse for black women" (p. 15). In other words, nuance theory constitutes black women's oppression as only an intensified example of (white) women's oppression, and is therefore used as the "ultimate example of how bad things [really] are" for all women (Harris, 1997, p. 15).

While we agree with the critique of nuance theory in feminist analyses that ignore the real experiences of black women, we argue in this chapter that CRF scholars deploy a similar analytical tactic through their (unconscious) nonanalysis of disability as it intersects with race, class, and gender oppression. In other words, we argue in this chapter that disability, just like race, offers not just a "nuance" to any analysis of difference. For example, one could argue that the outrage emanating from a heaving, black body wielding a knife sent a nervous (and racist) police officer into panic when confronted by his own racialized terror of otherness. But what about the other ideological terrors that loomed large in this encounter? Could the perception of Eleanor Bumpurs as a dangerous, obese, irrational, black woman also have contributed to her construction as criminally "insane" (disability) because her reaction to a "mere" legal matter of eviction (class) was murderous rage? And did our socially sanctioned fears of the mentally ill and our social devaluation of disabled (arthritic and elderly) bodies of color justify the volley of shots fired almost instinctively to protect the public from the deviant, the dangerous, and the disposable? We, therefore, argue that in the violent annihilation of Eleanor Bumpurs's being, disability as it intersects with race, class, and gender served more than just a "context" or "magnifier" to analyze the oppressive conditions that caused this murder.

In this chapter, we utilize both theoretical and empirical arguments to demonstrate the critical importance to engage disability in discourses of intersectionality by both disability studies and Critical Race Theory (CRT), because our failure to do so has disastrous and sometimes deadly consequences for disabled people of color caught at the violent interstices of multiple differences. From a theoretical standpoint, we note that CRT in recent years has expanded from its singular focus on the racial binary of Black/White to explore the complexities of racial identity (LatCrit, Asian American Crit) at the intersections of gender, class, and sexuality (Crenshaw, 1996; Wing, 1997b). At the same time, we also note that the social category of disability is prominently missing in CRT analyses, even though it plays a crucial ideological role in destabilizing normative discourses that construct difference in the first place (Erevelles, 2002; Watts & Erevelles, 2004). For example, a special issue in the *Journal of Educational Foundations* had called on critical race theorists in education to "address the educational inequalities and disparities for those whose identities place them in a double or tertiary bind with intersecting identities of race, class, gender, and/or sexuality". Significantly missing in this call for papers (CFP) was the social identity of disability, even though, particularly in educational contexts, poor disabled students of color often find themselves relegated to the segregated and alienating spaces of special education classrooms, alternative schools, and ultimately the school-to-prison pipeline (Artiles, 1998; Artiles, Harry, Reschly & Chinn, 2002; Dunbar, 2001; Watts & Erevelles, 2004).

In the first section of this chapter, we define the theoretical construct of intersectionality, as first proposed by Crenshaw (1996), and explore the different ways in which it can be utilized by both CRT and disability studies to analyze the experiences of people located at the interstices of multiple differences. Next, true to the CRT tradition, we will utilize two narratives to foreground the ways in which the inclusion of disability identity in discussions of intersectionality offers a more complex understanding of how race relations play out in contemporary life, both in educational institutions and in society at large. Both narratives that we draw upon are located in the southern United States—a social context that is still coming to terms with its violent history of racial oppression in social institutions such as state mental hospitals and public schools. The first narrative offers a synopsis of a recent historical work entitled *Unspeakable: The Story of Junius Wilson* (Burch & Joyner, 2007). In this narrative, an African American deaf man, Junius Wilson (1908–2001), was committed to a state mental hospital in North Carolina at age 17, following a false accusation of attempted rape from within his own community, imprisoned there for 76 years without ever having been tried or found guilty of a crime, and castrated, because he was deemed criminally insane by court officials unable to communicate with him. The second contemporary narrative is based on interviews we conducted with a 13-year-old African American girl, Cassie (pseudonym), who was unable to read and write, and her mother, Aliya Smith (pseudonym)—both of whom were battling a violent and uncaring special education bureaucracy that was threatening to expel Cassie from her middle school. Deploying the theory of intersectionality from within CRT and disability studies scholarship, we describe how both individuals located perilously at the interstices of race, class, gender, and disability were constituted as non-citizens and (no)bodies by the very social institutions (legal, educational, and rehabilitational) that were designed to protect, nurture, and empower them. Then, in the final part of the chapter, we explore the transformative implications of this intersectional analysis for both CRT and disability studies in education.

INTERSECTIONALITY AT THE CROSSROADS: THEORIZING MULTIPLICATIVE DIFFERENCES

With notions of essentialist identities being no longer tenable in critical analyses of difference, the challenge of how to theorize identity in all its complex multiplicity has preoccupied feminist scholars of color for quite some time (Anzaldua, 1990; Davis, 1983; hooks, 1985; Hull, Scott & Smith, 1982; Lorde, 1984). Kimberle Crenshaw (1996), one of the key proponents of the theory of intersectionality, has argued that "many of the experiences black women face are not subsumed within the traditional boundaries of race or gender oppression as these boundaries are currently understood" (p. 358). Part of the problem of "relying on a static and singular notion of being or of identity" (Pastrana, 2004, p. 75) is that the single characteristic foregrounded (e.g., female or black) is expected to explain all other life experiences of the individual or the group. Additionally, Crenshaw (1996) points out that social movements based on a single identity politics (e.g., the feminist movement, black power movement, or the LGBTQI movement) have historically conflated or ignored intragroup differences, and this has sometimes resulted in growing tensions between the social movements themselves.

Feminists of color have, therefore, had the difficult task of attempting to theorize oppression experienced at the multiple fronts of race, class, gender, sexuality, and disability (Anzaldua, 1990; Crenshaw, 1996; Harris, 1997; Lorde, 1984; Wing, 1997a). Thus, if one is poor, black, elderly, disabled, and lesbian, must these differences be organized into a hierarchy such that some differences gain prominence over others? What if some differences coalesce to create a more abject form of oppression (e.g., being poor, black, and disabled), or if some differences support both privilege/invisibility within the same oppressed community (e.g., being black, homosexual, and male)? What happens to the complexity of the analysis if "race" gets used as a stable register of oppression against which other discriminations gain validity through their similarity and difference from that register (Arondekar, 2005)? And would it not be problematic, if a gendered analysis only uses categories such as race and class to mark differences that continue to support stereotypic and problematic images that reproduce hegemonic portrayals of difference (e.g., working-class culture has more gender violence to preserve masculinity) (Bredstrom, 2006)? Intervening in this conundrum, therefore, becomes critical from an epistemological standpoint, because "representational practices often reflect and construct social and psychological reality" (Bredstrom, 2006, p. 85).

In the face of this theoretical challenge, intersectionality has been set up as the most appropriate analytical intervention expected to accomplish the formidable task of mediating multiple differences. For example, Patricia Hill Collins (1998) writes that "[a]s opposed to examining gender, race, class, and nation as separate systems of oppression, intersectionality explores how these systems mutually construct one another..." (p. 63). Pastrana (2004) emphasizes how the experiences of being Black are not only a matter of particularizing experiences of injustice and discrimination but also related to universalizing notions of stigma and oppression. And CRF scholar Adrienne Wing (Wing, 1997a) calls for a theory of intersectionality to engage in a multiplicative analysis for the following reason:

> We, as black women, can no longer afford to think of ourselves as merely the sum of separate parts that can be added together or subtracted from, until a white male or female stands before you. The actuality of our experience is multiplicative. Multiply each of my parts together, I X I X I X I X I, and you have *one* indivisible being. If you divide one of these parts from one you still have *one*. (p. 31)

But this is all much easier said than done. Attempts to deploy intersectionality as an analytic tool in academic research has taken on different forms with varying analytical outcomes—some more useful than others. McCall (2005), in an overview of how intersectionality has been utilized in women studies scholarship, has identified three different modes of theorizing intersectionality. The first mode of theorizing intersectionality uses an *anticategorical* framework based on the poststructuralist argument that social categories such as race, gender, sexuality, and disability are merely social constructions/fictions. Here, the very boundaries of identity have been challenged, with scholars arguing that we are no longer two sexes but five (Fausto-Sterling, 2000), or that race itself is ultimately indefinable because of multiracialism (Omi & Winant, 1994). CRF scholars have also tentatively embraced this framework by supporting critiques of identity as universal, bounded, coherent, and static. However, at the same time, they are unwilling to completely do away with the social categories that constitute identity in the first place. As Crenshaw (1996) explains:

> To say that a category such as race and gender is socially constructed is not to say that the category has no significance in our world. On the contrary, a large and continuing project for subordinated people...is thinking about the way in which power is clustered around certain categories and is exercised against others. (p. 375)

As a result, feminists of color are more apt to use an *intracategorical* framework in their theorizations of intersectionality (McCall, 2005). The intracategorical framework provides the middle ground between proponents of identity politics and proponents of the anticategorical framework. CRF scholars working within this framework have focused on "particular social groups at neglected points of intersection of multiple master categories" in order to reveal the complexity of lived experience in those groups (McCall, 2005, p. 1780). As Crenshaw (1996) explains:

> [W]omen of color are situated within two subordinated groups that frequently pursue conflicting political agendas...The problem is not simply that both discourses fail women of color by not acknowledging the "additional" issue of race or patriarchy, but rather that the discourses are often inadequate to the discrete tasks of articulating the full dimensions of racism and sexism (p. 360)...[I]ntersectionality provides a basis for reconceptualizing race as a coalition between men and women of color...Intersectionality may provide the means for dealing with other marginalizations as well. For example, race can also be a coalition of straight and gay people of color, and thus serve as a basis for critique of churches and other cultural institutions that reproduce heterosexism. (p. 377)

The intracategorical framework is especially promising to CRF scholars because it validates the reality of racism as it intersects with sexism and other social categories of difference (e.g., heterosexism, classism) in the everyday lives of women of color. This methodological approach "utilizes narratives and case studies to uncover the differences and complexities of experience embodied in [any particular social] . . . location [as well as] the range of diversity and difference *within* the group" (McCall, 2005, p. 1782). Although this framework appears promising, we are now faced with yet another challenge: How can the intracategorical framework address all differences when the list of differences seems endless and insurmountable (Ludwig, 2006)? For example, Yuval-Davis (2006) in her discussion on intersectionality includes a list of possible differences (potentially incomplete) that includes: "'race'/ skin color; ethnicity; nation/state; class, culture; ability; age; sedentariness/ origin; wealth; North-South; religion, stage of social development" (p. 202). Is it even conceivable to address all these possible social categories intersecting with a common master category (e.g., race or gender) at any given time? Do some differences acquire greater prominence than others (e.g., sexuality)? And are some "other" differences just added on to merely complicate and "nuance" this intersectional analysis (e.g., disability)?

If the intracategorical framework rejects tacking on another difference to its litany of categories (e.g., disability), it would have to, in effect, reject the additive approach to multiple differences, and instead utilize what Yuval-Davis (2006) has described as the constitutive approach to multiple differences. This approach, while foregrounding the actual experiences of women of color at the intersection of multiple social categories, also describes the structural conditions within which these social categories are constructed by and intermeshed with each other in specific historical contexts. McCall (2005) calls this third approach to theorizing intersectionality as the *intercategorical* framework that "adopt[s] existing analytical categories to document relationships of inequality among social groups and changing configurations of inequality along multiple and conflicting dimensions" (p. 1785). Yuval-Davis explains:

> The point of intersectional analysis is not to find "several identities under one" . . . This would reinscribe the fragmented, additive model of oppression and essentialize specific social identities. Instead the point is to analyse the differential ways by which social divisions are concretely enmeshed and constructed by each other and how they relate to political and subjective constructions of identities. (p. 205)

In this way, the intercategorical framework continues to insert complexity into analyses of multiple differences by examining the structural context where social categories are (re)constituted, without having to resort to an additive approach that will always be incomplete. Therefore, in the next section, rather than merely adding disability to nuance an intersectional analysis, we will foreground the historical contexts and structural conditions within which the identity categories of race and disability intersect.

POINTS OF CONTACT: AT THE INTERSECTION OF CRT AND DISABILITY STUDIES

In educational contexts, the association of race with disability has resulted in large numbers of students of color (particularly African American and Latino males) being subjected to segregation in special education classrooms through sorting practices such as tracking and/or through labels such as mild mental retardation and/or emotional disturbance(Artiles, 1998; Artiles, Harry, Reschly & Chinn, 2002; Connor & Ferri, 2005; Erevelles, 2002; Reid & Knight, 2006; Watts & Erevelles, 2004). The PBS film, *Beyond Brown: Pursuing the Promise* (Haddad, Readdean & Valadez, 2004) substantiates these claims with the following statistics:

- Black children constitute 17 percent of the total school enrollment, but 33 percent of those are labeled "mentally retarded."
- During the 1998–1999 school year, more than 2.2 million children of color in US schools were served by special education. Post-high-school outcomes for these students were striking. Among high school youth with disabilities, about 75 percent of African Americans, compared to 39 percent of whites, are still not employed three to five years out of school. In this same time period, the arrest rate for African Americans with disabilities is 40 percent, compared to 27 percent for whites.
- States with a history of legal school segregation account for five of the seven states with the highest overrepresentation of African Americans labeled mentally retarded. They are Mississippi, South Carolina, North Carolina, Florida, and Alabama.
- Among Latino students, identification for special education varies significantly from state to state. Large urban schools districts in California exhibit disproportionately large numbers of Latino English-language learners represented in special education classes in secondary schools.
- Some 20 percent of Latino students in grades 7 through 12 had been suspended from school according to statistics from 1999 compared with 15 percent of white students and 35 percent of African American students.

Clearly, the association of race with disability has been extremely detrimental to people of color in the United States, not just in education, but in society at large. In fact, historically, associations of race with disability have also been used to justify the brutality of slavery, colonialism, neocolonialism, and the continued exploitation of people of color in contemporary times (Baynton, 2005; Erevelles, 2002; Gould, 1981; Ladson-Billings & Tate IV, 1995). Thus, it is not surprising that CRT scholars would almost instinctively distance themselves from nurturing any alliance between race and disability. This is also because CRT scholars (like other radical scholars) have mistakenly conceived of disability as a biological category, as an immutable and pathological abnormality rooted in the "the medical language of symptoms and diagnostic categories" (Linton, 1998, p. 8). Disability studies scholars, on the other hand, have critiqued this "deficit" model of disability, and have argued instead for a *social model of disability* (Garland-Thomson, 1997; Linton, 1998; Oliver, 1990). The social model offers a sociopolitical analysis that describes disability as an ideological construction used to justify not only the oppressive binary cultural constructions of normal/pathological, autonomous/dependent, and competent citizen/ward of the state, but the social and racial divisions of labor as well (Erevelles, 2000; Russell, 1998). In other words, disability studies scholars have described disability as a socially constructed category that derives meaning and social (in)significance from the historical, cultural, political, and economic structures that frame social life.

It is here that both CRT and disability scholars meet at their first point of contact—both begin with the critical assumption that race and disability are, in fact, social constructs. Thus, Haney Lopez (2007) explains, "Biological race is an illusion...Social race, however, is not...Race has its genesis and maintains its vigorous strength in the realm of social beliefs" (p. 172). Similarly, Garland-Thomson (1997) describes disability as "the attribution of corporeal deviance—not so much a property of bodies [but rather]...a product of cultural rules about what bodies should be or do" (p. 6). At their second point of contact, race and disability are both theorized as relational concepts. Thus, CRT scholars argue that "[r]aces are constructed relationally against one another, rather than in isolation" (Haney Lopez, 2007, p. 168), such that the privileges that whites enjoy are linked to the subordination of people of color (Harris, 1995). Similarly, disability studies scholar Davis (1995) points out that "our construction of the normal world is based on a radical repression of disability" (p. 22), because "without the monstrous body to demarcate the borders of the generic...and without the pathological to give form to the normal, the taxonomies of bodily value that underlie political, social and economic arrangements would collapse" (Garland-Thomson, 1997, p. 20). Finally, at the third point of contact, both perspectives use stories and first-person accounts to foreground the perspectives of those who have experienced victimization by racism and ableism firsthand (Connor, 2007; Espinoza & Harris, 1997; Harris, 1997; Ladson-Billings & Tate IV, 1995; Linton, 1998; Parker, Deyhle & Villenas, 1999).

However, notwithstanding these commonalities, contemporary CRT/ CRF scholars have not perceived disability as a useful ally in their critique of social oppression. More often than not, disability had been usually added to the list of "other" social categories, sometimes (un)willingly, in an effort to be "politically correct." However, this is a serious omission. From a disability studies perspective, disability is much more than a descriptive biological category. Rather, the historian Catherine Kudlick (2005) argues that disability exposes the "implicit assumptions inherent in creating the social hierarchy that invest the list [of social categories] with meaning, [in the first place]" (p. 60). In fact, according to James and Wu (2003), since disability studies "calls attention to how built and social environments disenable those with physical, sensory, and cognitive impairments and privilege those who are normatively constituted" (p. 3), it follows then that disability could also be used to interrogate the normalizing discourses of racism, sexism, and heteronormativity—all of which generate the institutional exclusion of the deviant (read "disabled") Other. Put more simply, disability studies scholars argue that disability is, in fact, constitutive of most social differences, particularly race (Baynton, 2005; Erevelles, 2002; James & Wu, 2003).

One example to support the above claim lies in the historical narrative of eugenics that is especially significant in linking issues of race and class. In the more contemporary context of transnational capitalism, Erevelles (1996) writes that

> the "ideology" of disability is "essential to the capitalist enterprise because it is able to regulate and control the unequal distribution of surplus through invoking biological difference as the "natural" cause of all inequality, thereby successfully justifying the social and economic inequality that maintains social hierarchies... [D]isability... is [therefore] the organizing grounding principle in the construction of the categories of gender, race, class, and sexual orientation. (p. 526)

It is easy to dismiss eugenics as a relic of a bygone era, except that the continued association of race and disability in debilitating ways necessitates that we examine how eugenic ideologies continue to reconstitute social hierarchies in contemporary contexts by deploying the ideology of disability. To do so we draw on two narratives, one historical and one contemporary, to foreground the structural conditions that constitute inequalities at the intersections of difference. In the next two sections we will therefore narrate the life stories of our two protagonists, Junius Wilson and Cassie Smith, letting the stories speak for them. Then, in the final sections of the chapter, we will explain how the intercategorical framework is deployed to analyze these two narratives, and explore the implications this analysis has for CRT/F, disability studies, and theories of intersectionality in the context of education.

THE LIFE OF JUNIUS WILSON: THE "UNSPEAKABLE" NARRATIVE OF INTERSECTIONALITY

The first narrative that we draw upon to illustrate the intersectionality of race, class, disability, and gender is the story of Junius Wilson, poignantly told in Susan Burch and Hannah Joyner's (2007) book, *Unspeakable: The Life of Junius Wilson.* The reason this narrative is critical to CRT, disability studies, and Deaf Studies is because its life-altering events occurred at the intersection of disability, race, gender, and class, and because Wilson lived at the boundaries of all these communities. Junius was the third child born to Sidney and Mary Wilson in 1908 in the predominantly African American community of Castle Hayne on the outskirts of Wilmington, North Carolina. Burch and Joyner (2007) surmise that Junius Wilson must have lost his hearing as a toddler as a result of a childhood illness like scarlet fever, but the family only realized he was deaf much later. The poverty conditions within which his family lived, the tensions of raising a deaf child in these conditions, and the political context of racial violence in the community, all contributed to the breakdown of the Wilson family, and prompted Sidney Wilson to leave his wife Mary with her three children and find a new life for himself in Georgia. Mary Wilson was thus left to rely on the protection of a long-time family friend Arthur Smith and his family.

The Wilson family and their community were the inheritors of a "complicated legacy of freedom and horror" (Burch & Joyner, 2007, p. 10). Even though most African Americans were no longer slaves, the white powerful elite "[m]otivated by fears of black achievement and black sexuality" (p. 15) unleashed a wave of terror in black communities in North Carolina, which included lynching, forcing black families to provide their children with resources to survive Jim Crow. It was in this context that Junius Wilson, a deaf child, unable to always heed the warning calls of concerned family members, and therefore unable to understand and obey the brutal codes of the Jim Crow South, looked to be in particular jeopardy. It was perhaps for this reason that Mary Wilson was persuaded by her friend and mentor Arthur Smith to send her eight-year-old son, Junius, to the North Carolina School for the Colored Blind and Deaf in Raleigh.

In the segregated school in Raleigh, Wilson was initiated into a "black deaf community" that used "Raleigh signs" that were specific to the school, and a culture that included a " a rich heritage of folklore, humor, community heroes, social opportunities, and even a strong tradition of intermarriage" (Burch & Joyner, 2007, p. 4). Unfortunately, however, since this language and culture were particular to the school, it had almost no currency elsewhere—a fact that would later contribute to Wilson's social isolation in both the deaf and the black communities. Additionally, in line with racist ideologies of African American students' low mental capacities, the school encouraged vocational work over traditional classroom work, and so while Wilson could write his name out, he was unable to read and write anything else—another factor that impeded his ability to communicate with the outside world. Then, in 1924, Wilson was expelled from the school because of a minor infraction when he remained at a local fair for one night on a school trip, rather than return with his classmates. This infraction was costly because it catapulted Wilson into the most disastrous period in his life.

Returning home from Raleigh, Wilson experienced difficulties communicating with his family or his community. When he did try to communicate, he seemed especially disruptive and uncontrollable—perhaps because of his frustration of not being understood. Moreover, because of his deafness, Wilson's habits of "touching or holding people, stamping feet and waving arms" (p. 33) constructed him as a threatening figure who could inadvertently overstep the rigid boundaries of Jim Crow laws and compromise the safety of himself, his family, and his community. It was perhaps for all these reasons, and in an effort to protect his family and his community, that Arthur Smith, the family friend, accused the 17-year-old Junius Wilson of assaulting and attempting to rape his young wife, Lizzie. Thus, in August, 1925, Junius Wilson was arrested and taken to New Hanover County jail where he remained until the November term of the Supreme Court. Unable to communicate with Wilson, the court held a lunacy hearing, where it was concluded that Wilson was both "feeble-minded" and dangerous, and was therefore committed to the criminal ward of the North Carolina State Hospital for the Colored Insane in Goldsboro.

The State Hospital for the Colored Insane that was founded in 1877 accepted epileptics, "idiots," and other "mental defectives," in order to protect society from dangerous elements and "incapable" individuals from themselves, and it exerted more institutional control than practices of healing. Trapped in wards where he was unable to communicate, and faced with interminable days of supervised silence, Wilson may have become unusually hostile and unpredictable. Moreover, as mentioned earlier, eugenic ideologies dominant in the early twentieth century supported beliefs that inferior breeding created criminals, social deviancy, and impoverishment. Thus, fueled by these fears, social reformers turned to one means of effective social control of the criminally insane—castration, the surgical removal of the testicles. Thus, in 1932, Wilson became one of the first North Carolinians to be selected for this operation. Once castrated, Wilson was no longer perceived as a danger because he became "a submissive black man... [with] eyes downcast, silent, and reserved...a gentle childlike patient" (Burch & Joyner, 2007, p. 49).

According to a legal injunction, whenever Wilson was deemed legally sane, he was supposed to have been sent back to stand trial. However, the superintendent violated judicial procedure by not sending him to trial, on the grounds that his presumed mental retardation made him a better inmate rather than a free citizen. In order to ensure the "utmost efficiency at minimum cost" (Burch & Joyner, 2007, p. 42), inmates of the state hospital who behaved well and were deemed only minimally ill were forced to work in the farm colony (the farm attached to the hospital), and were also leased to private farmers. Wilson was identified as one such inmate who was taken out of the criminal wards to work in the farm colony. In 1937, Wilson's father and sister approached the hospital in an effort to procure his release, but this request was apparently rebuffed, and the family never approached the institution again. Thus, for the next two decades, Wilson lived out his placid and lonely existence at the farm colony.

By 1970, Wilson was transferred to a geriatric ward. Even though all charges against him were dropped by then, he continued to be incarcerated for another 20 additional years because it was conceived of as "the most benevolent course of action" (Burch & Joyner, 2007, p. 1). Paperwork from 1972 indicated that Wilson was given a variety of diagnoses. For example, in 1972, a New Hanover County judge committed Wilson as an involuntary patient describing him as a "deaf-mute" with "social maladjustment without psychiatric disorder" (p. 111). Later on in the decade, Wilson was described as having an "inadequate personality," and was said to have suffered from organic brain syndrome. Then, in 1980, when an opportunity to leave the institution arose, Wilson was given papers to sign where he unwittingly agreed to voluntarily remain at the institution. Two separate evaluations of Wilson in the 1980s by social workers who understood and could communicate in sign, however, described Wilson as both linguistically and intellectually competent, and lamented that he had been "systematically denied his rights for almost sixty years" (p. 118).

It was around this time period that disability rights became a civil rights issue, and in response to the Civil Rights of Institutionalized Persons Act, Carolina Legal Assistance (CLA), a group of attorneys in Raleigh, found scores of African American men and women "dumped in hospitals, abandoned by communities, and otherwise mislabeled as feebleminded" (p. 124). Junius Wilson was one of the inmates investigated, and he was assigned to the guardianship of John Wasson, a social worker, whose own investigation led him to a painful truth—that Junius Wilson had been "incarcerated in an insane asylum merely because he was deaf, poor and black, and bureaucratic inertia and staff paternalism kept him there for sixty-five years" (p. 129). Wasson, moved and angered by what he saw, contacted CLA and with the help of social workers and speech therapists who knew and understood sign language, started building a case that would enable Wilson to get resources that would allow him to communicate with others in the few years that he had left. Burch and Joyner (2007) describe the reaction of one of the American Sign Language (ASL) interpreters, Cathy Sweet, who was hired to assess Wilson's signing capacity:

> [S]he recognized the Raleigh signs that other African American deaf people had used around her when she lived in Winston-Salem. To Sweet's eyes, Wilson presented a culturally deaf man deprived of his natural community and language. After her first visit with Wilson, she walked back to her car, "I cried all the way home," she remembered. (p. 138)

After several years of lawsuits and the involvement of advocates and family members, Wilson was moved out to a cottage on the grounds of the hospital on February 4, 1994. He died on March 17, 2001. Hovering precipitously at the boundaries of race, class, gender, and disability, Wilson had been confined to the isolating confines of the institution for more than three-quarters of his life. Overwhelmed by the enormity of the crime committed against Wilson, Burch and Joyner (2007) ask, "How should a society—indeed, how can a society —make amends for past misdeeds?" (p. 3).

But society seldom makes amends for past misdeeds. On the contrary, it is often apt to repeat them. Junius Wilson's story took place in the early twentieth century. Our second narrative, Cassie Smith's story, takes place in the present, almost a century later. The terrifying aspect of Cassie's story is that it continues Wilson's narrative, becoming its unwilling sequel that once again foregrounds the violence that lies at the intersection of race, class, gender, and disability. Our decision to write up Cassie's story was serendipitous. One of the coauthors of this chapter, Andrea Minear, a former public school teacher had taught Cassie for one year in a home-school cooperative she was running for students who wanted out of the public school system, a project she had to abandon for financial reasons a year later. However, Cassie and her mother Aliya Smith maintained contact with Minear and often called on her to advocate for Cassie when dealing with the special education bureaucracy in the public schools. It was after one such request that Minear shared Cassie's story with the other coauthor, Nirmala Erevelles, the instructor in one of Minear's courses when she was a doctoral student. At that time, Erevelles who had been reading Burch and Joyner's book was struck by the similar themes in both stories. We met and decided we could interview both Cassie and her mother Aliya Smith and tell their story. After obtaining the Institution Review Board (IRB) approval, we conducted two interviews with Cassie and Aliya Smith. Drawing on critical events in the interviews, and interspliceing those events with Minear's own recollections of teaching the little girl, Cassie's story follows.

HER TIME IS UP! CASSIE GOTTA GO!: EXCLUSION AT THE INTERSECTIONS

She bounded through the door for her first day of middle school, ready to act grown up. Within the first month, she had been suspended at least twice for fighting. Middle school is tough. Girls, especially, are mean. They looked at her sideways. She lurched forward in an aggressive stance, teeth gritted, ready to pounce. Someone bumped her. She swung. "You ugly!" "You nasty!" "You stupid!" Insults were hurled at her! She hurled them back! They tore away at her self-esteem. Left her bleeding and raw. Before the semester had ended, she had been in trouble enough times to warrant alternative placement.

Alternative school. Not a separate building in another part of town. At least not this time. Instead, a large classroom at the back of the school, broken up into separate cubicles to minimize student contact. A teacher's desk positioned at the back of the room for maximum observation of all cells. Windows taped with paper to keep out the sunlight, the playground, and other children. In alternative school, students come to school late and leave early, in an effort to ensure that they are invisible to the rest of the school. All this is done to make sure that they NEVER forget that this seclusion is THE punishment. Cassie's only companions were kids just like her. All black. All poor. All labeled. Their badness now branded into their dark skin with a single word: TROUBLE.

Minear had met Cassie two years ago at the home-school cooperative, DAWN, that Minear had founded to help kids like Cassie, who did not seem to "fit in" public schools. Cassie and her mother came to DAWN, recommended by a neighbor. She came with no labels, no paperwork, no expectations. Just a 12-year-old girl who wanted desperately to belong to something, to someone, somewhere. Cassie's mother, Aliya Smith, a single mother on disability for the last 15 years, lived in public housing with her daughter and her then-six-year-old son, Charles, in a small southern town. Theirs was not a life of extravagances, because money was tight. Cassie's father lived close by but has been mostly absent from her life. She had been very close to her grandmother who had passed away a year earlier.

On her first day at DAWN, Cassie tried desperately to fit in with the other eight adolescent girls at the school. She was dressed neatly, as always, clothes clean and ironed. But she had severe eczema on her skin, and she was eyed suspiciously by the other girls as if her rash was contagious. Her hair was braided stylishly, but her braids were already loosening and falling out because she picked at her head continuously. Her big toothy grin gave way to raucous laughter, much louder than the children in the small school were used to. She tried so hard to be friendly, but she was met with wariness.

After barely less than a day of observation and evaluation, Minear realized that Cassie could not read—a fact that she had successfully hidden from even her closest friends. She could not read the simplest texts in DAWN's library. She struggled with letters and sounds. When asked to write a journal entry, her sentences contained a string of three-letter words that made little sense, such as "pig as you as zoo cat by as no as dog pig as zoo no by you as zoo as cat red." Cassie "pretended" very well, opening her book, following along, and even reading "along with" someone. Saying a word immediately after the other person began the word. Because she did not read, she had limited knowledge of other subject areas. She could barely add and could not subtract. She recognized some coins, but could not figure money. It was then that Minear realized with dismay that 12-year-old Cassie could not read or write.

When we interviewed Cassie and her mother, her turbulent and tragic educational history was slowly revealed. We learned to our horror that Cassie had been bounced around to a different school every year of her school life; two schools in some years. As a toddler, Cassie spent a lot of time with her grandmother because of Aliya's poor health. At age four, Cassie started out in a private preschool program at the Holy Trinity Baptist School. Without the benefit of records or firsthand knowledge, we wonder whether the fact that Cassie was an economically disadvantaged black child in an all-white school caused her to appear "behind" and uncontrollable. Aliya recalls:

> *Aliya*: She used to get temper tantrums and they told me if I couldn't get her straightened up, she gotta go!
> *NE*: Why did she throw tantrums?
> *Aliya*: She didn't want to do what they told her to do. Just wanted to do things her way.
> *Cassie* (interjects): Kicking, Hollering, Screaming. I was spoiled rotten and wanted to do things my way.

Thus, Cassie began her educational experience learning that she was not as good as the other children around her. And that they didn't want her around. She, therefore, fought back. Moved now to the Head Start program located at Main Street Elementary, a Title I school, Cassie was often placed outside the classroom and in the hallway as punishment, where she retaliated by kicking and spitting. Zoned to Horace Elementary for kindergarten, another Title I school, Cassie began to live up to her reputation, developing behaviors that were not conducive to a successful school experience. According to Aliya:

> She was doing the tantrums again. And then they [the school personnel] said that she needed help (Cassie interjects: "No, I don't!"). So I had to go through evaluations, meetings, and stuff. They tried to say that she was mentally retarded. (Cassie interjects, "I am not MR!")... [Aliya continues in response to Cassie's assertion] But she was then. So they sent her to *Sally's Corner*.

In this small southern town, *Sally's Corner* was touted as the haven for kids with severe emotional and behavioral problems. Its mission statement found on the school's website included the following description:

> [*Sally's Corner*] is a model treatment program for [State's] special needs children, adolescents and their families. Treatment is based on an interdisciplinary approach with psychology, education, nursing, psychiatry, social work and counseling comprising the professions that impact each client's treatment. All clients are provided individual services through directions from a program treatment team.

The website also included several testimonials from parents and one child that described *Sally's Corner* very positively. Cassie's memories of *Sally's Corner*, however, were very dark.

> *Cassie*: [*Sally's Corner*] is like a bad place. They put you there when you get in trouble. They restrain you. They put your arms like this...sit on you kinda and put you in a room where no windows at and a little time out room by yourself...And they come and look at you. And I say, "Let me out" and I kick the door
>
> *AM*: Cassie, What happens that you have to be restrained?
>
> *Cassie*: Um, If you spit on them or say shut up, you thing. Or I mean kinda fight. They'd do stuff
>
> *AM*: What makes you want to spit on them?
>
> *Cassie*: I don't know.
>
> *NE*: What is it that that gets you really angry for you to not know it and want to do that?
>
> *Cassie*: When somebody tries to fight with me and pull my hair.
>
> *NE*: But the teachers don't try to fight with you, do they?
>
> *Cassie*: Oh I'll still fight you the big ole fat ole...sit on me...Half ton white folks!...What time it is? I got to get ready for camp.

By Cassie's own admission, we can understand that she was no easy client, and it is reasonable to assume that Cassie was in need of some kind of program that would help manage her fits of rage so she could also learn. And surely, they had all that expertise from the multidisciplinary team to do something for her. But again, we do not really know what happened there except for this explanation from Aliya about why she wanted Cassie to leave *Sally's Corner* after only a couple of months there:

> *NE*: What kind of program did they have at *Sally's Corner*?
> *Aliya*: What did they have, Cassie?...They locked you up all the time. They had this jail cell. She had spit on the wall while she was in there. They called my mama [Cassie's grandmother]. I was sick at that time. My mama and my sister-in-law went. My mama was so mad when she went out there. She told them, "Open the door. Let that child outta there!" My mama did not understand. Actually she did not care. Like she [Cassie] was being treated like a dog or something...And then they said that before she left she had to scrub the room. My mama said, "Get that child outta there!" And they said, she could not leave before she did that. So my mom told Cassie what were the spots that she spit at. And to clean just them. They wanted her to clean the whole room! Then she got to get ready to go to...It was time for her to go...Kept on trying to get her out...They finally agreed and I got her to go to Woodberry Gardens.

Once again while we acknowledge that we have only one side of the story, there are aspects that still puzzle us. Surely, "a model treatment program" had more options for a small, angry FIVE-YEAR-OLD African American girl with anger-management issues than being thrown into a "jail cell!" What was it about that tiny enraged black body that terrified the staff so much that it threw all their knowledge out of the window, opting instead for the only behavioral strategy of "imprisonment?"

This was the educational legacy that Cassie would carry forward with her as she moved into the first grade at her new elementary school, *Woodberry Gardens*. Cassie remained at Woodberry Gardens for two "good" years in a special education classroom, and then Aliya was told that "[Cassie] had gone far enough with her behavior at *Woodberry Gardens* and then they said that it was time for her to go. She had progressed enough. At that school they were not calling her retardation [*sic*]." She was then sent to Spartan Elementary to another special education program, and according to her mother she spent another two good years there, even though she was still struggling as a reader. Then once again, at the end of the fourth grade, almost inexplicably, as Aliya put it, "It was time for her to leave there...Her time was up," and Cassie found herself in a new elementary school, Nottingham.

Apparently, at this time, Cassie no longer held the label of "mental retardation." Still, when asked, her mother just says, "She acted crazy!" She was now thrown into a regular program at Nottingham with no support. Once again her academic problems and her behavioral problems were exacerbated. Once again she was told by her teachers that she was not good enough. Once again she was teased and called names by her peers. Once again she fought back—this time cutting a classmate's hair. And once again she suffered the consequences of her negative behavior. Less than two months before her graduation from elementary school, Cassie was transferred to her eighth school, *Athena*. Aliya was livid:

> You talking about somebody was mad. No! I I could never understood why they sent her to *Athena*. I went over there and met with the teacher…It had something to do with her learning. There was a month and half to graduate and they sent her to *Athena*. Then that teacher was up there ill-treating her…They wanted her to graduate with her *Athena* class. And I said, "I didn't spend all that money and time at *Nottingham* for this. I was so mad. I told them that I would have her out of school if they would not let me take her out [of *Athena*]. Then they listened. When they figured out that I was not playing with them, they got those papers. Like they couldn't get them fast enough. They just moved them in the office. And I took her to *Nottingham* and she was there was for three days so that she could graduate with her class. And they did it [the graduation ceremony] in such a way, that she had to be escorted. Like she was such a bad child. Like she was coming from prison. Her last two teachers had to walk with her side by side. She was the last one to walk.

Thus, after being in eight schools in eight years, Cassie came to DAWN, the home-school cooperative as a sixth grader with a plethora of problems. With a brother in kindergarten, Cassie was embarrassed that he was beginning to read ahead of her. But with a great deal of one-on-one work, repetition, and the motivation to be like the others in the school, Cassie experienced a very good year, overall. Minear also, made sure that the students treated each other with respect. In this supportive context, Cassie made great leaps in her social behavior and even some academic headway. However, Minear was forced to close DAWN at the end of the year for financial reasons, and so Cassie prepared to reenter public school in the next fall. Armed with a narrative of her achievements of the past year and recommendations for a "least restrictive environment," which could help build on her new gains, she entered middle school. Minear assured her that she would be on call whenever she needed her. It was not long before the call came.

Eager to learn, but receiving very little help in school, Cassie soon got frustrated and got into fights again. She was sent to the alternative school, which, ironically, she actually liked because of the structure and the individual attention. According to Cassie:

> It's [Alternative School] helped. I did all my work in there…It's fun. We do PE. We do lunch in the classroom. Go to the bathroom twice a day.

Get to do games. Do our work and talk and watch movies and stuff and eat popcorn…No I didn't mind it. We didn't have a bunch of kids in our classroom.

But then, even this realm of contentment vanished one day—the day of the "incident." One spring day, six students (four boys and two girls) were left without supervision in a classroom for a few minutes while one of the teachers walked a student to his car to speak to his mother. The boys teased and taunted the girls making rude, sometimes vulgar suggestions, and then laughing them off. One of the boys told Cassie, "So-and-so thinks you're pretty. He wants you to suck his dick." And so, she went behind the cubbies and obliged.

By the next day, word spread all over the school. As the rumor gathered momentum, more and more people became aware, including the school counselor and the assistant principal. However, neither the classroom teacher nor the parents of the perpetrators were notified for nearly two or three weeks. According to the assistant principal, there was an ongoing investigation. The day Cassie's mother was summoned for what the school administration called a "manifestation determination," she stopped by Minear's house. Cassie was angry and extremely agitated, as was her mother. They talked for nearly an hour as they tried to sort out fact from fabrication.

At the meeting, the school officials, after determining the "facts" of the case, began to ask a barrage of questions. Cassie was uncooperative, often humming a tune when asked a question. Her mother tried to explain that she was embarrassed to talk about what happened publicly. But the "hearing committee" did not pay much attention, except for the young white male social studies teacher who seemed to empathize with Cassie. The question of the day was: Was it Cassie's "learning disability" that caused her to have oral sex with a boy in her class or was this done on her own volition? Following "procedure," each member concurred that her "learning disability" could not have caused her to perform oral sex. She knew what she was doing. Therefore she was GUILTY. Under the zero-tolerance policy, this called for expulsion.

Not once did the committee even bother to look at Cassie's painful history of exclusion, segregation, incarceration, and negation. It was lucky that Minear was there. Aliya was a poor advocate for her child. Intimidated, angry, confused, and defensive, she often ended up blaming her daughter for the "stupid thing she did." It was Minear who saved the day. Drawing on her experiences as a former special education teacher, Minear brought up Cassie's educational history of social isolation and low self-esteem that were the by-products of her "learning disability," and that may have influenced her decision to perform a sexual act that garnered her some form of warped recognition/respect/visibility among her peers. In addition, AM had to spell out the possible legal ramifications of leaving students unsupervised in a locked and isolated classroom for even a short period of time. We believe that it was the last statement that sealed the deal. It was the not the history of educational abuse, but the threat of legal ramifications that made the committee decide that they would not recommend expulsion. Cassie would have another chance at school. But whether she would have the supports that she needed to make it through another school year was still an open question.

The process of narrating Cassie's educational history during the interviews inadvertently produced an unpredictable benefit for Aliya. In a marked difference from the "professionals" who were reviewing Cassie's case, it was Aliya, confused, angry, troubled, and yet still hopeful, who was able to see how the different disruptive, demeaning, and punitive experiences that began early in Cassie's life were now responsible for the risky, sullen, and disorderly behaviors of her teenage daughter. Now with the gift of hindsight, and therefore conscious of her own disempowerment in the process, Aliya poignantly reflected:

> If I had known the system better, I would not have put her there [*Sally's Corner*]. But at that time I did not know the system. It seemed that they were trying to hurt me, rather than help me.

"UNSPEAKABLE OFFENSES": AN INTERCATEGORICAL ANALYSIS OF INTERSECTIONALITY

Just like Junius Wilson, Cassie and Aliya Smith are also located at the boundaries of race, class, gender, and disability. In fact, it is this precipitous location that is responsible for the tragic trajectory of Cassie's experiences of educational failure and devaluation of her personhood. Each of their stories brings to the forefront the central question that was raised at the beginning of this chapter: How does racism in its interaction with the inauspicious combination of class, gender, and disability oppression cohere to locate Wilson and the Smiths beyond the pale of appropriate interventions by the very institutions (legal, rehabilitational, and educational) that were designed to nurture and empower them? At which point did disability trump race? When did class become the critical influential factor? At what point did gender become the only perceivable threat? In each of the stories, it is very difficult to unravel and isolate the strands that played an integral part in weaving the violent tapestry of their broken lives.

For Junius Wilson, it was the sociopolitical context of racial terror and abject poverty in the Jim Crow South that constituted his deafness as "dangerous" difference that could only be contained within the institutional confines of a segregated residential school for the "colored" deaf. Ironically, this confinement provided Wilson with a cultural community of other deaf students of color, while at the same time it alienated him from his community outside the school. Additionally, unlike white deaf students, being black and deaf located him at the lowest rungs of the social hierarchy of the time, providing him with an inferior education that would also play a part in his continued social isolation. On returning home, his disability cast a shadow on his race and gender, and contributed to his construction as the dangerously virile young black male—images that led to the false accusation of sexual assault, his incarceration, and ultimately to the final violent act of his castration. Without financial resources and other social supports, his family could do little to intervene on his behalf, which resulted in him languishing in an institution for 76 years. The institution's refusal to release him even after all charges were dropped against him was justified under a mantle of benevolence. It was this same benevolence that allowed the institution to justify the unequal and oppressive conditions in the institution by arguing that "the lack of facilities are not due to racial biases but the fact Negro patients are willing to accept what is provided to them, 'which is more than they have at home'" (Burch & Joyner, 2007, p. 74).

In an earlier section of this paper, we wrote that Cassie Smith provided Junius Wilson's story with its unwelcome sequel. At first glance, this assertion may seem far-fetched in the contemporary historical context of the New South where Jim Crow (re)appears as only a distant and shameful memory. Yet, Cassie's story foregrounds an interesting twist to the continuing saga of racial segregation in the New South. In place of Jim Crow, Cassie's ever-changing labels of mental retardation/learning disability/attention deficit hyperactivity disorder (MR/LD/ADHD) were used as the justification for her continued segregation in an effort to protect the mainstream from a dangerous racialized Other—the economically disadvantaged disabled African American girl. Here, class and race also played a significant role in maintaining this segregation. As educators, we, the coauthors, have known privileged white students with similar behavioral problems, whose parents were able to corral the school's best resources, were able to access professional help outside the school, and, in the worst-case scenario, were able to transfer their child to a private school. Aliya Smith's economic and social disadvantages did not permit her these luxuries. Instead, her disadvantages proved to be a further liability, a signal to the school professionals that there was really no need to "fight" for her daughter Cassie. As a result, even though Cassie was supposed to have an individualized education program (IEP) replete with individualized goals to improve both her behavior and her learning, she never met most of those goals, and yet nobody cared. This was apparent in her seventh-grade report card that listed her as earning As and Bs, even though she was still unable to read and write, and still had little behavior control.

And finally, perhaps most telling is how disability as a "social" not a "physiological" condition was used to justify the benevolence of the special education bureaucracy, and in doing so masked the violence that became an inextricable part of Cassie's educational career. Cassie was first MR, then ADHD, and then LD—labels that ebbed and flowed with the passing tides in different contexts. Clearly, given its temporality, "mental retardation" cannot be a robust category. So, could it then be that the educational gatekeepers, when confronted with an allegedly undisciplined, economically disadvantaged, African American girl, fearfully sought the protection of the label "mental retardation"—a label that would justify her incarceration at the tender age of five, and continue to support her social isolation as it made its punitive march on the successive legs of her young educational career?

We argue here that an intercategorical analysis of intersectionality enables us to foreground the structural context where the social categories of race, class, gender, and disability are (re)constituted within the two narratives of Junius Wilson and Cassie Smith. First, we identify disability as the organizing ideological force that is deployed in both narratives as the means to organize the social hierarchies in their respective historical contexts. Here, we describe disability as the very embodiment of the disruption of normativity that is, in turn, symbolic of efficient and profitable individualism and the efficient economic appropriation of those profits produced within capitalist societies (Erevelles, 2000). In the early twentieth century, Jim Crow and eugenics served as the two principal mechanisms that patrolled the boundaries of society, in order to identify those individuals/communities who were seen as a threat to the normative social order (the status quo). The New South replaced those outmoded mechanisms of segregation with more modern systems that were more appropriately in keeping with the times. Thus, for example, in educational contexts, the special education bureaucracy with its complex machinery of pseudomedical evaluations, confusing legal discourses, and overwhelming paperwork, and administered by a body of intimidating professionals, now performs tasks that are not very different from Jim Crow and eugenic ideologies. To put it more simply, special education, instead of being used to individualize education programs to meet the special needs of students, is used to segregate students who disrupt the "normal" functioning of schools. While we do not deny that Cassie did have significant problems, we argue that the only intervention that was sought by the special education bureaucracy as the most effective was segregation. Moreover, on the few occasions when her mother, Aliya Smith, sought to confront them, they invoked their complicated bureaucracy (e.g., using words like "manifestation determination") to further confuse and intimidate her.

Educational institutions present themselves as agents of benevolence for the billions of students it purports to serve on a daily basis. However, these institutions, notwithstanding their "good" intentions, fail to educate "different" students such as Cassie, because they have transformed themselves into institutions of social control intent on following bureaucratic "procedures," where most of the time, these "procedures" are intent on propagating and preserving normativity rather than meeting the desperate needs of (Other) students. Cassie is, no doubt, difficult to manage, and perhaps even challenging to care about enough to help her conquer her barriers. However, it is her RIGHT that she NOT be made dispensable.

"SPIRIT MURDER" AND THE "NEW" EUGENICS: CRITICAL RACE THEORY MEETS DISABILITY STUDIES

The three stories of Eleanor Bumpurs, Junius Wilson, and Cassie and Aliya Smith, however poignant they may appear to be, are not unique. Police brutality, false imprisonment, and educational negligence are commonplace in the lives of people of color—especially those who are located at the margins of multiple-identity categories. So common are these practices that CRF scholar Patricia Williams (1997) has argued that these kinds of assaults should not be dismissed as the "odd mistake." On the other hand, Williams has argued that that these "mistakes" be given a name that associates them with criminality. Her term for such assaults on an individual's personhood is "spirit murder," which she describes as follows:

> I see spirit murder as no less than the equivalent of body murder...One of the reasons I fear what I call spirit murder or disregard for others whose lives qualitatively depend on our regard, is that its product is a system of formalized distortions of thought. It produces social structures centered around fear and hate, it provides a timorous outlet for feelings elsewhere unexpressed...We need to see it as a cultural cancer; we need to open our eyes to the spiritual genocide it is wreaking on blacks, whites, and the abandoned and abused of all races and ages. We need to eradicate its numbing pathology before it wipes out what precious little humanity we have left. (p. 234)

Clearly, in our educational institutions, there are millions of students of color, mostly economically disadvantaged and disabled, for whom "spirit murder" is the most significant experience in their educational lives. In fact, it is this recognition of "spirit murder" in the everyday lives of disabled students of color that forges a critical link between disability studies and CRT/F through the intercategorical analysis of intersectionality. In other words, utilizing an intercategorical analysis from the critical standpoint of disability studies will foreground the structural forces in place in schools that disregard students who are perceived as disruptive to the dominant ideologies that shore up the mythical norm. That most of the students are poor, disabled, and of color is critical to recognize from within a CRT/F perspective, because the implications these exclusions have on the community of color as a whole are disastrous. By failing to undertake such an analysis, we could miss several political opportunities for transformative action. For example, Connor and Ferri (2005) raise some critical questions regarding one of education's most famous court cases, *Brown v. Board of Education*:

> Why did supporters of Brown not recognize how the assigned status of "disability" could serve as a mechanism for resegregating students of color in otherwise desegregated schools? And why did special education fail to take into account the intersection of race and disability and, thus undermine the goals of the Brown decision? (p. 121)

Now that we have the benefit of hindsight, we need to move forward. Connor and Ferri's questions require that we pay close attention to reading race and disability not through an additive/comparative lens, but by deploying an intersectional analysis that seeks to understand and transform the structures where power coheres in complex yet dangerous ways. It requires that critical educators plant themselves firmly at the intersections of multiple differences to submit our educational institutions to a ruthless critique of the status quo.

In the context of our argument, these are some of the questions that should be raised by all critical educators: What role do disability labels play in public school settings? Why should parents and educators of color be active participants in advocating special education reform in public schools? Why should parents active in the disability rights movement also foreground the racial dimensions of special education reform? Why should parents of color, parents of students with disabilities, and parents from economically disadvantaged backgrounds, and parents who live at all these intersections work together to radically transform schools?

One of the largest problems in the special education movement is that parent advocates usually deploy the individualist model when fighting for their children. Both CRT/F and disability studies scholarship point to the social/political context in which families are situated in relationship to educational institutions. It is these contexts that have real effects on the families and those individuals caught at these intersections. The history of the civil rights movement was successful because of community advocacy. At the intersections of race, class, gender, sexuality, and disability, we will find that collective resistance is more fruitful than individualized forms of resistance.

The need for change has never been more pressing than now. Even as we write this chapter, there may be yet another Eleanor Bumpurs, Junius Wilson, or Cassie Smith, whose life is quite literally on the line. If we allow eugenic-like ideologies to continue to plague our institutions (legal, rehabilitational, and educational), we will be required to face the consequences. In the Nobel Prize winner Toni Morrison's famous book *Beloved*, she evocatively describes how we can never escape history because it will continue to speak to us in haunting tones until we listen, atone, and transform ourselves. Rather than viewing it as a threat, we argue that there is hope in this assertion. Patricia Williams (1997) herself also echoes Morrison's call to all of us educators to heed the voices of those who are innocently sacrificed at the altar of educational expediency. She writes:

> The legacy of killing finds its way into cultural expectations, archetypes, and "isms." The echoes of both the dead and deadly others acquire a hallucinatory quality; their voices speak of an unwanted past, but also reflect for us images of the future. Today's world condemns those voices as superstitious and paranoid. Neglected they speak from the shadows of such inattention, in garbles and growls, in the tongues of the damned and the insane...So-called unenlightened others who fail to listen to the voices of demonic selves, made invisibly uncivilized, simply make them larger, more barbarously enraged, until the nearsightedness of looking glass existence is smashed in upon by the terrible dispossession of dreams too long deferred. (Williams, 1997, p. 235).

CHAPTER 4

Embodied Antinomies: Feminist Disability Studies Meets Third World Feminism

> Refugees are the rest of the world...
>
> Those left to defend their human decency
> Against conditions the rich keep their animals from...
> Those who are forgotten in mean times
>   "Of Refuge and Language," Suheir Hammad

SINCE SEPTEMBER 11, 2001, IT HAS BEEN VERY DIFFICULT to engage issues of social difference because the obsessive focus on the Self in the United States has obscured the violence against the Other that has continued in its wake—first in Afghanistan, then Iraq, and now in a number of other countries in Europe, Africa, and Asia, as well as in the United States. I have found that many of my left-leaning colleagues and students, while eager to discuss the impact of this violence from the rather limited local standpoint of a specifically US-focused progressive liberalism, are, on the other hand, usually reticent, sometimes even hostile, and more often than not uninformed when urged to expand the locus of their discussions to engage the global contexts where much of this violence is both enacted and materialized. Part of the problem is that, to many of them, the local and the global exist as distinct and different entities such that any attempts to articulate analyses that foreground their commonalities run the risk of being viewed as metanarratives that are thought to consume all difference. In this chapter, I expose the dangers of this cavalier dismissal of the global. Rather, I invoke the global to foreground the complex ways in which the lived experiences of race, class, gender, sexuality, and disability in the national context of the United States exist in dialectical tension with similar lived experiences of race, class, gender, sexuality, and disability in global contexts.

To engage this dialectics of global politics, the locus of this chapter shifts to the Third World. In invoking the Third World, I reject traditional, ahistorical, and apolitical conceptualizations that geographically situate the Third World in the former colonies of Europe located in Asia, Africa, and South America, and that are perceived as underdeveloped in contrast to the industrialized nations in Europe, North America, and Australia. On the other hand, the conceptualization of the Third World that I take up is not restricted to national boundaries, but instead refers to the "colonized, neo-colonized, and decolonized countries (of Asia, Africa, and Latin America) whose economic and political structures have been deformed within the colonial process, [as well as] to black, Asian, Latino, and indigenous peoples in North America, Europe and Australia" (Mohanty, Russo, & Torres, 1991, p. ix). In other words, I deploy the term "Third World" in a much more expansive way to expose how the social, political, and economic conditions of global capitalism produce spaces of extreme exploitation and oppression in both the imperialist states and their former colonies. In the imperialist states, this exploitation is usually witnessed in zoned-off communities, sometimes densely populated areas commonly referred to as ghettos, inner cities, barrios, and reservations, forming what Frantz Fanon (1965) called "internal colonies." Given that the focus of this book is on disability, I expand Fanon's conceptualization of internal colonization to include disabled people, who have also historically been segregated in prison-like complexes such as special classrooms, sheltered workshops, nursing homes, and state institutions that have been very effective in rendering their denizens invisible (Watts & Erevelles, 2004).

The consequences of this invisibility are costly. To be invisible implies that for the Self, the (invisible) Other simply does not exist. In fact, in such a scenario, the very act of acknowledging that the Other exists evokes terror—a terror that demands a stifling silence; a desperate looking away; and an urgency to bury the evidence of the Other's existence. With the Third World already designated as a space of terror, disabled people who are confined to these spaces run the risk of almost complete erasure, and, subsequently, face the most extreme dehumanization on account of this non-recognition. To substantiate this claim, in this chapter, I will draw on two events in our recent history—Hurricane Katrina and the ongoing war in Iraq and Afghanistan—where disabled people living in spaces of terror are scarcely noticed by the mainstream media or even by the progressive segment of academia. I will foreground the significance of these invisibilities and reflect on why our terror of the Other forces us to look the other way.

Once again, I draw on feminist theory in this chapter, because of its significant contributions to theories of the body, but this time I focus specifically on the antinomies that exist between third world feminist theory and feminist disability studies. The antinomies arise because even though third world feminist theory and feminist disability studies espouse theories that should foreground crucial alliances, their nonrecognition of each other negates the possibility for opposition to their collective oppression. In an effort to foreground the conceptual pitfalls to which both theoretical frameworks fall prey, I draw on the political contexts that emerged in the aftermath of Hurricane Katrina and the wars in Iraq and Afghanistan. Thus, in the first section of this chapter, I explore the contradictory impulses that come to play in the media representations of the aftermath of Hurricane Katrina, when constructs such as Third World and disability deployed in these representations are placed under critical scrutiny. I will then identify both feminist disability studies and third world feminism as radical perspectives within the broad spectrum of feminist theory that are nevertheless analytically limited when engaging critical issues of gender and disability in post/neocolonial contexts. Next, shifting from the local terrain of the United States to a more global context, I will engage an often-ignored area in both feminist disability studies and third world feminism—the impact of war and disability on the lives of third world women. Emphasizing the dialectical relationship between the local and the global by drawing on a materialist disability studies framework, I conclude this chapter by mapping out the historical continuities and discontinuities that exist between racism, sexism, ableism, and heterosexism embodied in the eugenic practices of the early twentieth century and the contemporary context of neocolonialist policies, and their impact on disability, race, gender, and sexuality in both the imperialist states and the Third World. My purpose for writing this chapter is to foreground the repercussions of the invisibility of disability in global contexts, and to discuss its implications for the theory and praxis of what I term a *transnational feminist disability studies perspective*.

IN THE EYE OF THE HURRICANE

On August 28, 2005, due to the transnational reach of the US media, viewers from across the globe gathered around television sets to witness horrific scenes of despair, terror, and destitution as Hurricane Katrina launched itself on the US coastal towns and cities of Alabama, Mississippi, and Louisiana. In Louisiana's most famous city, New Orleans, the storm surge from 100 miles/hour winds caused the levees, which were supposed to protect this city lying below sea level, to break in three places, along the 17th Street Canal, the Industrial Canal, and the London Street Canal. We watched in disbelief as television screens replayed in horrific monotony the walls of water that crashed through the city, turning neighborhoods into a surging sea. We saw people stranded on rooftops, while others swam through brackish churning streets amid bloated bodies, animals, and sewage. We waited breathlessly for the help that came too late, while casting furtive glances at the crowded horror of the Superdome replete with rumor, fear, despair, and filth. And when the National Guard finally arrived on the streets fully armed with barbed wire and assault rifles to defend the wealth of the city from its impoverished residents (now refugees), and to perform daring rescues, we watched spellbound, unsure if our trembling was a result of our fear or our exhilaration.

Post Katrina, we are left with memories, analyses, recriminations, judgments, cynicism, and maybe, surprisingly, even some hope. News stories, documentaries, books, poetry, artwork, and television continue to keep alive these images through constant retellings urging us to never forget (Brinkley, 2006; Dallas Morning News, 2006; Dyson, 2006; Giroux, 2006; Lee & Pollard, 2006). In every one of these retellings, two discourses have consistently resurfaced, refusing facile erasure or trendy explanation—the obvious brutal reality of persistent poverty that had hitherto failed to gain center stage in national politics and its unremitting stranglehold on race. While these discourses relating race and poverty dominated the mainstream media coverage for a brief period of time, two other discourses, though significant, struggled for recognition, only to be recognized merely as subtext before being summarily ignored in any critical analyses. These two discourses were associated with the constructs "Third World" and "disability." I argue here that this oversight is partly because mainstream conceptions of both Third World and disability are already overdetermined by ideological discourses that constitute both constructs as "natural" conditions that defy any further explanation, treating the trope as if it is self-evident. As a result, the mere articulation of either of these terms is expected to instantaneously conjure up an imagery of such "abjection" that, with due apologies to a popular adage, a single trope is worth more than a thousand pictures.

Of the two, the construct of "Third World" enjoyed a dubious hypervisibility in mainstream media coverage of Katrina, used by journalists as a convenient sound byte to succinctly describe the widespread structural and social decay that the hurricane laid bare for all to see, and that all of them were astounded to confront for the very first time in New Orleans. Take, for example, the much-fabled image of the outraged and horrified Anderson Cooper from CNN (AC 360) standing amid the devastation in New Orleans, and gasping in horrified zeal while intoning, "Walking through the rubble, it feels like Sri Lanka, Sarajevo, somewhere else, not here, not home, not America" (Brinkley, 2006, p. 2004). This depiction of New Orleans as a "Third World" country was repeated by several others in the many retellings connected to the Katrina tragedy, and it necessitates some deconstruction. In describing a post-Katrina New Orleans as "Third World," was Cooper astounded that he was forced to use this phrase to describe an advanced industrial nation that was the presumed embodiment of the "free" world? What ideologies were at play to provoke this comparison? More importantly, why was he surprised to confront such destitution in his own backyard?

By raising these questions, my intent is to trouble the taken-for-granted assumptions that undergird the worldviews of journalists such as Cooper for whom the construct of the "Third World" serves merely as a metaphor for the "natural" state of utter destitution witnessed in nations overpopulated by people of color, whose "natural" conditions of despair, destitution, and dirt cause them to live out their lives in perpetual crises. This ahistorical and discursive conceptualization ignores an alternative conceptualization of the "Third World" as

> an analytical and political category [that represents an] "imagined community"...[that] links...the histories and struggles of third world [people] against racism, sexism, colonialism, imperialism, [ableism] and monopoly capital. "Imagined" not because it is not "real" but because it suggests potential alliances and collaborations across divisive boundaries and "community" because in spite of internal hierarchies within third world contexts, it nevertheless suggests a significant, deep commitment to what Benedict Anderson...calls horizontal comradeship.(Mohanty, 1991, p. 4)

The above definition of Third World replaces a metaphoric sound bite with a more concrete materialist definition, exposing the political and economic structures that contribute to the construction of the Third World as the very epitome of destitution. And it is specifically this reality of structural inequality created out of the violence of transnational capitalism that was forcibly exposed to public view by nature's fury. This was a story line that Cooper and his fellow journalists seemed reluctant to explore, and seemed even more bemused to encounter. Their bemusement was startling considering the statistics on poverty in the Deep South. Mississippi (with a 21.6 percent poverty rate) and Louisiana (19.4 percent) are the nation's poorest states, and New Orleans (with a 23.2 percent poverty rate) is the twelfth poorest city in the nation (Giroux, 2006). The city of New Orleans has had the third highest rate of children living in poverty in the United States. Its illiteracy rate was 40 percent, and almost 19 percent of New Orleans residents lacked health insurance (Giroux, 2006). Nearly one-third of the 150,000 people living in poverty were the elderly (Giroux, 2006).

Given that Cooper's show was called "AC 360," because it supposedly examined the news from all angles, how was it that Cooper and his colleagues had never encountered news stories (such as in the case of Katrina) where US citizens of color with and without disabilities had died/suffered because of poverty, lack of access to health care, environmental hazards, police brutality, or simply gross neglect—many of them in New Orleans and Mississippi in pre-Katrina times? Before Katrina, why did all these statistics not garner any attention in the news? Would exposing the failures of capitalism (otherwise touted as the best system there is) seem unpatriotic or heretical in this moment of national disaster? Was this why it was easier to have a discussion of "Third World poverty in the Ninth Ward" under the safe auspices of nature's fury? And what impact would this move to "naturalize" the disaster have for the "naturalization" of the relationship between poverty and race, and its "natural" association with the Third World?

Additionally, why did the hypervisibility of "third world" conditions cause Cooper and other journalists to render other aspects of this shameful moment in US history invisible? Why was the mainstream media not outraged that the bodies that kept surfacing in the brackish water, in abandoned houses, and on the streets, were mostly poor, black/brown, as well as elderly, critically ill, and/or disabled? Why did they not demand that state officials explain how this population did not figure in any official emergency evacuation plan? How did they imagine that a population, who, even in pre-Katrina times, were literally "confined" to their homes (because of inaccessible streets and public transportation) would find the means of transport to leave the city? Were there even shelters that were accessible to the varied needs of this population, if they actually heeded the warnings and left? Or did state authorities simply assume that since this population had seemingly survived their deplorable living conditions pre-Katrina, they would be able to do so once again? And if they did not survive, would anyone even notice?

The reality is that, in contrast to the hypervisibility of third world conditions, disability was surprisingly rendered invisible in these news reports. I describe this invisibility as surprising because usually in a sensation-driven media, the difference that disability embodies generally elicits intense attention. In fact, as Rosemarie Garland Thomson (2002) has remarked:

> The history of disabled in the Western world is in part the history of being on display, of being visually conspicuous while politically and socially erased...Disabled people have variously been objects of awe, scorn, terror, delight, inspiration, pity, laughter, or fascination—but they have always been stared at...Staring...creates disability as a state of absolute difference rather than simply one more variation in human form. At the same time staring constitutes disability identity by manifesting power relations between the subject positions of disabled and able-bodied. (pp. 76–77)

Now, in making this claim of disability's invisibility in media coverage, I am not asserting that it was impossible to stare at *disability* in the news coverage on Katrina. On the other hand, even though the media did not make much of it, such images were aplenty—a fact that disabled activist and author Anne Finger (2005) noted when she wrote:

> Throughout this week, I've been struck by the presence of disability... I read of a woman in the Superdome grabbing a reporter's arm, pleading for water for her daughter, a wheelchair user. "I'm afraid she's going to have a seizure," the mother cried. On NPR, I hear the voice of a man calling out, "Dilantin! I need Dilantin!" The president of Jefferson Parrish breaking down as he told of a man who'd been reassuring his mother, institutionalized in a nursing home, that help was on the way—only to learn that she had drowned—on Friday. And, of course, that image of the woman in the wheelchair dead outside the Convention Center. (para 2)

In the final sentence of the quote, Finger refers to the ubiquitous television still of an elderly woman crouched in her wheelchair outside the Superdome with a sheet covering most of her body, haunting us in her tragic stillness. The only image of disability flashed so often on our television screens, she served as the very embodiment of the metaphor for disaster, despair, and death—metaphors that have historically shaped and therefore naturalized the public's perception of disability and disabled people.

The ultimate symbol of pity, revulsion, and uselessness—it was an image that caused us to either turn away from our television sets, and/or startled many of us into a guilty charity. But as Anne Finger (2005) again notes, though

> the impulse to reach out and offer help [to] those in need is a generous and good one... charity keeps in place the notion that the "problem" is located in the bodies of disabled people; in the individuals who [died or who] have been displaced, rather than in social structures and in economic policies that often ignore and usually render the objects of charity as invisible. (para 6)

It is Finger's insightful comment about the materiality of disability that explains the nature of the stares we leveled at disabled bodies that appeared on our television sets. Our habitual staring at disabled bodies as the "natural" embodiment of intransigent physiological difference could no longer be sustained in the face of the actual social, political, and economic conditions that were laid bare as the real impediments to meaningful lives for disabled people. In other words, I am arguing here that the aftermath of Katrina became one of those truth-telling times when the ideology of disability as a purely "natural" phenomenon could no longer be sustained in the face of the obvious failure of social policy to support the survival of disabled people in their daily lives. Three years after Katrina, in September 2008, a report on a massive evacuation of the New Orleans on the eve of another threatening hurricane read:

> One local judge observed after days at the bus station, "It is unbelievable just how many disabled and elderly people actually live in our community. They just keep getting off these buses with their wheelchairs, their canes and crutches. Dozens, then hundreds, then thousands. Many must usually be housebound, because we rarely see them." (Quigley, 2008, para. 7)

It is in this context that the antinomies of Third World and disability become apparent. On the one hand, the hypervisibility of the Third World appeared in sharp contrast to the invisibility of disability only because the former could be safely invoked as a naturalized condition that could inspire emotion but not transformation. On the other hand, to acknowledge disability required the recognition of the material violence waged against disabled bodies—a recognition that would destroy the tropes that construct disability as the "natural" rather than a "political" (read materialist) embodiment of destitution. Thus, even though on the surface the two constructs, Third World and disability, experienced differential treatment in their representations, it is their commonalities that actually forced these differentiations—their commonality being the collective public effort to read them as "natural" rather than "political/materialist" constructs. And it is to this commonality that I turn to build my argument in the following sections of this chapter.

EMBODIED ANTINOMIES: THIRD WORLD FEMINIST THEORY AND DISABILITY STUDIES

In an essay that makes the case for the inclusion of feminist disability studies in mainstream feminist discourse, Rosemarie Garland-Thomson (2005) provocatively describes such scholarship as "academic cultural work with a sharp political edge and a vigorous political punch" (p. 1557). In another essay, Judy Rohrer (2005) echoes Garland-Thomson's vision when she asks that feminists formulate a "disability theory of feminism" (p. 40)—one that "upsets old frameworks and allows new questions to be asked" (p. 41). In Rohrer's view, the deployment of a disability analysis from within feminism deepens feminist analyses of the simultaneity of oppression, transgressive body politics, notions of interdependence and "choice," and the (re)visioning of ironic possibilities.

As a feminist who also works in the area of disability studies, I argue along with Garland-Thomson and Rohrer that feminist disability studies does have radical potential, though I will argue that contemporary scholarship in this field has not yet realized this potential. My critique of contemporary scholarship in feminist disability studies is that while it has been extremely effective in foregrounding the limitations of the universalizing category of "woman" that mainstream feminism continues to uphold (notwithstanding critiques from poor women, lesbians, women of color, and third world women), it falls prey to its own critique of normativity by failing to seriously engage "difference" within its own ranks along the axes of race, class, ethnicity, sexuality, and national difference. Thus, even though Garland-Thomson argues (and I agree with her) that disability as an analytical category can be useful in destabilizing static notions of identity, in exploring issues of intersectionality, and in investigating the complexity of (disabled) embodiment, I will argue that much of feminist disability studies is limited because of its overreliance on metaphor rather than materiality.

I want to state very clearly here that I am not dismissing the radical possibilities embodied in feminist disability studies, especially its critique of essentialist/static notions of identity. While I agree with disability studies scholars that in a dismodern[1] postidentity world (Davis, 2002), disability as a "heterogeneous and fluid category" embodies the "ultimate postmodern subjectivity" (Rohrer, 2005, pp. 41–42), I argue that the radical potential of this subjectivity can only be harnessed within certain privileged material contexts that these scholars appear to take for granted. By materiality I mean the actual historical, social, and economic conditions that impact (disabled) people's lives, and that are further mediated by the politics of race, ethnicity, gender, sexuality, and nation (Morris, 1991; Thomas, 1999). I am therefore arguing that, for feminist disability studies to make good its claims for transformative politics, it would have to expand its analytics from discursive interventions to a foregrounding of the materiality of structural constraints that actually give rise to the oppressive binaries of self/other, normal/disabled, and us/them.

For example, in a discussion on disabled identity from a feminist disability studies perspective, Garland-Thomson (2005) explains that disability is often presented "as an exceptional and escapable calamity, rather than as what is perhaps the most universal of human conditions" (p. 1568). She, therefore, argues that disability should be presented as "an integral part of one's embodiment, character, life, and way of relating to the world…as part of the spectrum of human variation" (p. 1568). While it is true that Garland-Thomson's argument from a feminist disability studies perspective poses a fundamental challenge to feminist concepts of the (ab)normal body, there is an implicit assumption in her argument that the acquisition of a disabled identity always occurs outside of historical, social, and economic contexts. This position becomes especially problematic when issues of race, class, gender, sexuality, ethnicity, and nation intersect with disabled identity—an argument I have consistently made in the previous chapters.

For example, how can acquiring a disability be celebrated as "the most universal of human conditions," if it is acquired under the oppressive conditions of poverty, economic exploitation, police brutality, neocolonial violence, and lack of access to adequate health care and education? What happens when human variation (e.g., race) is itself deployed in the construction of disabled identities for purely oppressive purposes (e.g., slavery, colonialism, immigration law, etc.)? How can cyborg subjectivities be celebrated when the manufacture of prostheses and assistive technology is dependent on an exploitative international division of labor? How does one "value interdependence" (Rohrer, 2005, p. 47) within imperialist/neocolonial contexts that locate consumers and producers of goods and services within a network of fundamentally unequal social relationships (Erevelles, 1996)? And finally, how do we build solidarity across difference even while we negotiate the distances that simultaneously separate and divide us within the contemporary context of transnational capitalism? Feminist disability studies has offered few responses to these questions.

Like feminist disability studies, third world feminism offers a critique of normative tendencies in (Western) mainstream feminism. Here, "western" is used to describe a certain normative construction of "woman" (read: educated, modern, having control of one's body, and the freedom to make one's own decisions) against whom the "average" third world woman is compared and found to be lacking. The "average" third world woman is generally represented as leading an "essentially truncated life on account of her gender (read: sexually constrained) and her being 'Third World' (read: ignorant, poor, uneducated, tradition-bound, domestic, family oriented, victimized, etc.)" (Mohanty, 1997, p. 80). These images constitute third world women as an embodiment of lack, and mirror ableist representations of disabled women who have also had to struggle against the stereotypical images of pathetic victimized femininity that justify patriarchal, imperialist, and ableist interventions (Fine & Asch, 1988; Garland-Thomson, 1997; Ghai, 2003; Morris, 1991; Thomas, 1999). And yet, notwithstanding the possibilities for a common platform of resistance, disability is conspicuously missing in third world feminist analyses of difference. For example, even though there are more than 35 million women who are disabled in India, disabled Indian feminist Anita Ghai (2003) reports that the National Women's Commission has testified that "disability is not an issue that attracts feminists" (p. 25).

This occlusion of disability issues in third world feminism is costly, especially when discussing (disabled) women's experiences in the specific context
of the patriarchal postcolonial state (Kaplan, Alarcon, & Moallem, 1999;
Mohanty, et al., 1991; Rai, 1996). Third world feminists have argued that
the postcolonial state, "the central site of 'hegemonic masculinity"'...[is
responsible for monitoring] the defining lines of citizenship for women,
racialized ethnicities, and sexualities in the construction of a socially strati-
fied society." In fact, the state "looms large in women's lives *only* [my empha-
sis] when women transgress the boundaries set by the state in various areas
of public and private life over which it has jurisdiction" (Rai, 1996, p. 36).
Since disabled women have historically been viewed as dangerous (Garland-
Thomson, 1997; Ghai, 2003; Morris, 1991; Thomas, 1999), the patriarchal
and ableist state closely patrols the boundaries of female bodily difference
as is evident in state practices that seek to control (disabled) women's reproduction (Ghai, 2003; Molina, 2006); (disabled) women's immigration and
citizenship rights (Molina, 2006); and (disabled) women's economic (in)
dependence (Chang, 2000; Erevelles, 2006; Livingston, 2006).

Additionally, notwithstanding "different histories with respect to the particular inheritance of post-fifteenth-century Euro-American hegemony—
the inheritance of slavery, enforced migration, plantation and indentured
labor, colonialism, imperial conquest, and genocide" (Mohanty, 1991,
p. 10)—third world feminists should have common cause around at least
one issue—that of disability, an inevitable repercussion of the violence of
such oppressive practices/structures. So then, in which spaces do disabled
third women claim sisterhood? How do they relate to their disabled sisters
who derive certain privileges from residing in the very imperialist states that
facilitated their becoming disabled in the first place? More urgently, how do
they challenge their invisibility among their third world sisters who, while
critiquing the imperialist state, refuse to foreground its ableist assumptions
that ultimately work against all third world women?

DISABILITY AS IMPERIALIST DISCOURSE: THE
POLITICS OF GENDER, RACE, AND NATION

I now turn to the very real and immediate context of war. Almost daily, on
the news, there are reports of roadside bombs detonating, the launching of
military offensives, the consistent regularity of power failures, and shortages
of food, drinking water, and fuel, in the "postwar" contexts of a devastated
Afghanistan and an occupied Iraq. Here, in the United States, a few news
media organizations keep a diligent count of the number of US soldiers
killed in the war—the most current count in Iraq being around 4,432, and
in Afghanistan being 1448 (iCasualties, 2011). Even more infrequently, and

almost always as a passing note, we hear a rare report of disabled US war veterans returning from combat—a probable count estimated at 32,049 from Iraq (iCasualties, 2011). In Afghanistan, the first country targeted in the "war on terror," the number of civilian deaths reported in the 2002 were 3,800 (Herold, 2002). More recently, Human Rights Watch (2008) reported that in 2006, the number of civilian deaths was 929, and in 2007 the number of civilian deaths was 1,163. On the Iraqi side, the number of civilian and military deaths reported is contested, with reports varying from 49,611 (iCasualties, 2011) to around 11,000 (Iraq Body Count, 2011). I was unable to find any statistics on Afghan and Iraqi civilians and members of the military (and now the insurgency) who have become disabled as a result of the war and the postwar conflict. I find this extremely troubling, since neither the alternative press nor radical scholars in the academy seem perturbed by these omissions.

In moving from a national context of Katrina to a transnational context of the wars in Iraq and Afghanistan, why has there been little outrage and protest not just by Anderson Cooper but also by his US audience, when for the last five years similar devastating accounts of death, destruction, and disability, from Afghanistan and Iraq have briefly appeared on television before disappearing forever with little debate and/or discussion? This is extremely problematic in light of the fact that this devastation was on a much larger scale and was a direct result of US imperialist policies. Even more troubling has been the unemotional response from both people of color and disabled communities in the United States. After all, this war has created more disability in people of color communities with very little or no social and economic support.

But it is not just the missing statistics of disability that is troubling in this time of war. What appears more troubling are the missing analyses of "disability and war" in the otherwise radical scholarship of both feminist disability studies and third world feminism, notwithstanding the relevance of this topic for both analytical frameworks. To put it simply, war is one of the largest producers of disability in a world that is still inhospitable to disabled people (Charlton, 1998; Russell, 1998) and their caregivers, most of whom are predominantly women (Chang, 2000; Glenn, 1992; Parker, 1993). In the advanced industrialized nations in Europe and the Americas, while upper- and middle-class disabled people may enjoy a certain level of social and economic accessibility, poor disabled people, and, in particular, poor disabled people of color, experience both social and economic oppression. This oppression is further exacerbated in third world contexts. Thus, while disabled US war veterans may be able to anticipate at least a minimal level of services and social support on their return from the war front, disabled veterans and civilians in the war-torn areas of the Third World may be in more dire straits because of an inadequate, overburdened, and/or nonexistent infrastructure in service provision for disabled populations. In contexts where subsistence is itself a struggle, third world disabled people, in general, and third world women, in particular, who are themselves disabled and/or who care for disabled family members/clients, face the social, political, and economic implications of being invisible (Chang, 2000; Erevelles, 1996; Ghai, 2003).

The intersections of gender, disability, and race within the neocolonial state are especially relevant in the contemporary context of war, because nationalist discourses use war as a rallying point to support their contradictory stance, where difference is simultaneously denied and yet at the same time universalized (Kaplan, et al., 1999). For example, post 9/11 US nationalist discourses, in an attempt to build an "imagined community" (Anderson, 1983) of patriots, sought to erase difference along the axes of race, class, gender, disability, and sexuality while at same time universalizing difference along the axes of a reified "U.S. citizenship." In this contradictory nationalist space of both denial and reification, the politics of race, gender, and disability are bound in relationships that are simultaneously both dangerous and transgressive.

But it is not just in times of war that the gendered aspects of the nation-state become apparent (Kaplan, et al., 1999; Mohanty, 1991; Rai, 1996). In fact, even in peacetime, the relationship of women to the state is mediated via their role as biological reproducers (mothers of the nation), as members of ethnic collectives, as participants in the ideological reproduction of the national collectivity, as transmitters of its culture; and as participants in national, economic, political, and military struggles (Waylen, 1996, p. 15). Seen as essential to the biological, social, and cultural reproduction of national identity, women are, therefore, often subject to the close scrutiny of the normalizing regime of the nation-state.

The disciplinary and regulatory functions of this normalizing regime are manifested in state policies that both feminist disability studies and third world feminism would find familiar. Waylen (1996) separates these policies into three categories: (a) policies aimed particularly at women via so-called protective legislation on reproduction (e.g., abortion, maternity leave); (b) policies that mediate the relationships between men and women (e.g., property rights, sexuality, family relations); (c) and policies that are not gender neutral because they subdivide into the public sphere (war, foreign policy, international trade, resource extraction) and the private sphere (welfare and reproduction), a space where women and children are both providers and recipients of these services, and are often forced to liaison with welfare services on behalf of their family members. Failure to adhere to the ideological norms of the nation-state has exacted severe material costs from certain classes of women who are then designated as deviant/abnormal citizens. I offer two examples to illustrate this point.

In the intersecting context of immigration legislation and reproductive rights, one of the central questions has historically been: Who may give birth to citizens (Molina, 2006)? Molina notes that prior to the 1924 Immigration Act, Mexican male laborers, whose physical bodies were seen to be uniquely equipped to perform physical labor in the agricultural, mining, and railroad industries, were not regarded as "diseased" even though the number of Mexicans who died of tuberculosis were almost double that of all other immigrant groups. On the other hand, Mexican women have consistently been subject to the close scrutiny of the state around the issue of reproduction, such that the high infant mortality rates in their communities were used as an indication not of poor economic conditions and inadequate prenatal care, but of Mexican women's ill-health, lack of education, and poor parenting skills. In this way, Mexican women were cast as diseased reproducers of unfit citizens and therefore undeserving of the privilege of legal immigration.

Similarly, Alexander and Mohanty (1997) describe how the colonial/postcolonial/neocolonial nation-state conflates (white)(hetero)sexuality with citizenship and organizes a "citizenship machinery" such that all those who deviate from this norm are seen as suspect. Thus, for example, while African American women's sexuality was effectively harnessed for the reproduction of slavery in the service of the colonial state, they were deemed as fit only for "a dehumanized reproduction" (Price & Shildrick, 1999, p. 80). This construction of African American women's sexuality and reproductive capacity continues to manifest itself in the neocolonial state via administrative (social) policies, where African American women with HIV/AIDS are represented as being both dependent and diseased, thereby denying them the right of access to resources that they need for their survival. Evelyn Hammonds (1997) describes how even though African American women's voices are not heard in discussions of HIV/AIDS, the intimate details of their lives while living with HIV/AIDS is often widely exposed and discussed in efforts to justify their victimization. In this way African American women living with HIV/AIDS are represented as "the victims that are the 'other' of the 'other,' the deviants of the deviant, irrespective of their sexual identities or practices" (Hammonds, 1997, p. 179).

In both of these examples, "disability" serves as the political and analytical category deployed by the colonialist state to patrol the boundaries of citizenship. Yet, notwithstanding the central role "disability" plays in the justification of nationalist discourses of colonialism/imperialism/neocolonialism, and the material consequences that (disabled) third world women of color experience as a result of such representations, both third world feminist theory and feminist disability studies have failed to explore the implications of interpreting disability in this way. This is perhaps because, as Stienstra (2002) reports, third world feminists uncritically accept disability as an issue of individual pathology/tragedy and therefore not a state responsibility, and by doing so, they problematically (re)locate disability in the "private" sphere. Similarly, feminist disability studies theorists, even though they argue that disability is not a "private" issue but a "public" social category, often fail to offer a sustained critique of the "public" context in which the neocolonial state is implicated in the pathologizing of not only disability but also of race, gender, and nation. An opportunity to do precisely this analysis within both third world feminism and feminist disability studies is possible when analyzing the intersection of gender, race, and disability in the context of war—a point I turn to in the next section.

MILITARIZING/MATERIALIZING DIFFERENCE: GENDER, RACE, AND DISABILITY IN WAR TIME

Third world feminists Jacqui Alexander and Chandra Talapade Mohanty (1997) argue that "militarized [hyper]masculinity" (p. xxv) has a strategic function in the reproduction of (neo)colonialism and the (re)organization of gendered hierarchies in the nation-state. For example, in the "patriotic" context of war, men's military service to the nation-state is both paid and honored, while women's service to their families is deemed as self-sacrifice and therefore unpaid (Haslanger, 2003). As a result, in wartime, the nationalist popular media creates a seemingly facile relationship between violent male behavior and hypermasculinity by glorifying tough, aggressive, and robustly masculine soldiers (Myrttinen, 2004), while ignoring women unless they appear in "recognizable and traditional roles such as the mourning widow or the all-feeling mother" (Lidinsky, 2005, p. 142). Moreover, in an effort to maintain its robustly masculine image, the military exists in persistent terror of being emasculated (Pin-Fat & Stern, 2005), fearful that an "effeminate masculinity" may be ineffectual in the critical task of loyalty and defense of the nation-state (Alexander & Mohanty, 1997, p. xxvi). Thus, even though both women and gay men serve in the US military, gay men, in particular, who represent a "feminized masculinity" in the popular imagination, had been required until very recently to maintain a "silent" presence, in order to sustain the mythical image of the hypermasculine imperialist army.

However, even tough and aggressive US soldiers are humbled while living through the actual materiality of war. War injuries produce disability—another threat to the hypermasculine imagery. Many of the soldiers who are diagnosed with depression, posttraumatic stress, and mental illness are afraid to admit their vulnerability and dependence on others—traits that appear so contradictory to their fictional ideal of masculinity because of their association with disability (Glasser, 2005). In Operation Iraqi Freedom, soldiers are reported to have access to the best emergency medical attention and advances in medical technology during the time period immediately after acquiring their injuries[2], especially in relation to prosthetics. Proud of its technology in this area, the military has announced new efforts to keep certain disabled personnel on active duty if they can regain their fitness after being fitted with a prosthetic (Hull, 2004). One such example is David Rozelle, who having been fitted with a prosthetic leg was redeployed to Iraq as commander of the Third Armored Cavalry Regiment. One of the few disabled soldiers celebrated in the mass media, Rozelle was portrayed as the very embodiment of the saying—"once a soldier, always a soldier"—because he was seen as the very embodiment of the fabled toughness and manliness of the US military.

In fact, disabled soldiers such as Rozelle could be seen to represent a new identity in contemporary military discourses—"the cyborg soldier...the juncture of ideals, metals, chemicals, and people who make weapons of computers and computers of weapons and soldiers" (Masters, 2005, p. 113). The cyborg soldier is the new posthuman subject who is intimately inter-connected with modern technologies of war (e.g., the Patriot missile, smart bombs, etc.) that are infused with the ability to reason and think without being interrupted by emotions, guilt, or bodily limitations. As a result, in this new cyborg militarism, the embodied human soldier is the weakest link. In fact, the cyborg soldier, in almost every way, is in constant battle against the normal human male body using "technological prostheses that repli-cate biological senses while circumventing human biological limitations: poor eyesight, hearing and discernment" (Masters, 2005, p. 122). Masters describes this cyborg soldier as "a much more resilient subject, a hegemonic technological subject animated by masculine subjectivity, effectively miti-gating against the imperfections of the human body while simultaneously [forging] a close identification with white, heterosexual, masculine subjec-tivity" (p. 121).

From a feminist disability studies perspective that draws on a discur-sive analysis, the cyborg soldier is a cause for celebration. The cyborg sol-dier as posthuman[3] subject troubles the boundaries of normal/abnormal humanity—creating a transgressive image of disabled subjectivity that mod-ernist discourses have historically denied. Whereas disabled subjectivity has historically been categorized as effeminate, disability as embodied by the body of the hypermasculine cyborg soldier challenges oppressive images of weak, pitiable, broken, and wounded human flesh, and offers more empow-ering and transgressive imagery of possibility and potential. Additionally, one of the benefits of militarism is that advanced technologies developed in the battlefield often trickle down to domestic markets (cell phones, video games, and now high-tech prostheses) to enhance the quality of (disabled) civilian life. Thus, some feminist disability studies theorists could argue that it is not just at the level of discourse but also at the level of materiality that the cyborg soldier can offer transgressive possibilities for the category of disability.

However, these transgressions and material possibilities when situated within the social, political, and economic context of an imperialist war foregrounds a more sobering scenario of violence, invisibility, and dehumanization. For example, Masters (2005) points out that one reason the modern battlefield can embrace the cyborg soldier is that the cyborg soldier may never have to actually be in the battlefield, and therefore may "never have to lay human eyes on the enemy because to kill in a battle is to aim at a blip in a radar screen or a heat sensored image" (p. 123). Thus, there is very little space to distinguish between what is simulation and what is reality. This, Masters argues, produces a kind of isolation from the material reality of the battlefield by making the body disappear from the war, resulting in the denial and suppression of embodiment. Masters reports that 23,000 cyborg-guided bombs were dropped in the early phases of Operation Iraqi Freedom as compared to 9,500 in Operation Desert Storm, an observation that seldom came to light in popular depictions of the war as "shock and awe" with limited collateral damage. Thus, within cyborg discourse, the other (enemy) is technologically dehumanized, now constituted as a "code problem in need of techno-scientific solutions" (p. 124).

But what if, we actually looked at the "other" face of disability—one that resists codification as cyborg because of actual social, political, and economic deprivation? As mentioned earlier, war produces disabilities that include loss of limbs, paralysis, emotional trauma—disabilities that challenge families, communities, and government agencies (Safran, 2001). For example, in Afghanistan, vast numbers of people have physical disabilities arising due to polio; blast injuries—visual disabilities from untreated eye diseases and blasts; mental disabilities associated with malnutrition, iodine-deficiency disorders, and trauma; and epilepsy associated with trauma or with untreated malaria (Miles, 2002). Moreover, Afghan refugees wounded and/or disabled as a result of "friendly fire" have had to depend on the meager resources of their families for survival. Miles (2002) has reported that access to disability services for women is very limited, and during Taliban rule these services ceased functioning. In addition, access to even community rehabilitation is restricted for women and children. In an interesting observation, the restriction of mobility of Afghan women has actually resulted in fewer women being killed or disabled by fighting, landmines, and unexploded bombs. Women also participate disproportionately in the informal home care and assistance—a major source of disability services in the country. Given these material realities, neither feminist disability studies nor third world feminism can dismiss disability in third world contexts as either a troublesome trope or an irritating detail.

In Iraq, the situation is even more sobering. Like Afghanistan, Iraq too has suffered 15 years of war, economic sanctions, and now the US invasion and ongoing occupation of Iraq. A study by the United Nations Development Program (UNDP) contained the following indices of what they term the "social misery" in Iraq:

- Nearly a quarter of Iraq's children suffer from chronic malnutrition;
- The probability of dying before 40 of Iraqi children born between 2000 and 2004 is approximately three times the level in neighboring countries;
- More than 722,000 Iraqi families have no access to either safe or stable drinking water;
- Forty percent of families in urban areas live in neighborhoods with sewage on the streets;
- More than 200,000 Iraqis have "chronic" disabilities caused by war (Walsh, 2005).

In addition, lessons learned from other war-torn countries such as Bosnia, Sierra Leone, and Kosovo demonstrate that there is also a proliferation of other invisible disabilities among civilian populations living through a war. For example, McKay (2004) reports that, in Sierra Leone, children participating in war return to rural communities with memories of terror and day-to-day suffering. Additionally, children exposed to war experience post-traumatic stress, anxiety and depressive symptoms, psycho-physiological disturbances, behavioral problems, and personality changes, in addition to physical traumas resulting from injury, physical deformities, and diseases such as tuberculosis, malaria, and parasites (Al-Ali, 2005; Kuterovac-Jagodic, 2003; McKay, 2004).

Ghobarah, Huth, and Russett (2004) describe some major influences wars have on public health infrastructures. First, as mentioned earlier, wars increase the exposure of the civilian population to conditions that increase the risk of disease, injury, and death as a result of displacement. Bad conditions of food, water, sanitation, and housing turn refugee camps into vectors for infectious disease. With the destruction of the health care infrastructure, prevention and treatment programs are weakened, and often in these circumstances new strains that are drug resistant (e.g., tuberculosis, HIV/AIDS) evolve. Second, wars reduce the pool of available resources for expenditure on health care for the general population, as well as constrain the level of resources allocated to the public health care system in their aftermath. Third, wartime destruction of the transportation infrastructure weakens the distribution of clean water, food, medicine, and relief supplies to both refugees and those who remain behind in these war-torn areas.

In citing these statistics, I am attempting to show how the proliferation of disability in war actively affects positive and negative meanings that are attributed to the category of disability. In third world contexts, international organizations such as the World Bank and the International Monetary Fund are often instrumental in defining and administering disability, with devastating consequences for disabled people themselves as exemplified by the use of the concept of the DALY—disability adjusted life years (Erevelles, 2006). According to the World Bank, the DALY is

> a unit used for measuring both the global burden of disease and the effectiveness of health interventions, as indicated by reductions in the disease burden. It is calculated as the present value of the future years of disability-free life that are lost as the result of the premature deaths or cases of disability occurring in a particular year. (Abbasi, 1999, para. 16)

Put more simply, using the DALY, the World Bank prioritizes health interventions by calculating their relative cost-effectiveness. In other words, cost-effectiveness is measured by the number of DALYs saved through each intervention, where the cost of each intervention is weighed against the person's potential "productivity" (i.e., contribution to economic growth) (Abbasi, 1999). Thus each disease, ailment, or disability is classified according to how many years of "productive" (disability-free) life the individual loses as a result, and is weighted against age and work potential. Hence, children and the elderly have lower value than young adults, and presumably disabled persons who are unable to work are awarded zero value and therefore have little or no entitlement to health services at public expense (Erevelles, 2006).

From a feminist disability studies perspective that examines disability in post/neocolonial contexts, such calculations can only be regarded as simply preposterous. In fact, scholars in the area of disability studies have already critiqued how ableist society has constructed disabled people as defective citizens incapable of contributing anything to society (Charlton, 1998; Garland-Thomson, 1997; Kittay, 1999; Russell, 1998). For example, Marta Russell (1998) has vividly exposed the brutal connection between capitalism and social Darwinism that is implicit in these arguments, and that constructs disabled people as "defective" and unproductive in the economy. However, as I have argued in previous chapters, productivity is not a transhistorical category, but is instead very much dependent on historical context. Under the present demands of (global) capitalism and US imperialism, an individual's productivity is not measured by his or her skill to produce goods and services that would satisfy social/human needs; rather, her or his productivity is based solely on the capitalists' exploitative demands for increasing profits. This logic under which capitalism and imperialism operates has deleterious effects on disabled individuals. Since most disabled individuals have physiological complications that prevent the efficient extraction of surplus value from their labor power, their labor power is accorded little value within the competitive marketplace, and they are, therefore, constructed as unemployable. Thus, the DALY constitutes disabled people as a liability to the state rather than as a valued investment.

However, it is not just the representational violence of the DALY that is significant in this analysis. From a third world feminist perspective that also engages disability in post/neocolonial contexts, the material implications of these representations on third world women's lives cannot be ignored. For example, disability policies implemented by international organizations such as the World Bank and the International Monetary Fund as part of their proposed Structural Adjustment Programs[4] have pushed for the increased privatization of health care and user-financed health services—a move that has served to transfer resources from poor clients to the wealthy investors of health care. This is evident in the Community Based Rehabilitation Programs (CBRs) that are actively supported by the World Bank and other international organizations such as ActionAid, and are perceived to be one of the most cost-efficient means to save on mounting staff costs, wastage of manpower, and the low efficiency of services (Thomas, 1992). Thus, in an attempt to ensure maximum cost-efficiency, policy makers assume that the primary support for these programs will come from the community, where parents and workers in the community supervised by a village rehabilitation worker (VRW) and a multipurpose rehabilitation worker (MRW)—(female) health volunteers living in the community—will provide more specialized services to disabled members of the community.

However, CBR only serves to transfer the costs of services to the community. Thus, for example, even one of its advocates, Maya Thomas (1992), director of the disability division, ActionAid, India, has admitted that "the trend of progressive impoverishment of rural dwellings and the growing abandonment of extended family systems leave little economic and manpower resources in families that continue to look after the needs of their disabled members" (p. 9). Further, in patriarchal contexts, the provision of rehabilitation services by the family predominantly implies the woman, and so this becomes another burden in the life of the rural housewife caught up in her struggle for day-to-day economic survival. At the same time, most of the rehabilitation aides who are low down in the occupational hierarchy and who receive pitiably low wages are once again predominantly poor women from the community. Therefore, what has happened is that these state-initiated policies that have been celebrated for their cost-effectiveness are actually geared to "[mobilize]...people's resources for government programs" (Kalyanpur, 1996, p. 125), where the additional costs of these services continue to be absorbed by both the lowly paid and unpaid labor of poor third world women. In a context where war is responsible for the proliferation of disability, it is critical that third world feminists examine the impact of disability on (both nondisabled and disabled) third world women's lives as they struggle against the oppressive policies/practices of the imperialist/neocolonial state.

TELLING IT LIKE IT IS: IMPERIALISM/NEOCOLONIALISM AS THE NEW EUGENICS

In earlier sections of this chapter, I have made the case for why it is critical that both feminist disability studies and third world feminism critically engage disability within the postcolonial/neocolonial, especially in the current context of war. In this final section of the chapter, I make the case for a *transnational feminist disability studies perspective*—a perspective that engages gender and disability and their intersection with race, class, and sexuality within the material context of the post/neocolonial state. Such a perspective is neither ahistorical, nor limited by national/ethnic boundaries. It is neither burdened by bourgeois interests nor restricted by normative modes of being. Rather, this perspective maps both the continuities and discontinuities across different historical periods that have both separated and connected women along the axes of race, class, disability, sexuality, ethnicity, and nationality, by foregrounding not just discursive representations but also the material (read actual) conditions of their lives.

To provide an example of a transnational feminist disability studies perspective, I link the discussion of disability and war to the oppressive practices of the eugenic movement within the broader transnational context of colonialism/neocolonialism. In other words, as I have already shown in the earlier chapters, it is possible to map out the historical continuities and discontinuities between racism, sexism, and ableism embodied in the eugenic practices of the early twentieth century and the contemporary context of neocolonialist wars and their impact on disability, race, and gender in the third world. The term "eugenics" was coined in 1883 in Britain by Francis Galton to describe a program of selective breeding. Within the imperialistic context of colonialism, eugenics thrived on the fear of racialized Others, fueled by racist associations of genetic degeneration and disease. Chamberlin and Gilman (1985) define degeneration as the losing of properties of the genus. The fear of the loss of this generative force encouraged typological as well as physical and biological speculation, and in doing so, supported the unscientific stereotyping of physiological differences. Degeneration became a compelling racial metaphor such that the colonized races were assumed to be intrinsically degenerate, and as a result could never be improved. By hinting at the imminent possibility of social decay if these degenerate "bodies" were not brought under control, the segregation and the destruction of the colonized races was regarded as necessary for the public good because maintaining biological distance was critical to preventing degeneracy—all practices that served to justify the violence of colonialism.

The association of degeneracy and disease with racial difference also translated into an attribution of diminished cognitive and rational capacities of nonwhite populations. Disability-related labels such as "feeble-mindedness" and "mental illness" were oftentimes seen as synonymous with bodies marked oppressively by race. Fearing that such characteristics could be passed down from generation to generation, and further pose a threat to the dominant white race, "protective" practices such as forced sterilizations, rigid miscegenation laws, residential segregation in ghettoes, barrios, reservations, and other state institutions, and sometimes even genocide (e.g., Holocaust) were brought to bear on nonwhite populations by bringing into play the oppressive practices of eugenics. Disability studies scholars Snyder and Mitchell (2006), in adapting race theorist Paul Gilroy's *Black Atlantic* to describe the trans-Atlantic cultural exchange in discourses of race in the early twentieth century, have identified what they term a "Eugenic Atlantic" in an attempt to demonstrate the parallel exchange in discourses of race and disability via the dehumanizing practices of eugenics. They, therefore, argue that eugenics needs to be understood as a trans-Atlantic ideology that used the social category of disability to produce constructs such as intelligent quotients (IQs), and practices such as institutionalization, sterilization, segregated education, and restrictive immigration policies that had detrimental effects not only on persons of color, but also on disabled people—all of whom were grouped under the limited but all-encompassing category of "defect."

While Snyder and Mitchell's argument is critical in foregrounding the discursive import of disability and race in eugenic ideologies, their conceptualization of disability mirrors that of feminist disability studies that I critiqued earlier in this chapter. For example, in the chapter entitled "The Eugenic Atlantic" in their book *Cultural Locations of Disability*, Snyder and Mitchell (2006) rightly castigate historians for ignoring the violence perpetrated against disabled people during the Nazi regime, while also making the ironic observation that "[e]ven among countries that were engaged military enemies at the time, scientific and cultural agreement about the menace of 'defectives' transcended battlefields and diplomatic impasses as an ideological function" (p. 104). In pressing this claim, Snyder and Mitchell are right on the mark in describing "the cultural groundwork of disability" as rooted in a transnational ideology of "in-built biological inferiority" (p. 128). However, it is precisely in this rendering of disability as an ideology rooted in culture, rather than as a historical materialist construct, that they inadvertently constitute disability as a ahistorical "naturalized" condition, where the operative assumption remains in the biological.

I offer this critique by drawing on the argument that I made earlier in this chapter (as well as in earlier chapters) that colonialism and neocolonialism along with the imperialistic practices that they sustain are not merely ideological in force. They are also material—namely economic. If these constructions were merely ideological, then it would be entirely possible to differentiate the good ideologies from the bad ideologies in an effort to bring about social transformation. However, my argument in this chapter points to a material base from which these ideologies stem. Thus, for example, I would argue that Nazism cannot be read merely as an aberrant ideology, but rather, it should be read as an aberrant ideology that was rooted in a particular social and economic order that depended on the devaluation of racial, female, and disabled bodies to sustain that order. Similarly, in the two examples of internal colonization (Hurricane Katrina and its aftermath) and neocolonialism/imperialism (wars in Iraq and Afghanistan) that I offered in this chapter, irrational though they may seem to the discerning public, they are really "rational" interventions by imperialist powers that exploit the bodies of the disenfranchised to support their aims for accumulation and profit. Thus, while I agree with Snyder and Mitchell's premise that disability offers a radical understanding of the cultural within a trans-Atlantic discourse, I call for an expansion of their argument into transnational contexts that will consider how the projects of colonialism, nation-building, and neocolonialism have historically been intimately intertwined with eugenic policies that have contributed to the social and material construction of people of color and people with disabilities as "unfit bodies" or "unworthy citizens."

Thus, drawing on the argument that I just made, discussions of war cannot be separated from the history of eugenics. Wars produce scarcity, and those who suffer the most as a result of scarcity are society's most vulnerable populations. For example, according to Mostert (2002), at the outbreak of the First World War, the material and logistic requirements of fighting had both social and material repercussions for asylum inmates. The wartime rationing of food, which resulted in the decreased caloric intake for inmates, as well as the provision of less heat, less clothing, shortage of medication, overcrowding, and poor sanitary conditions all led to increases in both communicable diseases and mortality rates among asylum inmates. Thus, even though caregivers acknowledged the deplorable state of affairs in asylums, it was also generally accepted that it was necessary to shift resources to those able to support the war effort rather than to those who were deemed unable to do so. It was these shifting ideologies that framed disabled people as "useless eaters," and justified the violent practice of euthanasia as the right to alleviate suffering for disabled people. Aided and abetted by sociobiological interpretations of Darwin, eugenic practices such as sterilization also became commonplace as the lives of disabled persons (and disabled women, in particular), came to be viewed as lives of little value—an argument that served as the justification for individual and state-sanctioned murder. Thus, Mostert's argument demonstrates how macro-political and social forces harnessed by eugenic ideologies came to have a detrimental effect in wartime on disabled persons as well as on poor people of color.

While some would argue that eugenics was an oppressive practice in the specific historical era of colonialism, I argue that eugenics continues as an oppressive practice in the contemporary context of the imperialist/neocolonialist "war on terror." To make this argument, I have drawn on transnational feminist disability studies as a perspective that foregrounds disability as a materialist rather than a discursive concept in its analysis of gender, race, and class in the colonial/postcolonial/neocolonial transnational economy. In other words, I argue here that it is only by foregrounding disability as an imperialist ideology that equates certain racialized, gendered, sexual, and class differences as "defect" that it is possible to also foreground the eugenic impulses articulated via the "war on terror" and that have oppressive implications for both poor nondisabled and disabled women of color living in both the First and Third worlds.

EMBODIED ANTINOMIES AND TRANSNATIONAL PRAXIS

In this chapter I have already provided several examples of both representational violence as well as material violence meted out against poor nondisabled and disabled third world women in the contemporary context of the war on terror. The most oppressive aspect of this violence is its invisibility and therefore its nonappearance in even the otherwise radical analyses of feminist disability studies and third world feminism. As I have already argued, the by-product of the war on terror is not just the disproportionate surge of death and destruction in the third world contexts of Afghanistan and Iraq, but also the disproportionate surge in the numbers of children and adults with disabilities as a result of war-related injuries, military torture, civil war, economic scarcities, and psychological trauma.

The sheer scope of this violence should be difficult to ignore, and yet it is ignored; its invisibility justified by the imperialist/neocolonial state through its claims of regulating and controlling differences that are seen as disruptive to the "natural" order of global civil society. This is where the echoes of eugenic policies of the late nineteenth and early twentieth centuries resonate in contemporary times. For example, Iraqis and Afghans who are killed or disabled in their "occupied" countries are not thought of as "civilians" resisting an imperialist force, but as "terrorists/insurgents"—a term that negates any rights to enfranchised citizenship. If civilian deaths and/or disabilities caused by the war are acknowledged, they are dismissed as collateral damage. When an odd discussion comes up regarding the meager pensions and lack of disability benefits made available to widows/mothers/caregivers that have lost family members as a result of the war on terror, it is explained away as a luxury they did not even enjoy prior to the occupation. And in spaces where concepts such as the DALY are deployed to determine who has access to health services at public expense, there will be oppressive outcomes for the thousands of civilians disabled on account of war and their caregivers, most of whom will be poor women of color. In each of these examples, I argue that eugenic ideologies that associate race, gender, and disability with disease, degeneracy, biological inferiority, and dependence have been deployed to justify both the representational and the material violence meted out against both disabled and nondisabled people of color, particularly women, by determining whether they can be designated as enfranchised citizens.

Persistent invisibility and occasional hypervisibility exact a heavy price from its victims. On February 1, 2008, for a brief moment race, disability, and gender claimed center stage in the news regarding the war in Iraq. The FOX news headline read, "Mentally Disabled Female Homicide Bombers Blow Up Pet Markets in Baghdad, Killing Dozens." The AOL news headline put it even more tersely and coarsely, "Mentally Retarded Pair Used in Bombing." Moral outrage is the only appropriate response to these headlines. But what exactly has caused our outrage? Was it the fact that the two women who literally exploded in the marketplace were "mentally retarded?" Were we outraged because we presumed they were unwilling pawns used by unscrupulous individuals for whom barbarism has no boundaries? Does our outrage reinforce our belief in the righteousness of our stance against the "terrorists?" Or do we give pause amid this moral outrage to reflect on several issues I have raised in this chapter that demonstrate that we have always used poor disabled third world women as pawns in our mythical struggles over good and evil—allowing them a "deadly" recognition—only when it suits our purposes. A transnational feminist disability studies perspective will force us to see that the embattled bodies of (disabled) (third world) women wear scars that speak of centuries of violence—representational, physiological, and material—and still live to tell their stories in the breathless whisper of exploding bodies and shattered bones. As witnesses to this violence, our only recourse is to forge a transnational theory and praxis that would work across the boundaries of race, class, gender, disability, and sexuality to end this violence now.

(IM)MATERIAL CITIZENS: COGNITIVE DISABILITY, RACE, AND THE POLITICS OF CITIZENSHIP

And now we are men, not minors and invalids in a protected corner, not cowards fleeing before a revolution, but guides, redeemers, and benefactors, obeying the Almighty effort, and advancing on Chaos and the Dark.

Ralph Waldo Emerson (1894)

Cast as one of society's ultimate "not me" figures, the disabled other absorbs disavowed elements of this cultural self, becoming an icon of all human vulnerability and enabling the "American Ideal" to appear as master of both destiny and self. At once familiarly human but definitely other, the disabled figure in cultural discourse assures the rest of the citizenry of who they are not while arousing their suspicions about who they could become.

Rosemary Garland-Thomson (1997)

TRANSFORMING INDIVIDUALS INTO CITIZENS HAS HISTORICALLY BEEN ONE OF the most important functions entrusted to educational institutions supported by the liberal state. Liberal theorists such as Locke, Rousseau, Dewey, and Rawls theorized the state as a collective creation of diverse individual members socialized via education to work toward the common good (social contract), while, at the same time, acting as autonomous agents to freely pursue their individual interests (Levinson, 1999). On the other hand, scholars such as Pateman (1988), Young (1990), and Mouffe (1996), among others, have challenged the universalism implicit in these formulations of citizenship by pointing out that notions of the "common good" and "equal treatment" presume a homogeneity among individuals and render difference invisible and/or unimportant. In fact, the historical struggles for the rights to citizenship by people of color, women, gays and lesbians, and disabled people[1] have demonstrated that citizenship, rather than being a universal category, represents "a terrain of struggle over the forms of knowledge, social practices, and values that constitute the critical elements of the [liberal democratic] tradition" (Giroux, 1988, p. 5).

Giroux's formulation is especially true in the aftermath of poststructural critiques of humanism, where identity no longer implies certain essential qualities/characteristics. Yet, much of citizenship education couched in liberal discourses belies these claims by reinscribing notions of the "good" citizen using humanist/essentialist traits of rationality, autonomy, and competence (Evans, 1998; Gutmann, 1987; Levinson, 1999). Take for example, Gutmann's careful theorization of how democratic citizens should be educated in a liberal society. While Gutmann's analysis envisions pedagogical possibilities for students differentiated on the basis of race, class, gender, sexuality, and (physical) disability, her argument stumbles when encountering "seriously handicapped children" (p. 149) or "children with brain damage" (p. 155). This is because, according to Gutmann, "even the best social services coupled with the best schooling may not give them [children with severe/cognitive disabilities] the capacity to deliberate and to participate effectively in democratic politics" (p. 155). Her response to this dilemma is to provide these students the kind of education that "will depend on their capacities to learn and our willingness to provide them with non-educational services as they grow older" (p. 155).

While I will not quarrel with Gutmann's sensitivity to difference when discussing the educational needs of children with cognitive/severe disabilities, I am much more critical of the humanist assumptions regarding rationality, autonomy, and competence that she invokes in her discussion of their educational capabilities. More importantly, I will argue here that not interrogating the essentializing tendencies in these concepts locates persons with cognitive/severe disabilities outside the margins of "active" citizenship. This has occurred even within the Disability Rights Movement, which is mostly dominated by persons with physical disabilities (Chappell, 1998; Ferguson, 1987; Goodley, 2001). Moreover, even though scholars in the interdisciplinary area of disability studies have (re)theorized disability as a social construction (Corker & French, 1999; Francis & Silvers, 2000; Linton, 1998; Oliver, 1990), these (re)theorizations continue to leave persons with cognitive/severe disabilities "out in the cold," as if to mark their biology as existing outside all modes of socialization (Goodley 2001; Chappell, 1998). It is in this context then, that despite several legislative interventions that purport to protect the rights of disabled people, there seems to be little interest in the citizenship rights of persons with cognitive/severe disabilities, except when discussing how severely disabled a fetus or a person should be before one is justified in preventing its (the fetus') birth or allowing the person to die (Fiser, 1994). More often than not, these death-invoking discourses constitute disability as marking the outermost limits of human existence, and therefore, never engage the everyday reality of what it means to be a citizen with a cognitive/severe disability. It is in this oppressive context that persons with cognitive/severe disabilities are perceived as (ir)rational and (non) autonomous—qualities that are then equated with noncompetence, nonstatus, and ultimately noncitizenship.

In this chapter, I explore why the above equations persist in the popular imagination, even after President George Bush Sr. signed the Americans with Disabilities Act (ADA) on July 26, 1990. Disability rights activists have celebrated the ADA's instrumental role in advancing disabled people "beyond confinement to a class subject(ed) to special treatment and joined them with other minorities as classes explicitly designated to command equal treatment" (Silvers, Wasserman & Mahowald, 1998, p. 4). While I concur with Silver's position that the ADA is designed to protect the rights of disabled citizens as a social class, I take a more critical approach regarding this celebration of formal justice for disabled people. To do so, I utilize cognitive/severe disability as the central analytical category to critically interrogate both liberal and poststructural theories of citizenship and citizenship education. For example, if persons with severe/cognitive disabilities are seen to represent inalienable Otherness in ableist contexts, then what effects does such alterity have on the "dilemma of difference"[2] (Minow, 1990) in liberal democratic society? In other words, will the application of citizenship rights and responsibilities to people with cognitive/severe disabilities further accentuate their difference or seek to ignore it? If democratic citizenship is about forging relationships between equal individuals, then, how does the difference embodied in people with cognitive/severe disabilities reconfigure notions of equality, especially when applied to the dual concepts of civil and social citizenship? If citizenship education involves teaching students to successfully negotiate the complexities of diverse identities in order to achieve the moral status of "abstract citizen" (Gordon, Holland & Lahelma, 1999), then how do persons with cognitive/severe disabilities disrupt this idealistic conceptualization? What implications will these disruptions have for traditional notions of citizenship and citizenship education?

While both liberal and postmodern theorists have critically engaged the "dilemma of difference" in ways that have challenged traditional conceptions of citizenship, I demonstrate in this chapter that these (re)theorizations continue to exclude people with cognitive/severe disabilities (Francis & Silvers, 2000; Minow, 1990; Mouffe, 1996; Young, 1990). In doing so, I will echo some of the arguments made by critical race theorists, who have foregrounded the limits of formal justice in the context of institutionalized racism (Crenshaw, Gotanda, Peller & Thomas, 1995; Delgado & Stefancic, 2000). Then, forging a linkage between Critical Race Theory (CRT) and materialist disability studies, I advance my own argument that both liberal and postmodern theories of citizenship serve as metaphors for control by masquerading as protector of citizenship rights. Expanding on this analysis, I argue that these disciplinary practices produced within the material conditions of late capitalism enact in complex and contradictory ways the "racialization of disability" and the "dis-abilization of race." Finally, I discuss the implications of this critique for an alternative theorization of citizenship and citizenship education that is not just inclusive of difference, but is also transformative in its intent and practices.

THE LIMITS OF FORMAL JUSTICE

Despite the fact that contemporary theory has celebrated the advent of the new post-al society, described as "post-production, post-labor, post-ideology, post-white, and post-capitalist" (Zavarzadeh, 1995, p. 1), the actual material reality of historically marginalized communities seems not to mirror these transformations. This is especially true for the nearly 49 million Americans with disabilities,[3] 24.1 million of whom have a severe disability (McNeil, 2000). This population has historically faced economic discrimination as is evidenced in the disparities in monthly income between the nondisabled and the disabled workforce (Trupin, 1997). For example, working-age nondisabled men (average income of $2970) and nondisabled women (average monthly income of $2775) earn more than twice the income of working-age disabled men (average monthly income of $1396) and disabled women (average monthly income of $1261). In light of these disparities, it is not surprising that 30 percent of disabled people who are employed live in poverty, a percentage that is three times higher (10.2 percent) than that of the nondisabled population. Among working-age people with severe disabilities who have been excluded from participation in the labor market, 38.3 percent of the population lives in poverty.

Disabled people also dominate the population of welfare recipients with nearly 30.7 percent living in subsidized housing, and nearly 48.2 percent collecting food stamps (McNeil 2000). However, even those who qualify for social security disability benefits can do little to raise themselves and their families out of poverty, because of the inadequate financial aid they receive from Social Security Disability Insurance (SSDI; men $634, women $425) and Supplemental Security Income (SSI; men $ 300, women $ 288) pay. Additionally, 52.7 percent of the households where disabled women are the main economic providers live below the poverty line. Such statistics only highlight the grim reality that disabled people (whose material needs far exceed those of the general population on account of their disabilities) are among the poorest of the poor in US society.

Additionally, dominant ideologies have utilized "the medical language of symptoms and diagnostic categories" (Linton; 1998, p. 8) to constitute disability as a pathological abnormality that has then been used to support the exclusionary, segregationist, and exploitative practices of an ableist society. Rejecting these ideological constructions of disability, disabled activists and their allies have sought to narrow "the gap between representation and reality" (Garland-Thomson, 1997, p. 12) by turning to what they have termed the "social model of disability" (Oliver, 1990; Linton, 1998; Thomson, 1997). The social model offers a sociopolitical analysis of disability that distances itself from the medical model, and instead, describes disability as an ideological construction that is used to justify not only the oppressive binary cultural constructions of normal/pathological, autonomous/dependent, and competent citizen/ward of the state, but also the social divisions of labor (Erevelles, 2000; Linton, 1998; Russell, 1998). It is in this context that the field of disability studies has gained impetus in the academy, where it has begun to challenge the naturalness of these constructions in the curriculum, in popular culture, and in politics. Interdisciplinary by necessity, disability studies has produced scholarship embedded in the material reality of the everyday experiences of disabled people that deconstructs ableist ideologies and works in concert with the Disability Rights Movement to support the interests of disabled people as a social class.

Ironically, even though the Disability Rights Movement has been active since the early 1970s, liberal and radical theorists who have generally been more responsive to conditions of alterity (e.g., race, class, gender, sexuality) have not included any sustained discussion of cognitive/severe disability in their contemporary theoretical work on citizenship[4]. More often than not, when liberal and radical theorists include disability in these discussions, they deploy certain concepts uncritically, which then prevents people with severe/cognitive disabilities from being perceived as citizens. Take, for example, the social contract theorist John Rawls (1998), who defined the citizen as "a fully cooperating member of society...[with] the capacity to understand, to apply, and to act from the public conception of justice...and to rationally pursue a conception of one's rational advantage or good" (p. 60). Then, Rawls offers a caveat to this definition, when he states that "for our purposes here I leave aside permanent physical disabilities or mental disorders so severe as to prevent people from being normal and fully cooperating members of society in the usual sense" (p. 60).

Rawls can justify the exclusion of persons with disabilities from his definition, because he relies on the humanist logic that emphasizes individual potential and its associated traits of autonomy, competence, and rationality as the necessary preconditions for being recognized as a citizen. This logic stems from the humanist ideology of liberal individualism that perceives the autonomous, competent, and rational Self as being housed in a body that is "a stable, neutral instrument of the individual will" (Garland-Thomson, 1997, p. 42). This autonomous, competent, and rational Self is a critical component that supports the laissez-faire economic policies of capitalist societies, and is based on the tenets of liberal individualism—faith in reason, belief in natural law, republican virtue, teleological progress, and individual [economic] freedom (Minow, 1990)[5]. On the other hand, Thomson describes the disabled body as representing "the self gone out of control, individualism run rampant...ungovernable, recalcitrant, flaunting in its difference, as if to refute the sameness implicit in the notion of equality" (p. 43). When brought face to face with this "unruly body" (Erevelles, 2000), humanism's only defense is exclusion—an exclusion that can only be achieved by a strict adherence to certain normative concepts that are narrowly defined, and that, if challenged, would topple the entire edifice on which liberal individualism and capitalism is erected.

At the same time, such exclusionary practices do not sit well with liberal theorists, who have historically prided themselves on their commitment to egalitarianism. Thus, when confronted with the issue of disability, philosopher Charles Taylor, for example, while once again privileging individual potential in humanist terms magnanimously proclaims that "our sense of the importance of potentiality reaches so far that we extend this protection [of liberal rights] even to people who through some circumstance that has befallen them are incapable of realizing their potential in the normal way—handicapped people...for instance" (as quoted in Silvers, 1997, p. 27). Silvers (1997) interprets Taylor's inclusive gesture to imply that disabled people are, in fact, inherently "defective agents," and it is only by extension, or derivation, or fiction that they can enjoy equal status as citizens, because given "normal" circumstances they will never be able to fulfill their potential. Silvers's critical reading of Taylor's position foregrounds yet another observation: liberal individualism needs the discourse of the "defective agent" embodied in the disabled Other in order to reify the humanist Self—the "normate" (Garland-Thomson, 1997, p. 8)—resplendent in his masculine, heterosexual, able-bodied, and propertied existence, and, of course, always magnanimous in his relationship to Otherness.

I want to emphasize here the poignant contradiction that minority groups face in their struggles against the oppressive structures that restrict their lives. Conscious of the limits of liberal discourses, they are, nevertheless, forced to appeal to these same discourses that dominate legal institutions in a liberal democracy. It is by marking these contradictions in the aftermath of civil rights legislation that CRT has gained prominence in the area of legal theory (Crenshaw, Gotanda, Peller & Thomas, 1995; Delgado & Stefancic, 2000). Similar issues have also arisen in disability studies scholarship, where its scholars are also wrestling with the best possible ways to realize the emancipatory potential of the Americans with Disabilities Act (Francis & Silvers, 2000; Silvers, Wasserman & Mahowald, 1998). Theorists in both areas of scholarship have critically confronted the dialectical complicity of liberal democratic law in upholding white supremacy and ableism, while, at the same time, acknowledging that it is these same laws that have, at least, opened opportunities for participation in civil society, which had formerly been denied them. Recognizing these contradictions, theorists in both areas are now grappling with the ideological terms and material conditions necessary to (re)negotiate their participation in civil society without reifying the hegemonic structures of white supremacy and ableism, which they argue still persist in liberal democratic society and that support limiting definitions of citizenship.

In the context of racial equality, according to the New Right, formal equality has finally been achieved for African Americans, apparent in the tangible progress made in the legal reforms pertaining to racial inequality over the past 40 years, and, as a result, they argue that US society is now ready to support color-blind politics. On the other hand, according to critical race theorist Kimberle Crenshaw (1995), the disjunction between the idealism of liberal legal reform and the actual materiality of the socio-economic living conditions of African Americans exists because of the pragmatic commitment of liberal politics to social reform rather than to social transformation. Additionally, Crenshaw argues that this tension is reflective of a similar tension in antidiscrimination legislation, between conceiving of "equality as process" and "equality as result."

Crenshaw describes the former as a restrictive view that downplays the actual outcomes of antidiscrimination legislation, but instead, focuses on preventing future wrongdoings that are primarily seen as "isolated actions against individuals, rather than as a social policy against an entire group" (p. 105). At the same time, when discrimination is identified, all efforts to redress such discrimination are meticulously careful in ensuring that the interests of the dominant group (e.g., white workers) are not to be overly burdened. Such a view, Crenshaw argues, does not recognize the historical reality that protecting the interests of the dominant class (e.g., white workers, nondisabled workers) is necessarily dependent on the creation and maintenance of oppressive practices that have required the continued subordination of the oppressed class (e.g., black workers, disabled workers).

On the other hand, according to Crenshaw, antidiscrimination law's more expansive view of "equality as a result" recognizes the structural bases of discrimination. This expansive view calls for the eradication of the substantive conditions of oppression on the basis of race and (in this context) disability. Such a position goes beyond the removal of formal barriers to advocate for the transformation of the normative structures that continue in an unspoken form the stereotypes used to legitimate both white supremacist and ableist society. Crenshaw's critique points to the limits of liberal citizenship that responds solely to the symbolic subordination of oppressed groups (formal denial of social and political equality through segregation), while paying scant attention to their material subordination. More specifically, Crenshaw's distinction between "equality as process" and "equality as result" foregrounds how formal justice, while seeking "equal opportunity," does so in a context that simultaneously naturalizes social and economic inequality.

Echoing Crenshaw, another critical race theorist Alan Freeman (1995) continues the critique of the liberal construction of formal justice. Freeman points out that the success of legal reform is more dependent on the point of view from which the legislation is written, rather than the actual legislation itself. Freeman argues that antidiscrimination legislation has traditionally taken on the perpetrator's perspective that is much more narrowly focused on neutralizing the inappropriate behaviors of "misguided" individuals. Here, too, discrimination is not viewed as structural, but rather, as a series of actions inflicted on the victim. Such a perspective is noticeably silent about concerns raised through the victim's perspective that would require antidiscrimination legislation to focus on transforming the social, political, and economic structures as well as the debilitating ideologies that justify discrimination by claiming "insufficient merit."

While Crenshaw and Freeman's arguments focus specifically on race, I argue here that both their critiques are especially relevant to legal scholarship in disability studies. For example, philosopher Anita Silvers views the American with Disabilities Act as significant in the lives of disabled Americans, because for the first time in history, social policy has sought to diminish their social isolation and further their equality "by removing obstructions to their social access rather than by correcting their personal flaws and failings" (Silvers, Wasserman & Mahowald, 1998, p. 5). She distinguishes this intervention from distributive discourses of justice as espoused by Amartya Sen, Richard Arenson, and Norman Daniels, among others, because these discourses often equate disability with incompetence in order to justify what she terms "extraordinary distributions" (p. 35). Put simply, Silvers's preference for formal justice over distributive justice lies in the distinction that, while the former constructs disability as "the *defective state of society* (my emphasis), which disadvantages disabled people," the latter constitutes disability as a "natural deficiency" or a "personal limitation," and thereby makes it difficult for disabled people to identify as a minority group. On the pragmatic level, Silvers believes that justice for disabled people will be served, not by providing them extraordinary resources, but by ensuring social access similar to nondisabled people, not in a compensatory but in an equal-opportunity fashion.

Arguing that "difference" is not synonymous with "defect," Silvers takes on the "victim's perspective" when she places her faith in formal justice and its legal instrument, the ADA, to demand structural changes in the social environment that will be responsive to the daily material reality experienced by disabled people. But herein lies the problem. The ADA (as both Crenshaw and Freeman would argue) is formulated from the perspective of ableist society (the perpetrator), and therefore only serves as the watchdog for inappropriate behaviors that can easily be proven in a court of law. What happens, however, when discrimination is a not a series of individual acts, but is, in fact, structural, institutional, ideological, and often not visible in concrete evidentiary form? What happens when the dominant assumptions that undergird the characteristics of rationality, autonomy, and competence that form the bulwark of liberal society contravene the very existence of the oppressed group? And more importantly, what happens when the very essence of the liberal humanist Self is necessarily predicated on the construction of the disabled Other as the embodiment of inalienable difference?

The challenges posed by the above questions become especially significant when examining the meaning of citizenship for people with severe/cognitive disabilities in a liberal democracy—an issue that even Anita Silvers pays insufficient attention to in her argument. While a liberal democratic society may (if sufficiently persuaded) be willing to transform the social environment so as to accommodate wheelchair access, support more widespread use of braille, sign language, and close captioning, and provide technology that will enhance the capabilities of persons with more severe physical disabilities, there is an almost palpable hesitancy when confronted with the similar challenge when responding to the specific needs of people with cognitive/severe disabilities. This hesitancy derives from dominant ideologies that, as I mentioned earlier, privilege a humanist logic—one that I will argue, in the next section, is limited in its ability to respond to the difference embodied in people with cognitive/severe disabilities.

REASON AS (IN)ALIENABLE DIFFERENCE:
THE CHALLENGE OF COGNITIVE DISABILITY

The limitations of formal justice as they apply to people with cognitive/
severe disabilities are foregrounded in Philip Ferguson's (1987) provocative
essay, "The Social Construction of Mental Retardation." In this essay, borrowing a phrase from historian E. P. Thompson, Ferguson argues that there
is "a poverty of theory," which has "increasingly shortchanged those people
with the most profound combinations of mental retardation and physical
impairment" (p. 52). These notions are so embedded in our ideological and
material realities that even the Disability Rights Movement has sometimes
excluded people with severe/cognitive disabilities from its vision of social
justice. This is because, as Ferguson (1987) explains:

> [To] be severely cognitively impaired is not a difference just like skin color or
> gender...It is easy to imagine a society where gender, skin color, age, nation-
> ality, and sexual preference have no social inequities attached. It seems much
> harder to imagine a world where it would not be preferable to be capable of
> abstract thought. The exclusion of people [especially those with severe/cognitive
> disabilities] from [even] the disability rights movement is not simply an over-
> sight or an understandable delay in fully implementing the theoretical guide-
> lines. The exclusion is also a logical concomitant of the conceptual base. (p. 54)

The "logical concomitant of the conceptual base" that Ferguson refers to in
his argument is tied to humanist ideologies that I have alluded to in this essay,
and that I argue need to be critically deconstructed because they continue
to exclude people with cognitive/severe disabilities. This, again, is ironic,
because even though poststructuralist critiques have shown Enlightenment
Reason to be a fiction, the Cartesian formula—"I think therefore I am"—is
still used to operate as the distinguishing moment in the discussion. For
example, philosopher Jeff McMahan (1996)'s article "Cognitive Disability,
Misfortune, and Justice" foregrounds some of the challenges faced by philosophers when attempting to locate persons with cognitive/severe disabilities within humanist discourses. McMahan writes:

> The common view is that the severely cognitively impaired [sic] are indeed
> badly off, or have lives that are deprived or below a decent minimum...They
> are wholly dependent on others for their continued existence and for what-
> ever other good their lives contain, and are therefore precariously vulnerable
> to neglect or abuse...The profoundly cognitively impaired [sic] are incapa-
> ble, for example, of deep personal and social relations, creativity and achieve-
> ment, the attainment of higher forms of knowledge, aesthetic pleasures, and
> so on. (p. 8)

Although McMahan concludes his essay by arguing that even people with cognitive/severe disabilities "possess properties and capacities that give their possessor a certain worth that demands respect" (p. 30), his argument, nevertheless, echoes the humanist commitment to Universal Reason that necessarily reinforces depictions of people with severe/cognitive disabilities as inherently defective.

However, even in spaces where this ideal of Universal Reason has been critiqued, people with cognitive/severe disabilities are often excluded from this discussion. Take, for example, feminist theorist Iris Marion Young's (1990) commitment to pursue a theory of justice that critically responds to the unique needs of disabled people. In her book *Justice and the Politics of Difference*, Young offers a rigorous critique of "the disembodied coldness of modern reason" (p. 125), exposing its complicity in generating "theories of human physical, moral, and aesthetic superiority... [that] made possible the objectification of other groups, and their placement under a normalizing gaze" (p. 130). Moreover, taking up the feminist standpoint, Young points out that the dichotomy maintained between the private (female) and public (male) spheres has the tendency to situate reason in opposition to desire, affectivity, and the body, and in doing so has excluded those "individuals and groups who do not fit the example of the rational citizen who is capable of transcending both body and sentiment" (p. 109). Here, Young claims to be broadly referring to groups and individuals oppressively marked by race, class, gender, sexual orientation, and (physical) disability. However, even though Young exposes Reason's claim to unity as a fiction, even though she argues for an alternative form of communitarian politics that can be inclusive of *all* difference, and even though she gestures toward people with cognitive/severe disabilities, she does not explicitly describe how this vision would translate for this particular group. This is because, as Ferguson observes:

> Retarded people in general, and severely retarded people especially, have always served as those falling beyond the pale of serious consideration. The current disability rights movement [and even Young, herself] reframes but does not remove the tendency to exclude categorically those with severe cognitive limitations. (p. 54)

If, however, Young were to seriously consider people with severe/cognitive disabilities in her discussions of social justice, then her critique of humanist ideologies would also have to include a more explicit critique of how persons with cognitive/severe disabilities fare within the oppressive logic of capitalist accumulation. This is the direction that feminist legal scholar Minow (1990) takes in offering her critique of liberal legal theory, even though her argument stops just short of implicating capitalism in her critique. In her book *Making all the Difference*, Minow's analysis of legal history describes a feudal legal system that supported different legal treatments for "normal" and "abnormal" populations—a legal distinction that Minow argues continues to this day.[6] While much has changed in how we distinguish between "normal" and "abnormal" classes since feudalism, one concept that has endured across several centuries and continues to mark the boundaries between the "normal" and "abnormal" classes is Universal Reason as is manifested in an individual's mental competence. In legal terminology, "mental competence signifies the ability to appreciate the consequences of one's actions, *to protect oneself from manipulation and coercion*, and to *understand and engage in transactions of property and commerce* (my emphasis)" (Minow, 1990, p. 126). For those who fail to meet the stringent conditions of this definition (e.g., people with cognitive/severe disabilities), how would formal justice resolve the dilemma of difference in the specific context of liberal legal theory? Or to pose the question in Minow's words: "How may advocates demand that law treat mentally retarded people [*sic*] the same as others for purposes of freedom from constraints and abuse but differently from others for the purpose of securing the attention, resources, and care that others do not need?" (p. 144).

My purpose in this essay, however, is not so much to resolve the dilemma of difference as manifested in legal theory, but to foreground the historical and material conditions that are instrumental in the social construction of Universal Reason, which is then used to distinguish people with cognitive/severe disabilities from "normal" citizens. This is a position that Minow leans toward when she argues that "[n]othing inherent in the idea of rationality requires such sharp distinctions between those 'with reason' and those 'without reason' . . ." (p. 150). In fact, Minnow argues, the universally accepted definition of what constitutes "reasonable" behavior is nothing but an ableist paradigm. In the specific historical context of laissez-faire capitalism, "rational" behavior represents those behavior traits that maximize benefits, minimize costs, and contribute to the efficient realization of profit. Those people who exhibit behaviors that prove to be counterproductive to the efficient logic of capitalism are marked as abnormal, and are either punished and/or segregated from the "normal" populations. In other words, I argue here that notions of autonomy and rationality are, in fact, closely tied to the historical and material conditions of capitalism, where certain definitions of reason and autonomy become more plausible than others.

Though Minow avoids the materialist argument I just made, she nevertheless persists in her critique of formal by arguing for a "social-relations approach" to law that recognizes the interdependent nature of human relationships. This notion of interdependency is critically examined by feminist philosopher Eva Feder Kittay(1999; 2000), who centers cognitive/severe disability in her analysis. Kittay critiques contemporary liberal theory for describing society as an association of equals and its citizens as fully cooperating members of society, as exemplified in John Rawls's characterization of social cooperation:

> The main idea is that when a number of persons engage in a mutually advantageous cooperative venture according to rules, and thus restrict their liberty in ways necessary to yield advantages for all, those who have submitted these restrictions have a right to a similar acquiescence on the part of those who have benefited from their submission. (Rawls as quoted in Kittay, 1999, p. 105)

Such a theory of social cooperation assumes that those involved in the dependency relationship are free and equal persons, who rationally contract with each other to work in equitable interdependent ways, and in doing so, earn the right to be regarded as equal citizens. As a mother of an adult daughter with profound physical and cognitive disabilities, Kittay is intimately aware that the dependency relationship between her daughter and herself, as well as other employed caregivers, is one that cannot meet Rawls's criteria of reciprocity that is essential in social cooperation. This is because, unlike other dependent populations (e.g., nondisabled children and the elderly) who will/have already demonstrate(d) their ability to reciprocate in kind to their caregivers, people with cognitive/severe disabilities may not be able to do so, and thus, according to Rawls will remain outside the scope of citizenship.

It is in this context that Kittay (2000) is critical of Silvers's commitment to the ideal of formal justice, which requires the removal of oppressive restrictions to allow disabled people to become self-sufficient, independent, and productive members of society. Kittay points out that her daughter (now 30 years old) may never become independent or self-sufficient, will always be a "burden" to any economic system, and no transformation of the social environment will ever change this reality. Then, in a theoretical move that is much more deliberate than that of any of the other theorists mentioned in this chapter, Kittay points out that reason is not what will define her daughter as "human." Rather, Kittay calls for an alternative retheorizing of dependency that replaces autonomy as one of the fundamental characteristics of what it means to be human. To pursue this, Kittay urges us to explore discursive notions of dependency that will include not only disabled people but also other citizens who find themselves inevitably located in dependent relations during the life stages of infancy, childhood, and the frailties of old age. This broadening of definition, Kittay argues, will reduce "the backlash and resistance" (p. 79) against issues of dependency, because we will then "allow ourselves to learn from those who are most dependent about the frailties that come with being human dependent animals . . . [and will enable us] to reappropriate our own resources and priorities so that meeting needs and granting rights are aligned in a just caring and effective manner" (p. 79).

While I will agree with Kittay's theoretical move to reimagine dependency within the "natural" continuum of human life, I am not convinced of the radical effects this discursive move may make on the liberal theories of citizenship. I am especially critical of the voluntarism explicit in Kittay's argument because it assumes that meanings of dependency can be renegotiated outside the material conditions within which it is situated. In saying this, I echo Silvers's ambivalence about Kittay's (re)conceptualization, when she writes:

> Political rearrangements meant to make dependence more desirable neither resolve the inherent power imbalance between caregiver and care receiver nor relieve its potential as a source of repression. . . . In a framework of moral relations in which some must make themselves vulnerable so that others can be worthy of their trust—that is, in paternalistic systems, in which those viewed as incompetent are coerced into compliance "for their own good"—people with disability are typecast as subordinate. (p. 100)

Despite Silvers's incisive critique, she continues to place her faith in Formal Justice, which she believes may offer disabled people "real" choices in their lives. On the other hand, I argue here that neither formal justice nor discursive interventions that deconstruct reason and privilege dependency over autonomy will prove to be emancipatory for people with severe/cognitive disabilities, because both reason and dependency are historically constituted within the laissez-faire economic structures of capitalist societies. Moreover, both liberal theory and its critical reformulations discussed earlier continue to define citizenship as constitutive of relationships between individuals rather than as embedded in inequitable institutional structures, an argument that both Crenshaw and Freeman make in the context of CRT. As a result, liberal theories of justice that privilege humanist discourses in their analyses limit the emancipatory possibilities for citizens with severe/cognitive disabilities.

PERFORMATIVITY AS POSTMODERN INTERVENTION FOR CYBORG CITIZENSHIP

My critique of the voluntaristic impulse in Kittay's retheorization of dependency is one that is also echoed by poststructuralists. Poststructuralists are

critical of voluntarism because it presumes the willful and instrumental subject of humanist discourses—one that, as I have argued in the previous section, is clearly inhospitable to difference, especially difference embodied in
people with cognitive/severe disabilities. Rejecting the troubling essentialisms embedded in liberal theories of citizenship, Laclau and Mouffe have
argued for a radical democratic conception of citizenship that supports "a
non-essentialist view of politics" (Mouffe, 1996, p. 24) without abandoning
the symbolic resources of the liberal democratic tradition (e.g., protection of
individual freedom in a pluralistic society).[7]

Within this paradigm, identity is described as "an ensemble of subject
positions that can never be totally fixed in a closed system of differences,
constructed by a diversity of discourses among which there is no necessary
relation, but a constant movement of overdetermination and displacement"
(Mouffe, 1992, p. 372). In such a context, binaries such as male/female, able
bodied/disabled, straight/queer are not boundary conditions but fluid concepts that tend to blur the defining limits of citizenship. More importantly,
unlike social contract theorists who attempt to consolidate difference by
using ethical principles to work toward the "common good," Mouffe (1996),
for instance, envisions

> all forms of agreement as partial and provisional and as products of a given
> hegemony. Its objective is the creation of a chain of equivalence among the
> democratic demands found in a variety of groups—women, blacks, workers,
> gays, lesbians, environmentalists—around a radical democratic interpreta-
> tion of the political principles of the liberal democratic regime... For it is not
> a matter of establishing a mere alliance between given interests but rather of
> actually modifying their identity so as to bring about a new political identity.
> (p. 24)

Even though Mouffe's delineation of different social groups continues to
exclude disability, I will argue that her position may assist in Silvers's commitment to (re)configure disabled citizenship in more empowering ways. In
fact, what is particularly appealing in Mouffe's argument is the need to constitute alternative political identities that do not reproduce the oppressive
binaries embedded in liberal theories of citizenship that continue to exclude
people with severe/cognitive disabilities. In particular, I turn to poststructuralist feminist Judith Butler's scholarship that has offered a compelling
critique of gendered identity—one that could be applied to disabled identity
as well.

Disability studies scholars will be especially interested in Butler's (1993)
critical treatment of the sex versus gender dichotomy—a dichotomy that
treats sex as nature, and gender as its associated socially constructed identity. Butler critiques feminists who support this dichotomous relationship

by pointing out that their essentialization of the concept "nature" is based on the assumption that nature has no history. Arguing from the poststructuralist premise that there is nothing outside discourse, Butler critiques the notion that "nature" is an objective fact (i.e., it has no value associated with it) because it is already constituted via discourse. In the context of the sex versus gender dichotomy, Butler argues that if gender is assumed to embody the social meanings attached to the "natural condition" of sex, it is not that gender serves as an additive property to provide social meaning to the concept "sex." On the other hand, according to Butler, "sex" is already imbued with meaning, which is exemplified in the medical interpellation that names the infant (it) as "she"—a process that Butler describes as "girling"—this naming that "is at once setting a boundary and also the repeated inculcation of a norm" (p. 8). This "girling" occurs, Butler argues, through incessant (re) iterations emerging out of a chain of foreclosures, erasures, and/or boundary conditions that "not only produce the domain of intelligible bodies [bodies that matter], but produce as well a domain of unthinkable, abject, unlivable bodies [those that do not matter in the same way]" (p. xi).

Butler's argument is appealing to disability studies scholarship because it problematizes our taken-for-granted interpretation of the natural. Disability studies scholars have also struggled with the nature versus culture debate, producing their own dichotomy of impairment versus disability that mirrors in many ways the feminist debates regarding sex versus gender (Corker & French, 1999; Linton, 1998). For disabled scholars, this differentiation brings with it its own unique problems. While on the one hand, disabled scholars have argued that disability is, in fact, a social construction, they are, on the other hand, eager to recognize their unique phenomenological experiences of having an impairment—experiences that mark their bodies as irreducibly different from "normal" bodies, and, yet, at the same time, are integral to their identity as disabled people. It is in this context that disabled scholars find themselves caught between a rock and a hard place, because while, on one level delinking disability from impairment will expose the social construction of their oppression, at another level this delinking will be unable to adequately account for the complexity embedded in the formation of disabled identity.

Butler's analysis becomes useful here. Impairment, just like sex, is associated with the medical interpellation of subjects into the semiotics of difference. In the process of this interpellation, impairment is discursively linked with defect that claims to be rooted in the "natural" terrain of the body. Just like the process of "girling," the "impaired" body is interpellated through a chain of incessant (re)iterations that stabilizes our notion of the natural, and this forms the boundary conditions between nondisabled bodies (bodies that matter) and disabled bodies (bodies that do not matter in the same way). But these boundaries that form identity are merely unstable discursive constructions that masquerade as the norm through the action of performativity. Performativity, according to Butler, is not constituted by a single voluntaristic act, but is, in fact, a series of (re)iterations that cite authoritarian conventions of normality that are themselves social constructions. Consequently, these normative constraints that map out the limits of the "natural/normal" body are now exposed as discursive constructions/performances, and in doing so, they simultaneously also support the possibilities for transgressing those limits that constitute humanist definitions of citizenship.

With identity stripped of its oppressive essentialisms, it is possible to read the disabled body as transgressive—for example, Haraway's theorizing of the blasphemous cyborg—"a hybrid of machine and organism, a creature of social reality as well as a creature of fiction" (Haraway, 1990, p. 191). Haraway's conceptualization of the "cyborg citizen" offers radical possibilities for people with severe/cognitive disabilities because it opens up spaces that liberal theories of citizenship have closed out. The cyborg citizen, unlike its humanist counterpart, "inhabits various bodies interfaced more or less intimately with various prosthetics... [and is] crucial in reconstructing the boundaries and technologies of daily life and the networks of power" (Gray & Mentor, 1995, p. 459). In a radical reconceptualization of the humanist citizen, Haraway (1990) asks: "Why should our bodies end at the skin or include as best other beings encapsulated by skin?" (p. 220). For people with cognitive/severe disabilities, whose bodies can often only be sustained with the help of a complex network of communication technologies, biotechnologies, and human caregivers, these dependencies can no longer signify a lack of autonomy, competency, and rationality, and can, therefore, no longer exclude them from rights to full citizenship.

The poststructuralist arguments of Butler and Haraway sharply contrast with liberal theories of citizenship that designate persons with cognitive/severe disabilities as dependent on extraordinary resources as well as the benevolence of their nondisabled citizens. On the other hand, Butler and Haraway's deconstruction of humanist subjectivity posits dependency as constitutive of human identity, and, therefore, removes it from both the normative constraints of liberal individualism and the voluntaristic paternalism of communitarian politics. In such a context, Haraway would argue that persons with cognitive/severe disabilities could be viewed as transgressive rather than defective citizens.

However, despite the radical possibilities that poststructuralist discourses offer the disabled citizen, I will insert a word of caution here. Even transgressive acts meet their limits in the brutal material conditions of everyday life. For example, even though Butler argues that the drag queens in the film *Paris is Burning*[8] are effective in denaturalizing the discursive limits of "sex," in the end, the materiality of compulsory heterosexuality and poverty claim its first victim through the brutal murder of one of the drag queens, Venus Extravaganza. People with severe/cognitive disabilities have had similar experiences—the one most telling being the controversy over facilitated communication. Adults and children with autism who use facilitated communication bring to mind Haraway's transgressive cyborg. Here, people with autism are dependent on the physical and emotional support of their (nondisabled) facilitators as they type or point to letters or pictures on a communication board (Biklen, 1993). Using this technique, people with cognitive/severe disabilities who had previously been perceived as severely developmentally disabled were now seen to display unusually high levels of literacy—an observation that seemed incredulous in light of the medical evidence that insisted on the impossibility of the act (Biklen, 1993; Biklen & Cardinal, 1997). Facilitated communication became especially controversial when questions were raised in legal contexts about the authenticity of the communications and the autonomy of the principal communicator (Green & Shane, 1994; Spitz, 1997; Twachtman-Cullen, 1997); on some occasions, proponents of facilitated communication were unable to prove the autonomy of the principal communicator, his/her communications were deemed inauthentic and the individual was not only denied a voice in a court of law, but was also denied the opportunity to communicate with the assistance of the facilitator.

I have argued elsewhere that the facilitated communication controversy arose as result of more significant political concerns rather than the simple disagreement of scientific methodologies (Erevelles, 2002). These significant political concerns are rooted in society's fears that the trangressive cyborg citizen may destabilize our ideological commitments to liberal individualism and its associated traits of rationality, autonomy, and competence. But, why these ideological commitments? Why are liberal theorists who espouse commitments to pluralist societies unwilling to disband these ideological barriers for persons with cognitive/severe disabilities? While poststructuralist theorists have been helpful in deconstructing humanist norms, they have not been able to explain why these normative structures persist? To respond to this "why" question, I turn to historical-materialist analyses that connect ideological constructions of difference to the economic conditions and social relations supported by capitalism.

ABILITY AS PROPERTY: TOWARD A HISTORICAL-MATERIALIST THEORY OF CITIZENSHIP

In this section of the chapter I will now elaborate on a materialist critique of citizenship. Specifically, I argue that notions of citizenship, rationality, and autonomy are ideological categories that are constituted within the historical and material conditions of capitalism. To do so, I critique theories of citizenship that continue their commitment to individualism and the associated traits of rationality, autonomy, and competence.

In the preface to *The Contribution to the Critique of Political Economy*, Marx (1859) wrote:

> The mode of production of material life conditions the social, political, and intellectual life process in general. It is not the consciousness of men that determines their being, but, on the contrary, their social being that determines their consciousness. (p. 4)

In the above quote, Marx highlights the importance of political economy in any analysis of identity. Drawing on this perspective, I argue here that a critical theory of citizenship for people with severe/cognitive disabilities would require a historical-materialist analyses that retheorizes citizenship within the historical context of US capitalism. Moreover, I will point out here that Marxism does not reject the possibility of human agency, rather it theorizes agency itself as historically constituted. As Marx (1871) himself pointed out, "men make their own history, but they do not make it just as they please, they do not make it under circumstances chosen by themselves, but under circumstances directly found, given, and transmitted from the past" (p. 595).

To demonstrate that citizenship is a historical-materialist category, I will now turn to the work of critical race theorist Cheryl Harris (1995), who maps out a critical relationship between citizenship and the economy. Engaging the dialectics of ideology and economics, Harris describes how rights in property are "contingent on, intertwined, and conflated with race" (p. 107). Property rights, she argues, are not "natural" but are, in fact, created by the law. More importantly, the notion of individual rights that emerged during the founding period of the New Republic was rooted in the protection of one's property, where property as described by John Madison "embraces every thing to which a man may attach a value and have a right" (as quoted in Harris, 1995, p. 279). According to Harris, the origins of property rights were instituted in racist institutional structures that only validated white possession and occupation of land, and permitted as an extension of these rights the hyperexploitation of black people and the claiming of Native American land. It is in this context that whiteness as property became significant, because it provided the ideological justification to exclude people of color from the privileges of owning property. Harris further points out that, because liberal legal institutions were constituted in a context that enforced and reproduced a property interest in whiteness, they contributed to the reproduction of black subordination. In this context, owning white identity as property affirmed the self-identity of whites, especially the dirt-poor white working class, who reveled in their privilege of racial superiority despite their exploitation at the hands of fellow whites. As a result, whiteness as property not only played a critical role in the racialization of identity, but also served as the ideological justification of the racial division of labor.

Extending this argument to the context of disability, I argue here that whiteness as property was an intrinsic part of the ensemble of discourses that upheld liberal individualism and that included the related discourses of competitive entrepreneurship, the work ethic, productivity, efficiency, and autonomy, among others. Whiteness as property was also the ideological discourse that has been used to justify the racial superiority of white people over people of color by using the logic of dis-ability (e.g., inferior genes, low IQ) to decide who has the rights to citizenship (Erevelles, 2001). In other words, I am arguing here that whiteness as property justifies and (re)iterates the centrality of the nondisabled white heterosexual male body as the most productive and profitable citizen for the burgeoning capitalist society. As such, it became critical that, in addition to whiteness, "ability" (both cognitive and physical) would also be an important property right that had to be safeguarded, protected, and defended in the effort to decide who could or could not be a citizen.

One of the principal contexts that safeguards, protects, and defends the property interest in "ability" is education. Just as in a market economy where property can be bartered for economic gain, in educational institutions, "ability" is bartered for social and economic status in the capitalist economy. Moreover, even though dominant ideologies represent the market as ostensibly a space where free exchange takes place, in both the economic and the educational contexts, it has become increasingly evident that the market has historically always benefited the ruling class. In the specific context of public education, "cognitive ability" is constituted, validated, and exchanged in the education marketplace through specific practices of schooling, for example, the national curriculum that supports the cultural capital of the white ruling class (Bourdieu, 1977); the evaluation strategies that include standardized tests that are biased against children of color and children living in poverty (Brantlinger, 2001); and the educational resources that are unequally distributed between the suburban and the "ghetto" schools (Anyon, 1997; Kozol, 1992). In each of these contexts, (cognitive) ability as property has provided the justification for segregating not only students with severe/cognitive disabilities, but also a disproportionate number of children living in poverty, children of color, and immigrant children with limited English proficiency—a segregation that has contributed to social and economic destitution of these populations (Brantlinger, 2001). Here, too, "ability" as property has played a critical role not only in constituting the disabilization of identity, but has also justified the oppressive logic of the social division of labor.

Of course, one could argue now that people of color, women, gays and lesbians, people with physical disabilities, and even some people with cognitive disabilities can enjoy the property rights accorded to all citizens, which could make Harris's argument outdated. However, what is rendered invisible by such assertions is the paradoxical process by which these rights were attained. In other words, because liberal individualism still rules the day, albeit in a more hospitable form, almost all of the oppressed groups listed above have earned the right of recognition as citizens by demonstrating their capacity for integration at whatever level into the labor force—the minimum qualification being the "ability" to contribute in some small way to the accumulation of profit. For those who are not considered naturally "able," liberal institutions support special education programs, rehabilitation programs, boot camps, etc., in an attempt to create "docile bodies" (Foucault, 1977, p. 136). Those "unruly bodies" who resist such "treatments" are relegated to the philanthropic protection of the welfare state whose mission is to protect its most vulnerable citizens from the excesses of capitalism.

The welfare state, however, foregrounds the crisis of liberal ideologies when it compels a certain section of the population to seek the protection of the welfare state. In this context, those individuals whose labor power cannot efficiently contribute to surplus accumulation (e.g., people with cognitive/severe disabilities) are excluded from participating in the market, and now become the property of state. As recipients of "special services" offered through social institutions such as schools, the welfare system, the health system, etc., they are labeled as "delinquent," "physically and mentally handicapped," "problem families," etc.. Located outside the discourse of property rights, this population reduced to the singular role as consumer, is deemed parasitic; their role as autonomous agent challenged; and therefore their right to citizenship.

It could be argued that my exclusive focus on civil and political citizenship ignores one other aspect—that of social citizenship. In fact, it could be argued that people with cognitive/severe disabilities are, in fact, guaranteed the rights of social citizenship that provides need-based social entitlements such as social security, health care, education, and so on. However, even though social welfare gets an aura of dignity when brought under the ambit of social citizenship, Fraser and Gordon (1997) argue that, within the United States, social citizenship is emphatically denied while civil citizenship is actively encouraged. In many ways, the differential status between civil and social citizenship mirrors the differential status between the public and private spheres, where the former is based on contractual property relations and the latter on voluntary/charitable associations. For example, Fraser and Gordon point out that, while "contract connoted equal exchange, mutual benefit, self-interest, rationality, and masculinity, charity took on contrasting notions of inequality, unilateral gift-giving, altruism, sentiment, and, at times, femininity" (p. 123). Thus, by once again reinvesting the two categories of public/private with differential status with respect to property, it is only "natural" that people with cognitive/severe disabilities will continue to be stigmatized as non-autonomous and dependent citizens. This logic is well represented in US Senator Patrick Moynihan's claims that

> the issue of welfare is an issue of dependency. It is different from poverty. To be poor is an objective condition; to be dependent, a subjective one as well... Being poor is often associated with considerable personal qualities, being dependent rarely so. [Dependency] is an incomplete state in life, normal in the child, abnormal in the adult. In a world where completed men and women stand on their own feet, persons who are dependent—as a buried imagery of the word denotes—hang. (as quoted in Fraser, 1997, p. 21)

In a context where people with cognitive/severe disabilities seem unable to be incorporated into the discourses of property rights, there is little choice left, but to hang.

It is important to note also, that if one is not worthy of owning property, it is quite possible that one can be transformed into property itself. Harris pointed to this in her argument when she described how whiteness as property was used to determine the legal status of a person as slave or free. In the current historical context, Mutua (2001) observes a similar trend in an ethnographic case study that "examine[s] the adverse effects of welfare reform policy on children and its intersections with school as a gate-keeping dispensary of identities of disability" (p. 289). In this study, Mutua describes "the pathologization of children of poverty" (p. 289) that occurs when they are labeled as mentally retarded and/or emotionally disturbed, in public schools contexts using evaluation tools that she argues are neither rational nor objective. Because the children in the study are from an African American family who receives welfare, food stamps, and cash benefits, there already existed a presupposition of "deviancy" even before the children entered school, and therefore school officials were already predisposed to referring these children to special education. Mutua further observes that this labeling process ensures the perpetual surveillance of this population by both special education and social welfare professionals—a process that denies even the most limited rights that formal justice promises its citizens. This "pathologization of children of poverty" has become over the years a lucrative business, where professionals interact with these children armed with a battery of tests, boot camps, and other behavior management programs that are more profitable to the professionals than humanizing to their clients.

In the context of the welfare state, a similar trend can be recognized in the increasing privatization of social welfare services and the move to support a more cost-effective and efficient organization of the surplus populations who are regarded as a drain on public resources. For example, sections of the prison system (public institutions that in the past year held about 2 million of the "surplus population," the majority of whom are poor and people of color) are privately owned, and derive their profits from the shipment of imprisoned bodies between facilities (Davis, 1998; Schlosser, 1988). In another example, the increased cuts in public spending for people with severe/cognitive disabilities have forced them and their family members to receive services from corporate conglomerates that have transformed the provision of health care and rehabilitation services into a profitable and ruthless business. In each of these contexts, it is possible to observe how the association of citizenship rights with property rights, as manifested in the material construction of whiteness and ability as property, now serves to "pathologize" certain individuals under the guise of social welfare and social citizenship. And it is these practices, I argue, that simultaneously support the *racialization of disability* and the disabilization of race in the construction of "immaterial citizens."

CITIZENSHIP AS SOCIAL TRANSFORMATION: A MATERIALIST DISABILITY STUDIES PERSPECTIVE

Poststructuralist feminist Chantal Mouffe has claimed that radical democracy is "the only viable alternative for the left today, and that it consists in trying to extend the principles of equality and liberty to an increasing number of social relations" (as quoted in Dhaliwal, 1996, p. 41). Yet, despite her argument and the creative theorizing by other poststructuralist feminists, cognitive/severe disability still continues to hover at the limits of even radical discourses of citizenship. This is because both liberal and poststructural theories of citizenship, by ignoring political economy, conceive of citizenship as a particular form of "lifestyle politics," which strengthens the basic ethical tenets of bourgeois individuals—"the ethical construct of capitalism where one has to be free to do what one wants, free to buy and sell, to accumulate wealth or to live in poverty, to work or not, to be healthy or to be sick" (Navarro as quoted in Doyal, 1981, p. 36). For people with cognitive/severe disabilities, for whom autonomy and choice are social rather than natural constructs, the freedom to choose in liberal society remains an idealistic construct rather than a material reality.

Amarpal Dhaliwal (1996), critiquing radical democratic politics, argues that, inclusion politics (notwithstanding their radicality), often "reaffirm a hegemonic core to which the margins are added without any significant destabilization of the core or continue to valorize the very center that is problematic to begin with" (p. 44). Dhaliwal defines this core as the hegemonic self "[that] always needs and is often manufactured in opposition to the 'othered' (the excluded)" (p. 44). She then locates her explanation for the construction of the "hegemonic self" and its despised "other" as it applies to racial oppression in the history of modernity, especially as it links up with the history of colonialism and imperialism.

Pursuing a similar trajectory with respect to cognitive/severe disability, I have attempted to explain in this chapter, how and why people with cognitive/severe disabilities have been constructed as the despised "other," and how this construction relates to the larger totality of social and economic structures. Further, even while I support liberal interventions that claim to protect the rights of citizens with severe/cognitive disabilities, I argue in this chapter that citizenship for these populations will only become meaningful in contexts where the material conditions of democracy are also realizable.

Feminist scholar Ruth Lister (1997) has argued that citizenship should be conceived of as a process rather than an outcome. On the other hand, I am arguing, in this chapter, that it may be necessary to examine the process in dialectical relationship to the outcome. From the critical standpoint of a materialist disability studies, the process of becoming a citizen is not rooted in the emergence of the autonomous individual, but is instead rooted in the historical and material conditions that nurture interdependence and community. In this context, rather than defining the freedom of individual citizens in negative terms (protecting individual rights from outside intrusion), citizenship rights should be articulated as positive rights that provide access to the social and material resources necessary for the achievement of both individual and communitarian purposes and plans. Additionally, the recognition of people with cognitive/severe disabilities as material citizens would require that liberal societies support the "the de-commodification of labor," which enables the decoupling of the living standards of citizens from their "market value," so that they are not totally dependent on selling their labor power in the market (Linton, 1998, pp. 16–17).

Mitchell and Snyder (2010), however, have argued that disabled people, rather than being labeled as "non-productive bodies" could, on the other hand, be (re)theorized in the words of Hardt and Negri as "'living labor' to suggest forms of creativity that cannot be reduced to an economic value" (p. 184). Rather than foregrounding only their exclusion, Mitchell and Snyder argue that these so-called non-productive bodies actually resist, and in doing so destabilize "the standardized demands of human value" (p. 184).

Moreover, this radical reunderstanding of nonproductive bodies recognizes *"forms of incapacity"* as the harbinger of radical change to come. However, even though I am sympathetic to Mitchell and Snyder's rearticulation of nonproductive bodies as living labor, I am not convinced that this conceptualization can actually support transformative possibilities—an argument I will continue in the next chapter where I will specifically engage the notion of affective labor as articulated by Hardt and Negri as it relates to the political economy of care.

CHAPTER 6

THE "OTHER" SIDE OF THE DIALECTIC: TOWARD A MATERIALIST ETHIC OF CARE

> To put it bluntly—because the need is blunt as it gets—we must have our asses cleaned after we shit and pee. Or we have others' fingers inserted into our rectum to assist shitting. Or we have tubes of plastic inserted inside us to assist peeing or we have re-routed anuses and pissers so we do it all into bags attached to our bodies. These blunt, crude realities. Our daily lives…We rarely talk about these things…Because let's face it: we have great shame about this need…If we are ever really home in the world and in ourselves, then we must say these things out loud. And we must say them with real language.
>
> (Cheryl Marie Wade as quoted in Siebers, 2008, p. 65)

IT IS NOT JUST THE "INADEQUATE" DEMONSTRATION OF RATIONALITY that is used against disabled subjects (especially those with severe and/or cognitive impairments) that prevents them from claiming the rights to full citizenship. It is also their perceived lack of autonomy on account of their dependence on their caregivers (paid and/or unpaid) for the social reproduction of their lives. In Chapter 5, I had briefly alluded to this dilemma through the critique offered by feminist philosopher Eva Feder Kittay, when she argued that her daughter's continued dependence on her caregivers even into adulthood does not cast her unequivocally as an undue burden on society because of the popular perception that such relationships are often incapable of being reciprocal. On the other hand, Kittay argues that there is much in this relationship that is reciprocal that may not have much economic value, but most certainly has affective value.

Echoing Kittay's claim, feminist scholar Sara Ahmed (2004) has argued that such relationships, in fact, form an economy—an affective economy. According to Ahmed, in affective economies, "emotions *do things* (author's emphasis), and they align individuals with communities—or bodily space with social space—through the very intensity of their attachments" (p. 119). Ahmed's definition enables a recognition of disabled subjects as social subjects located within reciprocal relationships that bind them to other bodies, and that, in turn, bind them to communities. This is because, according to Ahmed, emotions (affects) do not reside *in* bodies but *between* bodies, and therefore emotions become the critical building block of most social relationships. While Ahmed's theorization of affective economies may be especially useful for theorizing caring relationships with persons with severe/cognitive disabilities as having the potential for reciprocity, she conceives of the economics of affect solely in metaphorical terms. By doing so, Ahmed pays scant attention to the materialist context within which these relationships occur—a context that is instrumental in determining the nature of the relationship between caregiver and care recipient.

There has been an ongoing tension between feminists and disability studies scholars regarding the exact nature of this relationship between caregiver and care-recipient. Caring work has historically been considered women's work, and, as a result, even today, women are, for the most part, primary caregivers in both paid and unpaid caring work. In analyzing the social organization of caring, feminist Evelyn Nakano-Glenn (2010) has argued that underlying much of this caring work lie two specific forms of coercion—status obligation and racialized gendered servitude. Coercion via status obligation implies that, by virtue of one's gendered status (as wife, mother, daughter), it is generally accepted that one necessarily has to take on the role of caregiver. Here, it is not contractual relations entered into voluntarily that take precedence. Rather, as Nakano-Glenn argues, "women are charged with a triple status duty to care, on the basis of (1) kinship (wife, daughter, mother), (2) gender (as women), and (3) sometimes race/class (as members of a subordinate group)" (p. 7). Coercion as manifested in racialized gendered servitude refers to the sexual and racial division of labor, where through legal/social/economic mandates, those in power can command others to serve them. Referring to the historical practices of slavery, indentured labor, and debt bondage, where women of color were commandeered to perform caring work for their masters/bosses, Nakano Glenn argues that contemporary neoliberal political and economic trends continue to support similar practices (albeit in different forms), where race, class, and gender continue to remain the organizing principles of caring work.

While I am completely in agreement with Nakano-Glenn's argument regarding the politics invested in the social organization of caring, I am also painfully conscious that this argument situates disabled care recipients in an uncomfortable relationship with their caregivers. In foregrounding the forms of coercion present in caring work, does Nakano-Glenn implicitly situate disabled care recipients as the oppressive partner in this relationship? With disabled people increasingly arguing for choice in the context of care, does their right to seek affordable care within the market rather than the family reproduce unequal gender/race/class relations? In raising such questions are feminists implicitly designating disabled people as undue burdens in society, and what are the implications of such designations? Does the caring relationship always have to reproduce inequality? Are there examples of truly reciprocal relationships between nondisabled caregiver and disabled care recipient? Can affective economies enable us to navigate past these barriers to genuine reciprocity?

In this chapter, I raise the above questions in order to foreground the complex dialectical relationship between caregiver and care recipient. I use the term "dialectical" rather than "reciprocal" to highlight the complexities of this affective relationship. In doing so, I echo Anita Silvers's caution that a naïve celebration of the affective economy could possibly eclipse the power differentials between caregiver and care recipient and open up possibilities for abuse perpetrated by either the caregiver or care recipient. While Silvers's resolves this dilemma by arguing for "real choices" made by disabled care recipients to employ caregivers via the market, I argue that choice does not resolve the power relationships that are inevitable in a market economy crisscrossed by the racial, sexual, and transnational divisions of labor. In making this argument, I once again call into question Delueze and Guatarri's conception of affect, as unmediated by the material conditions of transnational capitalism—an argument I already made in Chapter 1 and will be extending in this chapter. On the other hand, in this chapter, I will locate the affective economy within the context of transnational capitalism to analyze the implications of the political economy of care for intercorporeal relationships imbricated within the constructs of race, gender, sexuality, and disability. By doing so, I will also attempt to articulate the conditions of possibility for a more transformative and/or emancipatory dialectic between caregiver and care recipient.

RELATIONAL ETHICS AND THE DIVISIVE POLITICS OF CARE

Traditional ethical theory has defined the "ethical" self as an autonomous, rational, moral agent, who independently judges the conflicting claims of others against an abstract and universal standard of equality or equal respect. Critical of this universalizing theoretical construction that negates difference, Nel Noddings (1990) has argued for a feminine ethics grounded in a relational ontology, where the "ethical" self is perceived as a product of relationships of caring with individual others (p. 124). This feminine ethics supports an alternative track of moral development for women that evolves from an initial stage where an egocentric form of self-care prevails, to culminate in a final stage that represents a self-chosen, self-reflective, self affirming form of mature caring (Gilligan, 1982, see chs. 3-4). As a result, unlike the individualism of traditional ethical theory that manifests itself solely in the public sphere, the feminine ethic of care emphasizes interdependence and the maintenance of relationships between family members and friends in the private sphere of female domesticity (Clement, 1996, p. 2).

This celebration of the ethic of care as a "feminine ethic" (Clement, 1996, p. 2) has been regarded with suspicion by other feminists, who have argued that women engaged in caring work are, in fact, exploited as carers (Bubeck, 1995). This exploitation occurs not only as a result of the sexual division of labor that designates caring work as domestic labor that is either unpaid or underpaid, but also occurs as a result of the peculiar logic of caring that requires certain skills and virtues that make women especially vulnerable to this exploitation (Bubeck, 1995; Dalley, 1988; Graham 1993, 1991; Parker 1993; Ungerson 1987). They have, therefore, argued that this formulation only serves to "[transform] victimization into virtue by merely saying it is so... [and] legitimizing subjugation to gender in a misguided attempt at self affirmation" (Puka, 1989, p. 19).

Notwithstanding their differing positions, both these schools of thought coalesce around their collective allegiance to a humanist conceptualization of autonomy for the female caregivers—the dominant presence in these analyses. Thus, for example, even though the feminine ethic of care emphasizes the interdependent relationship between the ethical self and its related others, this perspective continues to emphasize the motives, beliefs, values, self-conceptions, and feelings of a self-critical, rational, and autonomous agent—a definition that continues to reinstate the humanist subject, albeit in its "feminine" form. In a similar fashion, those feminists who have criticized the feminine ethic of care as being exploitative to caregivers have done so on the grounds that it requires women to take care of patriarchal interests at the expense of themselves and their own interests (Clements, 1996, p. 6). Such practices, they have pointed out, compromise the autonomy of the caregiver, where autonomy is once again conceived of in humanist terms as synonymous with rational and independent self-determination.

This foregrounding of humanist conceptions of autonomy for caregivers has almost always been done at the exclusion of any discussion of the care recipient, who is also a significant presence located at the other end of this dialectical caring relationship. Often, care recipients are only introduced into the debate when the discussion centers on autonomy, and where the portrayal of the caring relationship is such that the preservation of the autonomy for the female caregiver necessarily negates the possibility of ever applying a similar conceptualization to their disabled care recipients. In this chapter, I argue that such a conceptualization of the caring relationship is detrimental to most care recipients, especially those with moderate to severe, physical and/or cognitive disabilities.

Persons with moderate to severe disabilities have almost always required some form of personal assistance while meeting their basic needs, and this physical dependence on their care providers has often led to the common assumption that they are incapable of functioning as autonomous agents in other aspects of their lives. This is because when humanist notions of autonomy are privileged as normative in defining human subjectivity, persons with moderate to severe disabilities who radically differ from this norm have historically been labeled "deviant." Critical of these definitions several disability studies theorists have highlighted the limits of humanism in scholarship that "[has] denaturalize[d] the cultural encoding of extraordinary bodies (Garland-Thomson, 1997, p. 5), has exposed the notion of the norm as a "fictional" construction (Davis 1995, pp. 23–49), and has described how social, political, and economic structures contribute to the social construction of the "disabled" body (Oliver, 1990, pp. 25–42). While the feminist ethic of care, for the most part, would be supportive of such scholarship that deconstructs normative constructs of humanness, at the same time, its allegiance to humanist notions of autonomy intervenes as a critical tension between feminist theory and disability studies. Here, both sides struggle to preserve the autonomy of the female caregivers and the disabled care recipients, who are conjoined in a relationship that has been characterized as oppressive by both camps (Morris, 1991; Parker, 1993; Silvers, 1997; Ungerson, 1987). I, therefore, argue that when we examine both sides of the dialectic present in the relationship between caregiver and care recipient from the standpoint of a feminist materialist disability studies, such an analysis will expose the limits of the humanist conceptualization of autonomy. Moreover, I will argue here that an alternative reconceptualization of the concept of autonomy from the standpoint of disability will also trouble the limits of feminist ethical, social, and political theory when attempting to define the truly "moral" agent.

THE LIMITS OF FEMINIST CONCEPTIONS OF AUTONOMY

It is almost a truism to assert that the concepts of "autonomy" and "disability" have historically been regarded as binary opposites. This is especially evident in traditional Western ethical theory, which regards the "normal" person as autonomous, where autonomy is conceived of as a psychological disposition that upholds two standard conditions—the absence of coercion and the capacity for making independent critical decisions (Clement, 1996, pp. 24–35). Undergirding this definition of autonomy is the humanist vision of "naturalized 'man'... [whose] body... is a stable, neutral instrument of the individual will" (Garland-Thomson, 1997, p. 42). In stark contrast to this highly regulated and compliant "normal" body, the disabled body—unruly in its behavior, unpredictable in its demeanor, and disruptive in its difference—comes to represent "a social malady" (Murphy, 1987, p. 4), subverting the ideal, who appears as "master of both destiny and self" (Garland-Thomson, 1997, p. 41). It is for this reason that the disabled body is perceived as betraying the spirit of liberal individualism propagated in capitalist democracies because it calls into question "concepts [such] as will, ability, progress, responsibility, and free agency" (Garland-Thomson, 1997, p. 47)—concepts that form the bedrock of the autonomous humanist subject. As a result, within the popular imagination, disabled people are perceived as neither normal nor autonomous.

But disabled people are not the only population perceived as incapable of meeting the demands of autonomous humanist subjectivity. Women too, who were historically designated as inferior to men because their social and economic contributions to the production and reproduction of life, were seen as a function of their biology or "nature,"—a designation that justified the dominance of the (male) human being over (female) nature (Mies 1986, p. 45). Thus, for example, feminists have pointed out that when women enact their traditional social roles as primary caregivers to their husbands, parents, children, and other associates, they are perceived as violating the two standard conditions of autonomy. This is because when women attempt to fulfill their socially prescribed roles as caregivers, it is quite difficult to discern whether they perform these roles without coercion, and whether they are empowered to make independent critical decisions relating to their work.

For feminist theorists, who have struggled to equate the feminine ethic of care with its humanist (read masculinist) version of an ethic of justice, the dilemma regarding women's autonomy presents itself as a hurdle. In an attempt to resolve this dilemma, they have offered a critique of traditional definitions of autonomy that they claim are based on patriarchal constructs that do not accurately reflect the actual conditions of women's lives (Clement, 1996; Davion, 1993; Gilligan, 1982; Puka, 1989). Rejecting the individualism pervading the traditional definition, they have argued for an expanded definition that recognizes autonomy as a social competency that is not learned in isolation but through relationships with others. This is because, they argue, relationships with others actually support self-knowledge since "[personal uniqueness, creativity, expressiveness and self awareness...grow out of interdependence, and continually turn back to it for affirmation and continuation" (Code as quoted in Clement, 1996, p. 24). Therefore, in a context where autonomy has to take into account not only psychological but also social factors, it follows that the two standard conditions for autonomy should also be expanded to account for social conditions that can either impede or nurture the possibilities for autonomy (p. 26). It is for these reasons that feminists argue that caring relationships, in particular, serve as the necessary precondition for women's autonomy (Clement, 1996, p. 24).

The feminist redefinition of autonomy to include interdependent relationships that occur in historically specific social contexts could prove useful in redefining disabled people as autonomous agents. After all, disabled people rely on appropriate technology and personal assistance in their everyday lives such that their social identities are constituted in relationship with those on whom they rely for their daily care. Unfortunately, however, feminists have continued to balk at applying this expanded definition of autonomy to disabled people, especially when they occupy the role of care recipients conjoined in a relationship with their female caregivers. While feminist ethical theorists are willing to concede that even children, who have traditionally been perceived as nonautonomous care recipients, are actively promoted so that they appear autonomous, similar treatment is not meted out to adult disabled people, especially those with moderate to severe physical and/or cognitive disabilities. This is because, Clement points out, while caring for children will ultimately promote their eventual autonomy, "caring for individuals who are severely mentally retarded [will not yield similar results because]...often the[se] recipients of care are and will remain unavoidably non-autonomous" (p. 32).

Clement's argument reveals the limits of the feminist redefinition of autonomy that despite its expansion continues to be based on problematic assumptions—assumptions that, I argue, have their roots in humanist thought, albeit in the feminine form. Haunting Clement's argument is the assumption that while most "normal" care recipients (that include both men and women) may someday attain the humanist ideal of self-determination, this argument cannot apply to the disabled care recipient whose very existence renounces "the fiction of self improvement...and [therefore] presents the ultimate challenge to perfection and progress" (Garland-Thomson ,1997, p. 46). Thus, even though Clement argues that autonomy is not a precondition for a caring relationship, but is socially constituted through the caring relationship, her implicit commitment to the humanist ideal of "wholeness" only reinforces autonomy as an idealist and essentialist concept, which when applied to disability is, in the last instance, removed from the social and historical context in which it is located.

Even feminists who have rejected the idealist narrative in caring work and have opted for a materialist analysis continue to locate disabled people outside the ambit of their analyses. This is clearly evident in Diemut Bubeck's (1995) work, where she deploys a historical-materialist analysis to foreground the exploitation present in women's caring work. Bubeck's materialist analysis of the ethic of care makes a careful distinction between "service" and "caring," and she seeks to expose the latter as a source of exploitation. Bubeck explains:

> Since caring takes place as a response to a certain type of needs—that is needs the person in need cannot possibly meet herself—caring involves...a one-sided dependency of the person in need of care on the prospective carer. Their relationship is not one between equals or of equal bargaining strength since the carer has the power to withhold care and the cared for's needs have to be met. This power differential is irreducible since the needs to be met cannot be met by those in need themselves. I cannot talk to myself if I need to talk a problem over with somebody...nor can children bring themselves up, nor can a frail 90-year-old or a mentally disabled person survive without support by others. Again this assumption does not exemplify the usual assumptions made in liberal and political theory, where people are typically conceived of as (ideally) autonomous, independent agents in control of their choices and their life plans. (p. 141)

Bubeck's redefinition of caring to expose women's exploitation depends on the necessary construction of the care recipient—in this case, disabled people—as nonautonomous. This, Anita Silvers (1997) argues in response to another feminist philosopher Annette Baier's statement that "equality is not a even a desirable ideal in [caring] relationships" (as quoted in Silvers, 1997, p. 34), requires that "the very structure of helping or caring relationships invites the marginalization of whoever is consigned to a position of dependence...[such that] it becomes socially incumbent upon [the care recipients]...to profess incompetence even where they are more competent than [their care givers]" (Silvers, 1997, p. 33).

Then, in another curious twist to her argument, Bubeck points out that given the importance of care for those in need, the female caregiver, recognizing this dependence, finds it impossible to leave the relationship, and is therefore effectively coerced into continuing the caring work, even if she wishes to leave. This, Bubeck argues, implies that for a "good" carer, "the power she has over the person cared for is counteracted by her openness toward the person cared for which means that she reacts to a perceived need as a demand on her to care" (p. 143). Here, Bubeck's argument is contradictory, because the care recipient is located in a position of subordination (nonautonomous) to the female caregiver, only to have this position reversed so as to reveal his/her [the care recipient's] exploitative control over the caregiver. Interestingly enough, neither of these reversals of power is enacted through any act of volition from the care recipient, but occurs when the caregiver responds to the *innate* needs of the care recipient. Thus, even though Bubeck's text uses historical materialism to critique the idealism invested in women's caring work, she refuses to apply a similar analysis to the issue of autonomy as it relates to care recipients who are disabled people, and in doing so, continues to reify autonomy as an idealist and essentialist concept derived from humanist thought.

THE WELFARE STATE AND THE POLITICAL ECONOMY OF DEPENDENCY

As per the argument in the previous section, even though feminists conceive of gendered caring work as historical, they continue to regard disability as an innate biological quality that "unfortunately" causes disabled people to be dependent on others. Disability studies scholars, on the other hand, have been critical of this conceptualization arguing that disability is the embodied experience of social oppression constituted via the inhospitable social, cultural, and economic structures in mainstream society. By redefining disability in this way, much of the disability studies scholarship, especially in the United States, has focused on the cultural realm, and exposed how attitudes, discourses, and symbolic representations have played a critical part in the social construction of disability (Brueggemann, 1999; Davis, 1995; Garland-Thomson 1997; Mitchell & Snyder 1997). Their theoretical interventions have usually been discursive where they have attempted to creatively resignify both disability and autonomy in ways that are not oppressive to disabled people. While I consider their interventions useful to the project of disability studies, I argue that implicit in these retheorizations is the assumption that autonomy is a ahistorical concept—an essentialist characteristic utilized to define humanness. On the other hand, drawing on historical materialism from the standpoint of disability studies, I reject this implicit acceptance of the category of autonomy, and will instead explore why this category is significant in the historical context of late capitalism and how it is related to the social category of disability.

A historical-materialist view of disability argues that the social construction of the disabled body emerges from "the specific ways in which society organizes its basic material activities (work, transport, leisure, domestic activities)" (Gleeson, 1997, p. 194). Historical materialism begins with the presupposition that labor is the central organizing force in history, because human beings do not just live but instead "produce" their lives within specific historical contexts through their relationship to labor. In other words, the historical-materialist framework reads the subject—its body, consciousness, and meanings—as produced by and through labor. Thus, historical materialism is able to map out the dialectical relationship of individuals to social structures as determined by their locations in the social divisions of labor emerging from the social organization of the economy in specific historical contexts. In this way, such analyses explore how historical inequalities and social identities are related under capitalism (Hennessy, 1999).

As early as 1966, disability activist Paul Hunt argued that the exclusion of disabled people from the world of work, and their corresponding inability to "consume" the material and social benefits of modern society, has contributed to their experiences of oppression in society (Oliver, 1990). Farber (1968) explained this phenomena of exclusion by describing disabled people as located within the surplus labor market that supports specific levels of unemployment in an attempt to minimize production costs and maximize profits in capitalist societies. Farber further explained that allocating disabled people to the surplus labor market is justified via complex labeling and classificatory processes that designate them as dysfunctional because they fail to meet the so-called objective criteria of efficiency and productivity required in capitalist production. By certifying these populations as incapable of producing for exchange value, members of this surplus population are therefore certified as eligible to receive monetary aid as well as social services, and in return are subject to the regulatory and controlling benevolence of the welfare state (Stone, 1984).

It is in the context of the welfare state that the concept of autonomy becomes especially relevant. In capitalist societies, the commodification of labor necessitated "a social evaluation of work—the law of value...[that] appraise[s] the worth of *individual* (my emphasis) labor in terms of average productivity standards" (Gleeson, 1997, p. 195). On the basis of this social evaluation, "'slower', 'weaker,' and more inflexible workers were devalued in terms of their paid work" (p. 195), excluded from the labor market, and now, without the social means of economic survival, transformed into dependent clients of the welfare state. Here, the task of maintaining the nonworking populations falls on the welfare state, which utilizes its administrative machinery to supervise the transference of the social product from the productive population to those who are deemed unproductive to the economy (Gough, 1979).

However, a distribution system based on need is actually incompatible with a market economy because the guarantee of any sort of state assistance may actually serve as a disincentive to participation in the market. This is because a profit-oriented market economy is dependent on a large pool of cheap labor that has to be willing to work for any wage, and therefore cannot afford any other competing alternative. Thus, one aspect of the distributive dilemma under the purview of the welfare state has been to develop objective mechanisms by which to determine who among its needy citizens fall into one of the two categories, the "deserving poor" and the "non-deserving poor" (Ginsburg, 1979; Gough, 1979; Stone, 1984). Additionally, the welfare state has also been compelled to make clear to its clients that the benefits received through this need-based economy will not appear more lucrative than the wages received in the work-based economy. And finally, the third aspect of the distributive dilemma that continues to challenge the welfare state is the means to ascertain what kinds of needs are thought to be appropriate objects of social policy—a difficult dilemma because needs are in fact extremely subjective—based on "a complicated mixture of social resources and individual striving, of public expectations and private imagination" (Stone, 1984, p. 19).

With the advent of new scientific discoveries and modern medical technologies to combat the causes of ill-health, the medical profession has assumed an authoritative role by claiming to possess "pure, objective, unbiased expertise" (p. 107) to make clinical judgments about who legitimately "cannot" or "will not" work (Stone, 1984). Working in close association with the welfare state, the medical profession resurrected "disability" as a clinical concept that could be utilized as medico-scientific criteria to determine where the boundary lies between work and need. It was based on such assumptions that the American Social Security Disability Insurance (SSDI) Program in the 1950s was constructed, for example, to provide disability certification to those clinically identified as unable to work.

However, despite its claims to objectivity, the clinical method has continued to struggle to find an effective way to categorize "disability." This is because its claims to clinical objectivity have often concealed the possibility that eligibility decisions may not be safe from subjective manipulation. For example, how does one determine what levels of "pain" or "discomfort" can prevent people from working? Or to put it more broadly, how is one to ascertain what level of measurement is indicative of an individual's inability to function in the workforce? Such dilemmas, by demonstrating a failure to control the subjective dimension of the eligibility criteria, at the same time also expose the very instability of "disability" as an administrative category in the context of social welfare. In fact, it has been this instability of the definition of "disability" that continues to haunt the current welfare system, and that has contributed in some measure to the current crisis of the welfare state. This is because, as Stone (1984) points out, the popular conception of disability can be usually much broader than clinical definitions put forward by social policy, and as a result such loopholes make it very easy to cross officially created boundaries and make the task of gatekeeping extremely difficult. Further, this flexibility in the official criteria also appears to undermine the power of the state to control both its working and its nonworking populations.

Yet, ignoring this dimension of subjectivity in identifying disability, medical science constructed an etiology of deviance and derived diagnostic techniques to not only identify all such deviations as social difference, but to also demonstrate the "natural" inferiority inherent in these differences (Gould, 1981; Paul, 1995). Moreover, because of the elevated status that medical science acquired in the administrative hierarchy of the welfare state, its scientific assumptions regarding social difference carried over to the formulation and implementation of social policy. As a result, social problems of poverty, malnutrition, unemployment, prostitution, crime, etc., were "naturally" associated with populations identified as "deviant" on account of their "inherent" inferiority" (Gould, 1981; Jones, 1983; Mies, 1986). Thus, social welfare policy organized its so-called deviant clients into separate categories, labeled them as mentally/physically handicapped, mentally ill, juvenile delinquent, children at-risk, single parent, problem family, the elderly, etc., and offered clinical explanations to defend these classifications (Jones, 1983). However, what often got lost in this elaborate system of classification was the one striking similarity between all these groups—the overall class context of poverty, inequality, and powerlessness—that manifested itself, albeit differently for different groups, in "maladaptive" social and economic behaviors that characterized their daily lives.

Also, if social problems were assumed to have their roots in human biology, then it is only natural that social policy be inspired by clinical knowledge to seek solutions to these problems. One such solution is rehabilitation. The primary goal of rehabilitation is to "fix" the individual so that he/she can return as productive workers to the economy. Often, many of these clients, based on their assumed inherent inferiority, are tracked into programs that train people for low-skilled and low-waged jobs that most people would be unwilling to do. In this way, rehabilitation programs serve to socialize society's deviant populations into specific social divisions of labor—forming an industrial reserve army that the economy can draw from in its hour of need (Gough, 1979; Jones, 1983). However, in the current context of corporate downsizing and capital flight, there has been a steady decrease in the availability of low-waged, low-skilled jobs that the newly "rehabilitated" workers can fill. As a result, with very few alternative employment opportunities, many of these "rehabilitated" workers are returned once again to the state of poverty and their continued dependence on the welfare state (Abramovitz, 1996; Jones, 1983; Navarro, 1984). It is in this context then that rehabilitation, by seemingly failing to "fix" its clientele, is represented as an example of failed public policy, inspiring demands for cuts in services that are clearly identified as wastages and highlighting yet another factor that has contributed in some measure to the current crisis in the welfare state.

Curiously enough, even though the very construction of the welfare state and its attempts to organize and control "deviant" difference have been historically linked to the expansion of capitalism, most social policy has seldom questioned the part the capitalist economy has played in its constructions of social difference. Instead, the welfare state has directed its entire energies to monitoring the activities of its nonworking population, demonstrating its investment in placing limits on the life choices of these populations rather than placing limits on the economic conditions that have produced their experiences of deprivation in the first place. Thus, for example, while the welfare state has gone to great lengths to construct objective criteria to define the "disability" category, it has seldom taken the time to investigate the economic conditions that have rendered individuals "disabled" in relation to the market economy, based on the assumption that their exclusion from the economy is natural, inevitable, and self-induced. As a result, the current crisis in the welfare state is usually blamed on the parasitism of its clients, rather than on the exploitative conditions of late-capitalism.

The debates involving the current crisis of the welfare state have been dominated by conservatives who critique the welfare state for failing in its duty to successfully rehabilitate its "deviant clients," and have indicated that such failures only go to prove that it has outlived its usefulness and become obsolete (Murray, 1993; Taylor-Gooby, 1991). It is because of this political pressure that the earlier allegiances of the welfare state to support its own brand of distributive justice has all but been abandoned in many of the advanced capitalist countries. Instead, what has been instituted are several changes that have aimed to reform social welfare as we once knew it. First of all, educational and social security policies have been closely reexamined to see how best they can be adjusted to adapt the potential labor force more effectively to the needs of capital (e.g., the work fare programs in the United States). Second, there has been an increased enthusiasm to exert greater controls over other groups who are believed to pose a danger to the cohesiveness of society (e.g., the Defense of Marriage Act). Third, there have already been several budget cuts initiated that have attempted to tighten eligibility criteria and have downsized entire programs in an effort to ensure both profitability and efficiency. And finally, there has been increasing pressure on the welfare state to retain only its role as chief disburser of funds and diminish its role as welfare provider by reassigning the latter responsibilities to the voluntary, informal, and commercial sectors.

THE SEXUAL/RACIAL DIVISION OF (CARING) LABOR

Because women constitute the overwhelming majority of social welfare program recipients as well as employees, it is has usually been women and women's needs that are the principal stakes in the battles over public spending pertaining to the crisis of the welfare state (Ehrenreich, 1987; Fraser, 1993; Murray, 1993). And yet, social welfare scholars, for the most part, have paid very little attention to poor women, who have served both as clients and as workers for the welfare system (Abramovitz, 1996; Caplan, 1985b). More recently, however, feminists have highlighted a long term structural tendency—the feminization of poverty—a tendency that accounts for the increasing proportion of women included in the adult poverty population where many of them are the sole breadwinners in female headed households (Abramovitz, 1996; Caplan, 1985; Fraser, 1993; Glendinning& Millar, 1990). This seemingly natural association of women with poverty conceals the actual conditions of women's lives that are shaped by the historical structures of the sexual division of labor, such that even though women do 75 percent of the work, they earn only 10 percent of the wages, and own only 1 percent of the property (Pharr, 1988). As a result, it comes as no surprise to policy analysts that the poverty population dependent on social welfare in the United States, (the world's richest country), for example, would be dominated by women and children by the year 2000 (Abramovitz, 1996; Fraser, 1993).

Social welfare, in an effort to address women's needs, generally attributes the causes of poverty to their gender rather than to the economic and social processes that are based on this biological distinction (Caplan, 1985b; Glendinning & Millar, 1990; Kabeer, 1994). Moreover, they seldom question how the naturalization of the sexual division of labor produces the bifurcation of the public and the private spheres that has allowed for the male control of jobs and wages such that women get constructed as economically dependent members of the family (Caplan, 1985a; Kabeer, 1994). Thus, when policy analysts examine households, it is generally assumed that there is a degree of equality in the distribution of resources within households, and so they pay little attention to the dynamics of power and command that occur there (Glendinning & Millar, 1990). At the same time, welfare scholars problematically assume that marriage is one social institution that protects women against poverty, which once again reaffirms the dependent status of married women. Thus, when women undertake paid work outside the home, their wages are assumed to only supplement the male breadwinner's wages, and at the same time does little to override their primary housewifely and maternal responsibilities (Fraser, 1993; Kabeer, 1994). It is in this context that women's largely hidden and unpaid position in the domestic sphere and their secondary position in the labor market has often got translated into and reflected in the private, occupational, and public systems of welfare provision. It is these structural practices that enact what Fraser (1993) has called "public patriarchy" that refers to the systems by which while men are treated as right bearers and purchasing customers of social services, women, on the other hand, are regarded as members of "failed families," and constructed as deviant and dependent clients of the welfare system. As a result, the inequalities that women experience in both the labor market and the welfare systems are underpinned and legitimated by the ideology of dependency (Glendinning & Millar, 1990).

One of the major factors attributed to the cause of women's poverty in global contexts is their lack of access to education that, in turn, dis-enables women. First, the limited opportunities for girls and young women to hold high-skilled jobs that require training are often minimal, and their "natural" skills are often deemed more useful to perform the unpaid social labor that is necessary for the survival of the family unit. As a result, young girls, in particular, are often kept away from school so that they are better able to fulfill some of the household duties such as caring for very young children while the older women leave to perform waged labor. Second, much of the paid employment these women participate in depends on the "natural" skills that draw upon their capacities for domestic labor, and which is located predominantly in both the formal and informal service sector, which has also historically been the low-waged sector. Given the fact that these jobs do not require any specialized training and at the same time do not substantially benefit the family income, education for women seems a useless investment to be made in contexts of economic scarcity.

Another problem that arises is that very rarely do any of these literacy and/or educational programs focus their energies on meeting the specific needs of women. Because the cult of domesticity continues to be the dominant ideology in the framing of public policy, the central motive of supporting the education of women as formulated in world development reports argue that "women are to be educated because they will benefit the health of their families; they are to have incomes so that their children's health improves; and more importantly, in the context of diminishing availability of resources, women's 'natural' abilities to cope with limited resources must be enhanced" (Rao, Nayar, Rama & Priya, 1995, p.1158). As a result, most of the developmental agencies offer women training in nutrition, home-economics, maternal and child health, and family planning, in keeping with their domestic roles of social reproduction in society (Caplan, 1985a; Kabeer, 1994).

While feminist critiques of the development programs have urged that women be included be in the economy as productive members of society, the official response has been to institute income-generating projects that demonstrate some compatibility with women's reproductive and domestic roles. More recently, though supporters of the Structural Adjustment Programs (SAPS) have claimed that the generation of low-paying jobs will not only increase production but also the participation of women in market, and help in the general alleviation of poverty, these programs have only served to shrink women's employment opportunities in the organized sector since new employment opportunities for women are predominantly in the export-processing zones (Feldman, 1992). Further, under the SAPs, real wages have declined as a whole such that women continue to earn extremely low wages. Therefore, while there has been a greater increase in the female participation rate in the labor force than men, this has occurred in a context where the work is more decentralized, wages are lower, and contracts are temporary and irregular. As a result, it becomes increasingly evident that social welfare programs, particularly in education and employment, have continued to maintain women's devalued status in society, the market, and the family (Caplan, 1985a; Kabeer, 1994).

But women are associated with social welfare not only as clients; they are also its principal workers serving in different capacities and occupying different locations in its occupational hierarchy. Women outnumber men as providers of health care in roles both within the private space of the family as well as in the public context of social welfare (Nakano-Glenn, 2010). Much of this labor that women perform within the context of the welfare state is "caring work," which includes tasks such as teaching, healing, nursing, tending—work that was formerly done in the family primarily by women for no wage because it was assumed that such work came naturally to women and did not require much skill (Caplan, 1985b; Mies, 1986; Nakano-Glenn, 1992; Pascall, 1986). While much of this labor occurs within the private domain of the family, when this labor is moved out into the market, it is still primarily the domain of women, characterized as unpaid voluntary labor or as low-waged and insecure employment (Nakano-Glenn, 1992; 2010).

In her most recent book, *Forced to Care*, Evelyn Nakano-Glenn (2010) argues that caring work, either paid or unpaid, has actually increased in recent years such that in 2009 there were nearly 43.5 million Americans involved in caring of an aging family or friend. Moreover, Nakano-Glenn points out that those caregivers who were employed full time put in about 16 hours of unpaid care work, while those employed part time put in an average of 21 hours. Employed caregivers often had to miss work, work after hours, and/or make compromises regarding their career, such that they often suffered a mean loss of $566,443 in wages, $25,494 in social security benefits, and $67, 202 in pension wealth. Moreover, women who were carers at an early age were 2.5 times more likely to end up in poverty (p. 2–3). Additionally, in the United States, for instance, average median wage for paid workers was $9. 22 an hour—a wage that placed a two-person household below the poverty line; and these wages came with no health insurance

despite the high incidence of work-related injuries or even retirement benefits because they were not considered full-time jobs.

These statistics frame the backdrop for Western feminist critiques of community care policies that have moved disabled people out of institutions and
into the community (Dalley, 1988; Graham, 1991; Morris, 1995; Parker,
1993; Ungerson, 1987; Thomas, 1993). Feminist critiques have highlighted
the gendered nature of community care policies that rest on the assumption
that women, particularly, mothers, daughters, and wives will be the most
important providers of care to their dependent family members (Baldwin &
Twigg, 1990; Traustadottir, 1988). In part, this argument has been based
on an almost universal but false premise of "maternalism," a uniquely feminine value system based on care and nurturance, where women perform a
service to the state by raising its citizens (Ladd-Taylor, 1994). This has been
supported by some feminists, who have attributed such understandings to
the assumption that caring work does indeed define both the identity and
activities of women (Land, 1990; Parker 1993; Puka, 1989; Traustadottir,
1988)—a perspective drawn from Gilligan's argument that the formation
of the female gender identity and role exhibits a spontaneous expression of
a "relational social perspective, [that] places care as central to the feminist
ethic of choice" (Puka, 1989).

At the same time, without dismissing caring work as either "natural" or
as coercion, Devault (1991) suggests it may be more useful to examine the
complex ways in which women are drawn into participation within prevailing relations of inequality, such that it will be possible to examine how their
everyday lives are shaped by larger social relations. Much of the feminist
research that is carried out in this manner has focused predominantly on
the unpaid voluntary work performed by middle-class women, who enjoy
relative privilege on the basis of their race, caste, and class (Caplan, 1985b;
Parker, 1993; Traustadottir, 1988; Ungerson, 1983; Wendell, 1996). As a
result, in a critique of the exploitation of upper-class women's labor through
the discourse of voluntarism, feminists have argued that the provision of
such services be moved from the private sphere of the family into the public
space of the market, where at least those who perform that labor would
receive a wage.

But, what if such labor was moved out into the market? In what ways
would the exploitative conditions surrounding the sexual division of labor
be mitigated? Who then would perform this labor, and what value would
be placed on this labor? Moreover, in what ways can this work, centered as
it is on disabled individuals whose labor power has very little value in the
economy, be deemed as productive, given that it can do little to replenish
the labor force as other reproductive labor has been able to do? Such questions force us to reflect on whether domestic labor as waged labor "is a step

forward or backwards, is beneficial or exploitative, is a break with tradition, or merely an extension of it, is good or bad for helpers or helped, for volunteering or for the welfare system" (Baldock & Ungerson, 1990, p. 136).

Nakano-Glenn's (1992) study of paid service work within the United States is a partial response to these questions. In her study, this paid reproductive labor under the rubric of service jobs (e.g., nurses' aides) is performed by mostly poor women of color, most of them being new immigrants, who also experience the exploitation of low wages and poor working conditions. Further, Nakano-Glenn points out that this labor is able to relieve bourgeois women from the drudgery of caring work to perform productive labor for the capitalist economy. Therefore, through her analysis, Nakano-Glenn is able to effectively demonstrate how the unpaid reproductive labor of bourgeois white women within the private sphere of the home is inextricably bound to the paid reproductive labor of poor, women of color within the public sphere of the market. And while this labor still remains the same, the only difference is that the work that was once done at home has also been subsequently taken over by capitalism (the state and the market), where the relationship between the care provider and the care recipient is one structured by the consumer relations of the market (Glazer, 1984). Thus, it is only because of the persistence of the historical sexual division of labor in the family with the corresponding sex, race, and class segregation of the labor force that women still continue to bear much of the burden of reproductive labor.

However, even in their more expanded analyses of caring work, feminist scholars (Glazer, 1984; Graham, 1993; Nakano-Glenn, 1992, 2010) have continually failed to address in any meaningful way the social category of disability. In fact, in highlighting the exploitative nature of caring work and its implications on race, caste, class, and gender, such analyses have placed disabled persons, who are of course central to this debate, as antagonistic to the interests of the class, race, and gender politics. Thus, in offering critiques of community care policies, feminist scholarship has seldom addressed disabled people as anything but dependent entities with no political stakes in the entire debate (Nakano-Glenn, 1992; Ungerson, 1983). Morris (1995), a disabled feminist, has pointed out that much of the feminist bias regarding disability stems from an apolitical understanding of "independence" in Western culture, which demands that an individual be at all times self-sufficient and self-supporting. Thus, in a context where disabled people need physical assistance in their daily lives, they become dependent on their carer, who is therefore in control of their lives. On the other hand, Morris points out that a materialist understanding of disability would indicate that dependence is constructed as a result of economic poverty and oppressive social structures—conditions that may simultaneously be responsible for contributing to the dependence of poor women in the welfare state. However, these possible interconnections have not been adequately explored in feminist research.

AFFECTIVE LABOR AS POSSIBILITY FOR GLOBAL CORPOREALITIES

Perhaps the one feminist scholar who has attempted to bring together the politics of feminism and care within transnational contexts is Margrit Shildrick (2009). Because much of Shildrick's work is a rejection of humanist notions of autonomy for posthumanist notions of intercorporeality, her arguments resonate well with the conceptual and political issues regarding the dialectics of care. Shildrick, however, rejects a materialist analysis, embracing instead Deleuze and Guattarri's notions of rhizomatic dispersals, nomadic wanderings, and hybrid associations. As a result, she is explicit that her project is not to highlight the social, political, and economic inequities of globalization, but rather to critically engage globalization as "the experiential nature of living-in-the-world-with others" (p. 149).

It is not that Shildrick does not recognize the inequities that globalization engenders, obvious as they are, especially in the context of care. Shildrick, however, is specifically focused on the corporeal networks that globalization has spawned, especially in light of how the new technologies of communication and networks of global capital have quite literally shrunk the globe, such that bodies are enabled to both metaphorically and literally "touch" each other in most unexpected ways. Shildrick (2009) explains:

> [M]y concern is...with the no less important task of thinking through the phenomenological significance and implications of intercorporeality. If the capacities of any one body alter in relation to any other body—a disabled women's mobility in response to a Filipino women's manual dexterity; her diet in response to the Westerner's reliance on a specialist car—then it can no longer be assumed that bodies exist in discreet spaces. (p. 155)

As noted in this quote, Shildrick recognizes the unequal distances that separate and still connect the nondisabled Third World woman and her disabled First World counterpart. But, Shildrick's focus is on the productive possibilities in these associations rather than on the obvious inequalities. Here, echoing Deleuze and Guattari's emphasis on "the positivity of desiring production" (Shildrick, 2009, p. 157), her focus is on the affective relationships that arise out of these intercorporeal associations because she argues they open up spaces to reimagine more ethical possibilities.

To illustrate her argument, Shildrick shares a narrative of her partner, Janet Price, who needed the use of a caregiver to assist her while she was experiencing some temporary paralysis as a result of a recurrence of multiple sclerosis. Many of the caregivers in the agency that she employed were immigrant women, often refugees, and Price celebrates the new relationships that are forged with women she would never ever have had the opportunity to relate to with such intimacy. Price describes one such encounter here:

> One of the care workers, for example, a Sri Lankan woman, once asked whilst she was showering me, 'Why don't you cut your pubic hair?' Although we were undoubtedly intimately connected intercorporeally—her hands on my naked body—her words had a profound affect, making me feel anxious and disturbed. What for me brought up questions of whether I would ever be able to be sexually active again, probably seemed to her—coming from a different cultural context—a straightforward query about the maintenance of bodily hygiene and propriety. For both of us the moment caught the strangeness of coming together, the instant at which self-familiarity is unsettled and opened up new modes of becoming otherwise. (as quoted in Shildrick, 2009, pp. 161–162)

I quoted this narrative at length because I thought it captured very well the dilemma of difference that often rudely emerges in the intimate context of care. Here, the nondisabled care worker, a stranger, but for the intimacy of the caring work she did, felt enabled to ask a very personal question that caused the recipient of her care much existential anxiety. At the same time, Price is aware that the intrusive question is actually merely a pragmatic one: how can this caring work be done most efficiently? In fact, Price reflects that by raising this question, both care worker and care recipient, are forced, in that unsettling moment, to learn something new about each other—their intercorporeal interaction forging a bond that transforms them—making them become somebody different as a result of this encounter. It is such becomings that, Shildrick argues, can transform this intercorporeal (caring) caring relationship from lack into amazing possibility.

In the above example, Shildrick is referring to what Michael Hardt (1999) has called "affective labor," or what feminist scholars have called caring work, which I have described in much detail in the earlier sections of this chapter. However, while my representation of caring work foregrounded the possibilities of exploitation that are inherent in this work because of the racial and gendered divisions of labor as well as its representation as nonproductive labor within capitalism, Hardt, however, argues that this formulation of caring work or reproductive labor as existing outside the purview of capitalist accumulation is outdated and does not account for the many transformations that capitalism has undergone over the past several decades. This is because the manufacturing industry is now being replaced by the service industry that includes health, education, finance, transportation, entertainment, and advertising; all of which involve immaterial labor—"labor that produces an immaterial good such as service, knowledge, and communication" (Hardt, 1999, p. 94). Immaterial labor includes on the one hand symbolic analytical service tasks (e.g., computer programming, data management) and on the other hand, affective labor that thrives on human contact and interaction. Immersed in the corporeal, this labor is immaterial because what it produces are social networks and forms of community, or, in other words, biopolitical production.

One example of affective labor is most definitely caring work. And it could be argued that Hardt's conceptualization of affective labor may augur well for persons with severe and cognitive disabilities, because it enables a form of reciprocity that is emotional rather than economic. In contexts where persons with severe/cognitive disabilities are conceived of as unworthy of all the rights of citizenship on account of their dependence on caregivers, the recognition of affective labor brings forth a concomitant recognition of affective citizenship (Johnson, 2010), where intimate relationships between people are recognized and celebrated in social contexts. Thus, for example, Wolff (2010) argues that in order to realize social citizenship for persons with severe/cognitive disabilities, it is essential to enable them to renegotiate their place in the world. Here, Wolff's reference to place does not necessarily refer to the spatial. Rather, what Wolff is referring to is the goal of generating the largest number of social relationships with other bodies, disabled and nondisabled. This is because, such an ethic of care, according to Wolff, would, thereby, enhance the conditions for persons with severe/cognitive disabilities to actively claim affective citizenship.

What affective citizenship essentially achieves is that it offers an alternative to liberal citizenship that I had discussed in Chapter 5, by celebrating interdependence rather than independence. Remember Ahmed's argument, earlier in this chapter, which argued that affect does not lie within a body but between bodies. Basically, affective citizenship enables encounters between a diverse range of bodies, who, as a result of globalization, are brought in contact with each other in reciprocal relationships of interdependence. Thus, for example, the encounter between Price and her Sri Lankan care worker exemplifies their interdependence around issues of personal care and economic survival. Extrapolating from this example, Shildrick (2009) writes:

> The intercorporeal care and assistance that many disabled people experience in daily life has significance far beyond the confines of personal comfort. Those encounters stage a process of becoming that speaks to a rhizomatic proliferation of connections, situated in nodular global networks coalescing in temporary points of assemblage. Regardless of how any one of us may be socially located,

such interactions—direct and indirect—profoundly reshape our subject being, and ultimately the dimensions of the worlds we inhabit. (p. 163)

For Shildrick, then, the analysis of exploitation though present must be abandoned in order to pursue the exciting possibilities of the encounter itself. In making this argument, Shildrick echoes Deleuze and Guattari in their rejection of the "modernist discourse of political struggle" for the "move to promote dis-organ-ization in all its aspects and to offer a virtual model of 'desiring production'" (p. 164). Here, production is disassociated from the concrete activities of labor (the materiality of caring work) and reattached to affective relationships that emerge as a result of the activities of consumption (receiving care). And it is this collapsing of the practices of production and consumption in the dialectics of care that has profound implications for not only articulating an ethics of care, but also for articulating a transformative theory of disabled subjectivity.

RECOGNIZING THE OTHER SIDE OF THE DIALECTIC

I have much admiration for Margrit Shidrick's work in feminist disability studies, but I was very disappointed in her specific argument regarding the ethics of care in transnational contexts. Notwithstanding the radical possibilities inherent in theorizing caring work as affective labor, I argue that affective labor does not critically engage the dialectic of care. In fact, it actually dissolves it. Here, the assumption is that the very possibility of intercorporeal relationships, while not necessarily dissolving social inequalities, opens up contexts that enable the collective thinking of other/more transgressive possibilities. Essentially then, Shildrick joins with Hardt and Negri to envision an ethics of encounter that transcends the problematic inequalities that might arise as a result of these intercorporeal encounters between caregiver and care recipient. In fact, that very dialectic is dissolved, and in its place are anomalous intercorporeal bodies that become a crucial site of positive resistance. According to Hardt and Negri, such intimacies of affective labor may therefore produce

> a body that is completely incapable of submitting to command...a body that is incapable of adapting to family life, to family discipline, to the regulations of a traditional sex life, and so forth. (If you find your body refusing these "normal" modes of life, don't despair–realize your gift!). (as quoted in Shildrick, 2009, p. 167)

My problem with Hardt and Negri's analysis is that once again this argument is idealist rather than materialist. It suggests that we can imagine our way toward an emancipatory existence. But we know that this is not true, and Shildrick herself admits that there is indeed a depth of material oppression associated with global capital. Moreover, as my argument in Chapter 4 demonstrated, it is neither easy to dissolve the dialectic nor is it ethical to do so. Hardt and Negri (2000), however, justify their argument by pointing out thus:

> Today the social institutions that constitute disciplinary society (the school, the family, the hospital, the factory) which are in large part the same as or closely related to those understood as civil society, are everywhere in crisis. As the walls of these institutions break down; the logics of subjectification that previously operated within their limited spaces now spread generalized across the social field. (Hardt and Negri, 2000, p. 329)

Here, Hardt and Negri celebrate the power of capitalist markets to break down the boundaries of social institutions such as the nuclear family, and to open up the social field for more transgressive couplings (Torrant, 2002). But as Julie Torrant rightly points out this argument fails to conceive of the bourgeois family as a political and economic institution that is constituted within the dialectic relationships of wage-labor and capital. Here, Torrant is arguing that the family is not just an ideology but an economic unit that still continues to be a site of unpaid/underpaid reproductive labor that is either way appropriated as profit by capitalist markets. Much of the earlier discussions in this chapter (as well as in the discussion in Chapter 4) supports Torrant's claim. Additionally, Torrant perceptively points out that affective needs can be realized if and only if basic needs are met. In the current economic context and as per the statistics I shared earlier in this chapter, we know that families continue to struggle to meet their basic needs. It is in the context of these struggles to meet basic needs that caring work for disabled people becomes an undue burden within the familial context.

Additionally, the definition of immaterial labor that Hardt and Negri (2000) deploy claims that

> cooperation is completely inherent in the labor itself. Immaterial labor immediately involves social interaction and cooperation. In other words, the cooperative aspect of immaterial labor is not imposed or organized from the outside as it was in previous forms of labor, but rather *cooperation is completely immanent to the laboring activity itself.* (p. 294)

However, once again, the continued existence of the racial and gendered division of labor that I have referred to earlier in this chapter, disputes this claim. Robert McRuer (2006), refers to Grace Chang's work on "disposable domestics"—women populating both the formal and informal economy in search of work, displaced from their homelands as a result of colonial and neocolonial legacies, and offered the only jobs that continue to be both gendered and raced, and, as a result, continue to remain low-waged jobs. That they live their lives in immense jeopardy as undocumented migrant workers, as a result of their nonrecognition as citizens, and as potentially disabled people, as a result of real physical injuries that occur on the job, is no cause for celebration. In fact, in many ways their experiences reflect the experiences of the slave women I began this book with, whose becomings have always been mediated via the social constructs of race, gender, sexuality, and disability. Thus, as Silvia Fedirici (2006) has argued, introducing "affective labor" into this discussion transforms the necessary reproductive labor that women have historically done for centuries into a "labor of love" that exists outsides capitalist relations. Here, Federici repeats the materialist feminist argument that "capitalism is built on an immense amount of unpaid labor, that is not built exclusively or primarily on contractual relations: that the wage relation hides the unpaid slave-like nature of so much of this work upon which capitalist accumulation is premised" (p. 7).

But I want to take Federici's argument even further. Neither Federici nor Torrant nor most feminists have taken disability into account in their analyses. In fact, when feminists have engaged disability, as is evident in this chapter, disabled people are located mostly within the context of consumption, and seldom if ever located within the context of production. However, throughout this book, I have demonstrated that disability is a materialist construct because becoming disabled is an historical event. Moreover, in Chapter 1 I have argued that the use value of disability lies in its deployment as a commodity fetish in transnational capitalism. In other words, I am arguing here that disability plays a critical part even within the relations of production. Whether it is the context of slavery, the sex curriculum, segregated institutions, the justification of war, or the politics of care, the disabled body is deployed as a commodity fetish to enable capitalist accumulation of profit and justify the social organization of difference in oppressive ways in transnational contexts.

In arguing that disability is a commodity fetish, I can foresee the critique that I have once again theorized disability as lack. In response, I argue that it is not disability that is inherently lacking, it is the material conditions of transnational capitalism that produce disability as lack. In other words, instead of dissolving the dialectic, I have argued that most posthumanist analyses have focused only on one side of the dialectic—that of the bourgeois Self (even when the Self is marked by race, gender, and disability). On the other hand, I argue that an examination of the other side of the dialectic foregrounds in searing reality the actual violence of economic exploitation that produces difference that refuses to disappear notwithstanding the most transgressive discursive imaginaries that are summoned up by posthumanist theories.

And so, what are the implications of the argument I have just put forth? Throughout this book, in almost every chapter, I have argued that any analysis of disability has to be relational. More urgently, I argue that any analysis of disability will also have to be dialectical. I therefore want to end by raising an interesting question Federici raises in her essay: How do we struggle...without destroying the people you care for?" (p. 7). This question echoes Titchkosky's question about not seeing disability as the limit, and McRuer's question about imagining that another world is possible. My answer is quite simple. We need to always foreground the material conditions of transnational capitalism that enable the specific relations of production and consumption that construct social difference in order to transform the body politic. In other words, Hardt and Negri's (2004) notion of the "multitude" can only be possible within nonexploitative relations of production and consumption in transnational capital.

We know through anthropologist Nancy Schepper-Hughes (2001) work that one aspect of the underside of care includes the trafficking of body parts from across oceans lapping against barren lands to enable a desperate but privileged patient in affluent contexts get a new lease on life. We know through medical anthropologist and physician Paul Farmer's (1999) work that, "local and global inequalities mean that the fruits of medical and scientific advances are stockpiled for some and denied to others" (p. 1488). We know that on a daily basis we produce disability as a result of war, environmental hazards, social conservatism, economic exploitation, segregated/ghetto schooling, and simply just hate. We know this. So, then, how do we forge a collective struggle without destroying the people we really care for? It is possible. But we need to collective will to do so.

Notes

Chapter 3

1. A shorter version of this article was originally published in the *Journal of Literary and Disability Studies* 4, no. 2 (2010). The original article can be accessed at http://liverpool.metapress.com/content/121628/.

Chapter 4

1. Lennard Davis (2002) in his book *Bending over Backwards*, uses the term "dismodern" to distinguish it from the term "postmodern." Davis argues that postmodernism is still based on humanist notions of the subject. According to Davis, the dismodern subject is a far more radical theorization of the subject that is "partial and incomplete...whose realization is not autonomy and independence but dependency and interdependence" (p. 30). Davis's argument is a good example of a disability studies perspective that privileges the metaphorical without really examining the material conditions within which such metaphors gain prominence—an argument I will be making in this chapter.

2. Here I am referring only to the emergency care that soldiers receive at the military bases and at hospitals such as Walter Reed in Bethesda, Maryland. Follow-up medical care and access to medical benefits that occurs in VA hospitals in the months following emergency care are reported by several news media sources to be far from satisfactory.

3. Judith Halberstam and Ira Livingston (1995) define posthuman bodies as "the causes and effects of postmodern relations of power and pleasure, virtuality and reality, sex and its consequences. The posthuman body is a technology, a screen, a projected image; it is a body under the sign of AIDS, a contaminated body, a techno-body...a queer body." (p. 3)

4. Structural Adjustment Programs (SAPs) are economic restructuring programs ordered by the World Bank and the International Monetary Fund, and they are implemented in those countries that could not meet their debt obligations. This stabilization was also seen as a critical precondition for third world nations to qualify for loans needed in the future. SAPs requirements of deflation, devaluation, decontrol, and privatization (Elson, D. (1992).

From survival strategies to transformation strategies: Women's needs and structural adjustment. In L. Beneria, and S. Feldman (eds.) *Unequal burden: economic crises, persistent poverty, and women's work*. Oxford: Westview Press) resulted in the following economic reforms in third world nation-states: trade liberalization, which required a more focused export policy on "cash crops" and other raw materials, and import substitution for all other goods that were not manufactured in the nation-state's economy; increased dependence on international financial resources; and reductions in public spending, which included reduction in public sector employment, limitations on food and agricultural subsidies, denationalization of public sector enterprises, and reduction in public expenditures in the areas of health, education, and social welfare (Feldman, (1992). Crisis, Islam and gender in Bangladesh: The social construction of a female labor force, in L. Benera, and S. Feldman (Eds.), *Unequal burden: Economic crises, persistent poverty, and women's work* (Boulder, CO, Westview Press, 1992). In addition to these austerity measures, borrowing countries were encouraged to promote private investment, to support trade and tariff reforms that benefited the donor nations, and to construct export-processing zones (EPZs) for multinational companies to produce goods tax-free using cheap labor from the host country—mostly third world women.

CHAPTER 5

1. I use the terminology "disabled people" rather than people with disabilities to foreground disability as a political category. However, at other times, I have used the terminology "people with cognitive severe/cognitive disabilities" to illustrate the social constructionist nature of these categories. Also, in the text of the essay, I included a discussion on the critical relationship between impairment and disability—and therefore refrain from pursuing the discussion in this footnote.

2. According to Minow (1990) the "dilemma of difference" raises the following question: "[W]hen does treating people differently emphasize their differences and stigmatize and hinder them on that basis and when does treating them the same become insensitive to their difference and likely to stigmatize or hinder them on that (emphasis in text) basis?" (p. 20).

3. This number does not include the nearly 2 million disabled people, many of them with the most severe disabilities, who live in institutions.

4. Martha Minow's work is one notable exception.

5. On pages 123–124 of her book, *Making all the difference*, Minow locates the origin of liberal politics in the historical conceptual shift from notions of fixed and assigned status to notions of individual freedoms and rights. More importantly, Minow asserts that "[r]eciprocal—and non-hierarchical—obligations, freely chosen by self-defining beings, became the central pattern underlying economic transactions and political action... [and were predicated on] the new economic order [that] rested on private property and

the market." This clearly foregrounds the commitment of liberal politics to capitalism.

6. In a chapter entitled "Different histories" (pp. 121–145), Minow argues that though scholars have depicted Western intellectual and legal histories as making the radical shift from notions of fixed and assigned status to notions of individual freedom and rights, this shift has in fact been incomplete. This is because, Minow points out that, when legal theory supports what she calls the "abnormal-persons approach" (an approach that support restraints on the autonomy and rights of those populations considered "incompetent" and therefore "abnormal," e.g., persons with cognitive/severe disabilities), then legal theory has acted on the basis of social status rather than on notions of individual rights. Thus, Minow writes, "Cast in this light, doctrines about incompetence reveal areas that a liberal legal order does not reach, area where an older notion of law continues to operate" (my emphasis) (p. 126). How much more feudal can we get!

7. Here one can see how poststructuralist theory is also committed to some of the precepts of humanism even while critiquing that position.

8. *Paris Is Burning* is a documentary on drag queens directed by Jenny Livingstone.

BIBLIOGRAPHY

Abbasi, K. (1999). The world bank and world health: Under fire. *British Medical Journal*. Retrieved from http://www.bmj.com/cgi/content/full/318/7189/1003.

Abramovitz, M. (1996). *Regulating our lives: Social welfare policy from the colonial times to the present*. Boston, MA: South End Press.

Adams, R. (2001). *Sideshow USA: Freaks and the American cultural imagination*. Chicago, IL: University of Chicago Press.

Addlakha, R. (2007). How young people with disabilities conceptualize the body, sex, and marriage in urban India: Four case studies. *Sex and Disability, 25*: 111–123.

Agamben, G. (1998). *Homo sacer. Sovereign power and bare life*. Stanford, CA: Stanford University Press.

Ahmed, S. (1998). Animated borders: Skin, color, and tanning. In M. Shildrick & J. Price (Eds.), *Vital signs: Feminist reconfigurations of the bio/logical body* (pp. 45–65). Edinburgh: Edinburgh University Press.

Ahmed, S. (2004). Affective economies. *Social Text, 22*(2), 117–139.

Al-Ali, N. (2005). Reconstructing gender: Iraqi women between dictatorship, war, sanctions, and occupation. *Third World Quarterly, 26*(4–5), 739–748.

Alexander, M. J., & Mohanty, C. T. (1997). Introduction: Geneaologies, legacies, movements. In M. J. A. Alexander & C. T. Mohanty (Eds.), *Feminist geneaologies, colonial legacies, democratic futures* (pp. xiii–xlii). New York: Routledge.

Allen, L. (2008). "They think you shouldn't be having sex anyway": Young people's suggestions for improving sexuality education content. *Sexualities, 11*(5), 573–594.

Anderson, B. (1983). *Imagined communities: Reflections on the origin and spread of nationalism*. London: Verso.

Anyon, J. (1997). *Ghetto schooling: A political economy of urban educational reform*. New York: Teachers College Press.

Anzaldua, G. (1990). *Making face, making soul/Haciendo Caras: Creative and critical perspectives by women of color*. San Francisco, CA: Aunt Lute Books.

Arondekar, A. (2005). Border/Line sex: Queer positionalities, or how race matters outside the United States. *Interventions, 7*(2), 236–250.

Artiles, A. J. (1998). The dilemma of difference: Enriching the disproportionality discourse with theory and content. *Journal of Special Education, 32*(1), 32–37.

Artiles, A. J., Harry, B., Reschly, D. J., & Chinn, P. C. (2002). Over-identification of students of color in special education: A critical overview. *Multicultural Perspectives, 4*(1), 3–10.

Ashcraft, C. (2006). "Girl, you better go get you a condom": Popular culture and teen sexuality as resources for critical multicultural curriculum. *Teachers College Record, 108*(10), 2145–2186.

Aunos, M., & Feldman, M. A. (2002). Attitudes towards sexuality, sterilization, and parenting rights of persons with intellectual disabilities. *Journal of Applied Research in Intellectual Disabilities, 15*: 285–296.

Baldock, J., & Ungerson, C. (1990). "What d'ya want if you do want money?": A feminist critique of "paid volunteering." In M. Maclean & D. Groves (Eds.), *Women's issues in social policy* (pp. 136–157). New York: Routledge.

Baldwin, S., & Twigg, J. (1990). Women and community care: Reflections on a debate. In M. Maclean & D. Groves (Eds.), *Women's issues in social policy* (pp. 117–135). New York: Routledge.

Barker, C., & Murray, S. (2010). Disabling postcolonialism: Global disability cultures and democratic criticism. *Journal of Literary and Cultural Disability Studies, 4*(3), 219–236.

Barnes, C., Mercer, G., & Shakespeare, T. (1999). *Exploring disability: A sociological introduction.* Malden, MA: Polity Press.

Baynton, D. (2001). Disability and the justification of inequality in American history. In P. K. Longmore & L. Umansky (Eds.), *The new disability history: American perspectives* (pp. 33–57). New York: New York University Press.

Baynton, D. (2005). Slaves, immigrants, and suffragists: The uses of disability in citizenship debates. *Publication of the Modern Language Association (PMLA), 120*(2), 562–566.

Becker, H. (1964). *The other side: Perspectives on deviance.* New York: Free Press.

Begum, N. (1992). Disabled women and the feminist agenda. *Feminist Review, 40*: 70–84.

Biklen, D. (1993). *Communication unbound: How facilitated communication is changing views of autism and ability-disability.* New York: Teachers College Press.

Biklen, D., & Bailey, L. (1981). *Rudely stamp'd: Imaginal disability and prejudice.* Washington, DC: University Press of America.

Biklen, D., & Cardinal, D. (1997). *Contested words, contested sciences: Revisiting the facilitated communication controversy.* New York: Teachers College Press.

Block, P. (2000). Sexuality, fertility, and danger: Twentieth century images of women with cognitive disabilities. *Sexuality and Disability, 18*(4), 239–254.

Blumer, H. (1969). *Symbolic interactionism; perspective and method.* Englewood Cliffs, NJ: Prentice-Hall.

Bogdan, R. (1988). *Freak show: Presenting human oddities for amusement and profit.* Chicago, IL: University of Chicago Press.

Bogdan, R., & Taylor, S. (1982). *Inside out: The social meaning of mental retardation.* Toronto; Buffalo: University of Toronto Press.

Bogdan, R., & Taylor, S. (1987). Toward a sociology of acceptance: The other side of the study of deviance. *Social Policy, 18*(2), 34–39.

Bogdan, R., & Taylor, S. (1992). The social construction of humanness: Relationships with severely disabled people. In P. Ferguson, D. Ferguson & S. Taylor (Eds.), *Interpreting disability: A qualitative reader* (pp. 275–294). New York: Teachers College Press.

Bordo, S. (2003). *Unbearable weight: Feminism, Western culture and the body.* (10th anniversary ed.). Berkeley: University of California Press.

Bourdieu, P. (1977). *Outline of a theory of practice.* New York: Cambridge University Press.

Bourke, J. (1996). *Dismembering the male: Men's bodies, Britain, and the Great War.* Chicago, IL: University of Chicago Press.

Boyd, T. D. (2009). Confronting racial disparity: Legislative responses to the school-to-prison pipeline. *Harvard Civil Rights-Civil Liberties Law Review, 44*(2), 571–580.

Braidotti, R. (1989). Organs without bodies. *Differences: A Journal of Feminist Cultural Studies, 1*(1), 147–161.

Brantlinger, E. (2001). Poverty, class, and disability: A historical, social, and political perspective. *Focus on Exceptional Children, 33*(7), 1–19.

Bredstrom, A. (2006). Intersectionality: A challenge for feminist HIV/AIDS research? *European Journal of Women's Studies, 13*(3), 229–243.

Brinkley, D. (2006). *The great deluge: Hurricane Katrina, New Orleans, and the Mississippi Gulf Coast* (1st ed.). New York: Morrow.

Brown, T. M. (2007). Lost and turned out: Academic, social, and emotional experiences of students excluded from school. *Urban Education, 42*(5), 422–435.

Brueggemann, Brenda. (1999). *Lend me your ear: Rhetorical constructions of deafness.* Washington, DC: Gallaudet University Press.

Bubeck, Diemut E. (1995). *Care, gender, and justice.* New York: Oxford University Press.

Burch, S., & Joyner, H. (2007). *Unspeakable: The life of Junius Wilson.* Chapel Hill: University of North Carolina Press.

Butler, J. (1993). *Bodies that matter: On the discursive limits of "sex."* New York: Routledge.

Callinicos, A. (1993). *Race and class.* Chicago, IL: Bookmarks.

Campbell, F. K. (2009). *Contours of ableism: The production of disability and abledness.* New York: Palgrave Macmillan.

Caplan, P. (1985a). *Class and gender in India: Women and their organizations in a South Indian city.* New York: Tavistock Publications.

Caplan, P. (1985b). Women's voluntary social welfare work in India: The cultural construction of gender and class. *Bulletin of Concerned South Asian Scholars, 17*(1), 20–31.

Centers for Disease Control (2008). Health, United States, 2008 with special feature on the health of young adults. Retrieved from http://www.cdc.gov/nchs/data/hus/hus08.pdf.

Chamberlin, J. E., & Gilman, S. L. (1985). *Degeneration: The dark side of progress.* New York: Columbia University Press.

Chang, G. (2000). *Disposable domestics: Immigrant women workers in the global economy.* Cambridge, MA: South End Press.

Chappell, A. L. (1998). Still out in the cold: Persons with learning disabilities and the social model of disability. In T. Shakespeare (Ed.), *The Disability Reader: Social Science Perspectives* (pp. 211–220). New York: Cassell.

Charlton, J. I. (1998). *Nothing about us without us: Disability oppression and empowerment.* Berkeley: University of California Press.

Clement, Grace. (1996). *Care, autonomy, and justice: Feminism and the ethic of care.* Boulder, CO: Westview Press.

Cohn, J. (2007). *Sick: The untold story of America's health crisis—and the people who pay the price.* New York: Harper Perennial.

Connor, D. J. (2007). *Urban narratives: Portraits in progress—Life at the intersections of learning disability, race, and class.* New York: Peter Lang.

Connor, D. J., & Ferri, B. A. (2005). Integration and inclusion—A troubling nexus: Race, disability, and special education. *Journal of African American History* *90*(1/2), 107–127.

Corker, M., & French, S. (1999). *Disability discourse.* Philadelphia, PA: Open University Press.

Corker, M., & Shakespeare, T. (2002). *Disability/Postmodernity: Embodying disability theory.* London: Continuum Publishing House.

Crenshaw, K. (1996). Mapping the margins: Intersectionality, identity politics, and violence against women. In N. G. K. Crenshaw, G. Pellar, & K. Thomas (Eds.), *Critical race theory: The key writings that formed the movement* (pp. 357–383). New York: New Press.

Crenshaw, K., Gotanda, N., Peller, G., & Thomas, K. (1995). *Critical race theory: The key writings that formed the movement.* New York: New Press.

Dallas Morning News. (2006). *Eyes of the storm: Hurricane Katrina and Rita: The photographic essay.* Dallas: Taylor Trade Publishing.

Dalley, Gillian. (1988). *Ideologies of caring.* London: Macmillan Education

Davion, Victoria. (1993). Autonomy, integrity, and care. *Social Theory and Practice,* *19*(2), 161–183.

Davis, A. (1998). Masked racism: Reflections on the prison industrial complex. *ColorLines, Fall,* 1–5.

Davis, A. Y. (1983). *Women, race, and class.* New York: Vintage.

Davis, L. J. (1995). *Enforcing normalcy: Disability, deafness, and the body.* New York: Verso.

Davis, L. J. (2002). *Bending over backwards: Disability, dismodernism, and other difficult positions.* New York: New York University Press.

Deleuze, G., & Guattari, F. (1983). *Anti-Oedipus: Capitalism and schizophrenia.* Minneapolis: University of Minnesota Press.

Deleuze, G., & Guattari, F. (1987). *A thousand plateaus: Capitalism and schizophrenia.* Minneapolis: University of Minnesota Press.

Delgado, R., & Stefancic, J. (2000). *Critical race theory: The cutting edge.* (2nd ed.). Philadelphia, PA: Temple University Press.

Devault, M. (1991). *Feeding the family: The social organization of caring as gendered work.* Chicago, IL: University of Chicago Press.

Dhaliwal, A. (1996). Can the subaltern vote? Radical democracy, discourses of representation and rights, and questions of race. In D. Trend (Ed.), *Radical democracy: Identity, citizenship, and the state* (pp. 442–461). New York: Routledge.

Doyal, L. (1981). *The political economy of health.* Boston, MA: South End Press.

Dukes, E., & McGuire, B. E. (2009). Enhancing capacity to make sexuality-related decisions in people with an intellectual disability. *Journal of Intellectual Disability Research, 53:* 727–734.

Dunbar, C. (2001). *Alternative schooling for African American Youth: Does anyone know we are here?* New York: Peter Lang.

Dyson, M. E. (2006). *Come hell or high water: Hurricane Katrina and the color of disaster.* New York: Basic Civitas.

Eagleton, T. (1983). *Literary theory: An introduction.* Minneapolis: University of Minnesota Press.

Ebert, T. (1996). *Ludic feminism and after: Postmodernism, desire, and labor in late capitalism.* Ann Arbor: University of Michigan Press.

Edgerton, R. (1967). *The cloak of competence: Stigma in the lives of the mentally retarded.* Berkeley: University of California Press.

Ehrenreich, B. (1987). The new right attack on social welfare. In F. Block, R. Ploward, B. Ehrenreich & F. Piven (Eds.), *The mean season: The attack on the welfare state.* New York: Pantheon Books.

Elson, D. (1992). From survival strategies to transformation strategies: Women's needs and structural adjustment. In L. Beneria, and S. Feldman (Eds.), *Unequal burden: Economic crises, persistent poverty, and women's work.* Oxford: Westview Press.

Erevelles, N. (1996). Disability and the dialectics of difference. *Disability and Society, 11*(4), 519–537.

Erevelles, N. (2000). Educating unruly bodies: Critical pedagogy, disability studies, and the politics of schooling. *Educational Theory, 50*(1), 25–57.

Erevelles, N. (2001). In search of the disabled subject. In J. C. Wilson & C. Lewiecki-Wilson (Eds.), *Embodied rhetorics: Disability in language and culture* (pp. 92–111). Carbondale: Southern Illinois University Press.

Erevelles, N. (2002a). (Im)Material citizens: Cognitive disability, race and the politics of citizenship. *Disability, Culture, and Education, 1*(1), 5–25.

Erevelles, N. (2002b). Voices of Silence: Foucault, Disability, and the Question of Self-determination. *Studies in Philosophy and Education, 21*(1), 17–19.

Erevelles, N. (2006). Disability and the new world order. In Incite! Women of Color Against Violence (Ed.), *Color of violence: The Incite! Anthology.* Cambridge, MA: South End Press.

Erevelles, N., & Mutua, K. (2005). "I am a woman now!": Rewriting the cartographies of girlhood from the standpoint of disability studies. In P. Bettis & N. Adams (Eds.), *Geographies of girlhood: Identity in-between* (pp. 253–270). New York: Lawrence Erlbaum.

Erickson, K. T. (1964). Notes on the sociology of deviance. In H. S. Becker (Ed.), *Perspectives on deviance: The other side* (pp. 9–22). New York: Free Press.

Espinoza, L., & Harris, A. P. (1997). Afterword: Embracing the tar-baby—LatCrit theory and the stick mess of race. *California Law Review, 88*(5), 499–559.

Evans, K. (1998). *Shaping futures: Learning for competence and citizenship.* Aldershot, Hampshire: Ashgate.

Ewart, C. (2010). Terms of disappropriation: Disability, diaspora and Dionne Brand's "What we all long for." *Journal of Literary and Cultural Disability Studies, 4*(2), 147–161.

Fanon, F. (1965). *The wretched of the earth.* New York: Grove Press.

Farber, B. (1968). *Mental retardation: Its social context and social consequences.* Boston, MA: Houghton and Mifflin.

Farmer, P. (1999). Pathologies of power: Rethinking health and human rights. *American Journal of Public Health, 89*(10), 1486–1496.

Farmer, P. (2004). *Pathologies of power: Health, human rights and the new war on the poor.* Berkeley: University of California Press.

Farmer, P. E., Nizeye, B., Stulac, S., & Keshavjee, S. (2006). Structural violence and clinical medicine. *PLoS Medicine* (October), 1686–1691.

Farrelly, C., O'Brien, M., & Prain, V. (2007). The discourses of sexuality in curriculum documents on sexuality: An Australian case study. *Sex Education, 7*(1), 63–80.

Fausto-Sterling, A. (2000). *Sexing the body: Gender politics and the construction of sexuality.* New York: Basic Books.

Featherstone, M. (1992). The body in consumer culture. In M. Featherstone, M. Hepworth, & B. S. Turner (Eds.), *The body: Social processes and cultural theory.* London: Sage Publications.

Federici, S. (2008). *Precarious labor: A feminist viewpoint.* Paper presented at the In the Middle of a Whirlwind.

Ferguson, P. (1987). The social construction of mental retardation. *Social Policy, 18*(1), 51–56.

Ferri, B. & Connor, D. (2006). *Reading resistance: Discourses of exclusion in desegregation and exclusion debates.* New York: Peter Lang.

Fine, M. (1988). Sexuality, schooling and adolescent females: The missing discourse of desire. *Harvard Educational Review, 58*(1), 29–53.

Fine, M., & Asch, A. (1988). *Women with disabilities: Essays in psychology, culture, and politics.* Philadelphia, PA: Temple University Press.

Fine, M., & McClelland, S. I. (2006). Sexuality education and desire: Still missing after all these years. *Harvard Educational Review, 76*(3), 297–338.

Finger, A. (2005). Anne Finger reflects on Hurricane Katrina. Rolling Rains Report. Retrieved from http://www.rollingrains.com/archives/000644.html

Finkelstein, V. (1980). *Attitudes and disabled people: Issues for discussion.* New York: World Rehabilitation Fund.

Finkelstein, V. (1993). The commonality of disability. In J. Swain (Ed.), *Disabling barriers: Enabling environments.* London: Sage Publications.

Fiser, K. (1994). *Defending diversity: Contemporary philosophical perspectives on pluralism and multiculturalism.* Amherst: University of Massachusetts Press.

Fisher, C. M. (2009). Queer youth experiences with abstinence-only-until-marriage sexuality education: "I can't get married so where does that leave me?" *Journal of LGBT Youth, 6*: 61–79.

Folbre, N. (1994). *Who pays for the kids? Gender and the structures of constraint.* New York: Routledge.

Foucault, M. (1965). *Madness and civilization: A history of insanity in the age of reason.* New York: Pantheon Books.

Foucault, M. (1977). *Discipline and punish: The birth of the prison.* New York: Random House.

Foucault, M. (1980). *The history of sexuality: An introduction.* New York: Vintage.

Foucault, M., & Gordon, C. (1980). *Power/knowledge: Selected interviews and other writings, 1972–1977.* Brighton, Sussex: Harvester Press.

Fox, N. J. (1994). *Postmodernism, sociology, and health.* Toronto: University of Toronto Press.

Francis, L., & Silvers, A. (2000). *Americans with disabilities: Exploring implications of the law for individuals and institutions.* New York: Routledge.

Fraser, N. (1993). Women, welfare and the politics of need interpretation. In L. Richardson & V. Taylor (Eds.), *Feminist frontiers, III* (pp. 447–458). New York: McGraw-Hill.

Fraser, N. (1997). *Justice interrupts: Critical reflections on the "postsocialist" condition.* New York: Routledge.

Fraser, N., & Gordon, L. (1997). A genealogy of "dependency": Tracing a keyword of the US welfare state. In N. Fraser (Ed.), *Justice interruptus: Critical reflections on the "postsocialist" condition* (pp. 121–150). New York: Routledge.

Freeman, A. D. (1995). Legitimizing racial discrimination law: A critical review of Supreme Court Doctrine In K. Crenshaw, N. Gotanda, G. Peller & K. Thomas (Eds.), Critical Race Theory: The Key Writing that Formed the Movement (pp. 29–46). New York: The New Press.

Garland-Thomson, R. (1996). *Freakery: Cultural spectacles of the extraordinary body.* New York: Columbia University Press.

Garland-Thomson, R. (1997). *Extraordinary bodies: Figuring physical disability in American culture and literature.* New York: Columbia University Press.

Garland-Thomson, R. (2002a). Integrating disability, transforming feminist theory. *National Women's Studies Association Journal, 14*(3), 1–32.

Garland-Thomson, R. (2002b). The politics of staring: Visual rhetorics of disability in popular photography. In S. L. Snyder, B. J. Brueggemann, & R. Garland-Thomson (Eds.), *Disability studies: Enabling the humanities* (pp. 56–75). New York: Modern Language Association of America.

Garland-Thomson, R. (2005). Feminist disability studies. *Signs, 30*(2), 1557–1587.

Gates, H. L. (1988). *The signifying monkey: A theory of Afro-American literary criticism.* New York: Oxford University Press.

Ghai, A. (2003). *(Dis)embodied form: Issues of disabled women.* New Delhi: Shakti Books.

Ghobarah, H. A., Huth, P., & Russett, B. (2004). The post-war public health effects of civil conflict. *Social Science and Medicine, 59*(4), 869–884.

Gibson, B. (2006). Disability, connectivity and transgressing the autonomous body. *Journal of Medical Humanities, 27*(3), 187–196.

Gilligan, C. (1982). *In a different voice.* Cambridge, MA: Harvard University Press.

Gilman, S. (1986). Black bodies, white bodies: Toward an iconography of female sexuality in late nineteenth-century art, medicine, and literature. In H. L. Gates (Ed.), *"Race," writing, and difference* (pp. 223–261). Chicago, IL: University of Chicago Press.

Ginsburg, N. (1979). *Class, capital, and social policy.* London: Macmillan.

Giroux, H. A. (1988). *Schooling and the struggle for public life: Critical pedagogy in the modern age.* Minneapolis: University of Minnesota Press.

Giroux, H. A. (2006). Reading Hurricane Katrina: Race, class, and the biopolitics of disposability. *College Literature, 33*(3), 171.

Glasser, R. J. (2005, July). A war of disabilities. *Harper's Magazine,* 59–62.

Glazer, N. (1984). Servants to capital: Unpaid domestic labor and paid work. *Review of Radical Political Economy, 16*(1), 61–87.

Gleeson, B. J. (1997). Disability studies: A historical materialist view. *Disability and Society, 12*(2), 179–202.

Gleeson, B. J. (1998). *Geographies of disability*. New York: Routledge.

Glendinning, C., & Millar, J. (1990). Poverty: The forgotten Englishwoman. In M. Maclean & D. Groves (Eds.), *Women's issues in social policy* (pp. 20–37). New York: Routledge.

Glenn, E. N. (1992). From servitude to service work: Historical continuities in the racial division of paid reproductive labor. *Signs, 18*(1), 1–43.

Goffman, E. (1963). *Stigma: Notes on the management of spoiled identity*. Englewood Cliffs, NJ: Prentice Hall.

Goodley, D. (2001). "Learning difficulties," the social model of disability and impairment: Challenging epistemologies. *Disability and Society, 16*(2), 207–231.

Goodley, D. (2007). Becoming rhizomatic parents: Deleuze, Guattari and disabled babies. *Disability and Society, 22*(2), 145–160.

Goodley, D. (2009). Bringing the psyche back into disability studies: The case of the body with/out organs. *Journal of Literary and Cultural Disability Studies, 3*(3), 257–272.

Goodley, D., & Roets, G. (2008). The (be)comings and goings of "developmental disabilities": the cultural politics of "impairment." *Discourse: Studies in the Cultural Politics of Education, 29*(2), 239–255.

Gordon, A. (1997). *Ghostly matter: Haunting and the sociological imagination*. Minneapolis: University of Minnesota Press.

Gordon, T., Holland, J., & Lahelma, E. (1999). *Making spaces: Citizenship and difference in schools*. New York: St. Martin's Press.

Gough, I. (1979). *The political economy of the welfare state*. New York: MacMillan Press.

Gould, S. J. (1981). *The mismeasure of man*. New York: Norton.

Graham, H. (1991). The concept of caring in feminist research: The case of domestic service. *Sociology, 25*(1), 61–78.

Graham, H. (1993). Social divisions of caring. *Women's Studies International Forum, 16*(5), 461–470.

Graham, Linda J. (2007). (Re)Visioning the centre: Education reform and the "ideal" citizen of the future. *Educational Philosophy & Theory 39*(2), 197–215.

Gray, C. H., & Mentor, S. (1995). The cyborg body politic: Version 1.2. In C. H. Gray (Ed.), *The cyborg handbook* (pp. 453–467). New York: Routledge.

Grealy, L. & Patchett, A. (2003). *Autobiography of a face*. New York: Vintage.

Green, G., & Shane, H. (1994). Science, reason, and facilitated communication. *Journal of the Association for Persons with Severe Handicaps, 19*(3), 151–172.

Groce, N. (1985). *Everyone here spoke sign language: Hereditary deafness on Martha's Vineyard*. Cambridge, MA: Harvard University Press.

Grosz, E. A. (1994). *Volatile bodies: Toward a corporeal feminism*. Bloomington: Indiana University Press.

Gutmann, A. (1987). *Democratic education* (pp. xii, 321 p.). Princeton, NJ: Princeton University Press.

Haddad, L., Readdean, C., & Valadez, J. J. (2004). *Beyond brown: Pursuing the promise* (Motion Picture).

Hahn, H. (1987). Advertising the acceptably employable image: Disability and capitalism. *Policy Studies Journal, 15*(3), 551–570.

Hahn, H. (1988). Can disability be beautiful? *Social Policy, 18*(3), 26–27.

Hammonds, E. M. (1997). Toward a genealogy of black female sexuality: The problematic of silence. In M. J. Alexander & C. T. Mohanty (Eds.), *Feminist genealogies, colonial legacies, democratic futures* (pp. 170–182). New York: Routledge.

Haney Lopez, I. F. (2007). The social construction of race. In R. Delgado (Ed.), *Critical race theory: The cutting edge* (pp. 163–175). Philadelphia, PA: Temple University Press.

Haraway, D. (1989). The biopolitics of postmodern bodies: Determinations of self in immune system discourse. *Differences: A Journal of Feminist Cultural Studies, 1*(1), 45–65.

Haraway, D. (1990). A manifesto for cyborgs: Science, technology, and socialist feminism in the 1980s. In L. Nicholson (Ed.), *Feminism/Postmodernism* (pp. 190–233). New York: Routledge.

Hardt, M. (1999). Affective labor. *Boundary 2, 26*(2), 89–100.

Hardt, M., & Negri, A. (2004). *Multitude: War and democracy in the age of Empire.* New York: Penguin Press.

Harris, A. (1997). Race and essentialism in feminist legal theory. In A. K. Wing (Ed.), *Critical race feminism* (pp. 11–26). New York: New York University Press.

Harris, C. (1995). Whiteness as property. In N. G. K. Crenshaw, G. Peller, & K. Thomas (Eds.), *Critical race theory: Key writings that formed the movement* (pp. 276–291). New York: New Press.

Harry, B., & Klingner, J. K. (2006). *Why are so many minority students in special education? Understanding race and disability in schools.* New York: Teachers College Press.

Haslanger, S. (2003). Gender, patriotism and the events of 9/11. *Peace Review, 15*(4), 457–461.

Hassouneh-Phillips, D., & McNeff, E. (2003). "I thought I was less worthy": Low sexual and body esteem and increased vulnerability to intimate partner abuse in women with physical disabilities. *Sexuality and Disability, 23*(4), 227–240.

Hennessy, R. (1999). Book review of *Justice interruptus*: Critical reflections on the "postsocialist" condition. *Hypatia, 14*(1), 126–133.

Hennessy, R. (2000). *Profit and pleasure: Sexual identities in late capitalism.* New York: Routledge.

Herold, M. W. (2002). A dossier on civilian victims of United States aerial bombing of Afghanistan: A comprehensive accounting. Retrieved from http://www.cursor.org/stories/civilian_deaths.htm

Herrnstein, R. J., & Murray, C. A. (1994). *The bell curve: Intelligence and class structure in American life.* New York: Free Press.

Hevey, D. (1992). *The creatures time forgot: Photography and disability imagery.* New York: Routledge.

Hill Collins, P. (1998). It's all in the family: Intersections of gender, race, and nation. *Hypatia, 13*(3), 62–82.

hooks, b. (1985). *Feminist theory: From margin to center.* Cambridge, MA: South End Press.

Holmes, S. E., & Cahill, S. (2004). School experiences of gay, lesbian, bisexual, and transgender youth. *Journal of Gay and Lesbian Issues in Education, 1*(3), 53–56.

Hughes, B., & Paterson, K. (1997). The social model of disability and the disappearing body: Towards a sociology of impairment. *Disability and Society, 12*(3), 325–340.

Hull, A. (2004). Wounded or disabled but still on active duty. *Washington Post.* Retrieved from http://www.washingtonpost.com/ac2/wp-dyn/A23345 -2004Nov30?language=printer

Hull, G. T., Scott, P. B., & Smith, B. (Eds.). (1982). *All the women are white, all the blacks are men, but some of us are brave.* Old Westbury, NY: Feminist Press.

Human Rights Watch. (2008). Afghanistan: Civilian deaths from airstrikes. Human Rights Watch. Retrieved from http://www.hrw.org/en/news/2008/09 /07/afghanistan-civilian-deaths-airstrikes

iCasualties. (2011). Iraq coalition casualty count. From http://icasualties.org/

Ingstaad, B. & Whyte, S. R. (Eds.). (1995). *Disability and culture.* Berkeley: University of California Press.

Ingstaad, B. & Whyte, S. R. (Eds.). (2007). *Disability in local and global worlds.* Berkeley: University of California Press.

Iraq Body Count. (2011). Database: Documented civilian deaths from violence. Iraq Body Count, from http://www.iraqbodycount.org/database/

Isler, A., Tas, F., Beytut, D., & Conk, Z. (2009). Sexuality in adolescents with intellectual disabilities. *Sex and Disability, 27*: 27–34.

James, J. C., & Wu, C. (2003). Editor's introduction: Race, ethnicity, disability, and literature: Intersections and interventions. *Multi-Ethnic Literature of the United States (MELUS), 31*(3), 3–13.

James, J. C., & Wu, C. (2006). Editors' introduction. Race, ethnicity, disability, and literature: Intersections and interventions. (Editorial). *MELUS, 31*(3), 3(11).

Janssen, D. F. (2009). Sex as development: Curriculum, pedagogy, and critical inquiry. *Review of Education, Pedagogy, and Cultural Studies, 31:* 2–28.

Johnson, C. (2010). The politics of affective citizenship: From Blair to Obama. *Citizenship Studies, 14*(5), 495–509.

Kabeer, N. (1994). *Reverse realities: Gender hierarchies in development thought.* New York: Verso.

Kafer, A. (2003). Compulsory bodies: Reflections on heterosexuality and able-bodiedness. *Journal of Women's History, 15*(3), 77–89.

Kalyanpur, M. (1996). The influence of Western special education on community based services in India. *Disability and Society, 11*(2), 249–270.

Kaplan, C., Alarcon, N., & Moallem, M. (1999). *Between women and nation: Nationalisms, transnational feminism, and the state.* Durham, NC: Duke University Press.

Kittay, E. F. (1999). *Love's labor: Essays on women, equality, and dependency.* New York: Routledge.

Kittay, E. F. (2000). *At home with my daughter.* New York: Routledge.

Kozol, J. (1992). *Savage inequalities: Children in America's schools* (1st Harper Perennial ed.). New York: Harper Perennial.

Kristeva, J. (1982). *Powers of horror: An essay on abjection.* New York: Columbia University Press.

Kudlick, C. J. (2005). Disability history, power, and rethinking the idea of "the other." *PMLA, 120*(2), 557–561.

Kuppers, P. (2009). Toward a rhizomatic model of disability: Poetry, performance, and touch. *Journal of Literary and Cultural Disability Studies, 3*(3), 221–240.

Kuppers, P., & Marcus, N. (2008). *Cripple poetics: A love story.* Ypsilanti, MI: Homofactus Press.

Kuterovac-Jagodic, G. (2003). Posttraumatic stress symptoms in Croatian children exposed to war: A prospective study. *Journal of Clinical Psychology, 59*(1), 9–25.

La Paperson, (2010). The postcolonial ghetto: Seeing her shape and his hand. *Berkeley Review of Education, 1*(1).

Ladd-Taylor, M. (1994). *Motherwork: Women, child welfare and the state—1890–1930.* Chicago: University of Illinois Press.

Ladson-Billings, G., & Tate IV, W. F. (1995). Toward a critical race theory of education. *Teachers College Record, 97*(1), 47–68.

Lamb, D. (2010). Toward a sexual ethics curriculum: Bringing philosophy and society to bear on individual development. *Harvard Educational Review, 80*(1), 81–105.

Land, H. (1990). Time to care. In A. Gitlin (Ed.), *Power and method: Political activism and educational research* (pp. 227–238). New York: Routledge.

Lecercle, J-J. (2005). Deleuze, Guattari and Marxism. *Historical Materialism, 13*(3), 35–55.

Leder, D. (1990). *The absent body.* Chicago, IL: University of Chicago Press.

Lee, S., & Pollard, S. (Writer). (2006). *When the levees broke: A requiem in four acts* (Motion Picture).

Lehr, C. A., & Lange, C. M. (2003). Alternative schools serving students with and without disabilities: What are the current issues and challenges? *Preventing School Failure, 47*(2), 59–65.

Lehr, C. A., Tan, C. S., & Ysseldyke, J. (2009). Alternative schools: A synthesis of state-level policy and research. *Remedial and Special Education, 30*: 19–32.

Levinson, M. (1999). *The demands of liberal education* (pp. ix, 237 p.). Oxford: Oxford University Press.

Lidinsky, A. (2005). The gender of war: What "Fahrenheit 9/11's" women don't say. *International Feminist Journal of Politics, 7*(1), 142–146.

Linton, S. (1998). *Claiming disability: Knowledge and identity.* New York: New York University Press.

Lister, R. (1997). *Citizenship : Feminist perspectives.* Washington Square, NY: New York University Press.

Livingston, J. (2006). Insights from an African history of disability. *Radical Review of History, 94*: 11–126.

Lofgren-Martenson, L. (2009). The invisibility of young homosexual women and men with intellectual disabilities. *Sexuality and Disability, 27*(1), 21–26.

Longmore, P. K. (2005). The cultural framing of disability: Telethons as a case study. *PMLA: Publications of the Modern Language Association of America, 120*(2), 502–508.

Lorde, A. (1984). *Sister outside: Essays and speeches*. Berkeley, CA: Crossing Press Feminist Series.

Lorde, A. (2006). *The cancer journals: Special edition*. San Francisco: Aunt Lutes Books.

Ludwig, A. (2006). Differences between women? Intersecting voices in a female narrative. *European Journal of Women's Studies, 13*(3), 245–258.

Markula, P. (2006). The dancing body without organs. *Qualitative Inquiry, 12*(1), 3–27.

Marshall, C. (1997). *Feminist critical policy analysis*. Washington, DC: Falmer Press.

Marx, K. (1859). Preface to *A contribution to the critique of political economy*. In R. C. Tucker (Ed.), *The Marx-Engel's reader (1972)* (pp. 3–8). New York: Norton Press.

Marx, K. (1871). The eighteenth broodmare of Louis Bonaparte. In R. C. Tucker (Ed.), *The Marx-Engel's reader (1972)* (pp. 594–617). New York: Norton Press.

Marx, K., Engels, F., & Tucker, R. C. (1978). *The Marx-Engels reader* (2nd ed.). New York: Norton.

Marx, K., Engels, F., & Arthur, C. J. (1989). *The German ideology*. New York: International Publishers Company.

Masters, C. (2005). Bodies of technology: Cyborg soldiers and militarized masculinities. *International Feminist Journal of Politics, 7*(1), 112–132.

Mbembe, J. A. (2003). Necropolitics. *Public Culture, 15*(1), 11–40.

McCall, L. (2005). The complexity of intersectionality. *Signs, 30*(3), 1771–1800.

McKay, S. (2004). Reconstructing fragile lives: Girls' social reintegration in Northern Uganda and Sierra Leone. *Gender and Development, 12*(3), 19–30.

McMahan, J. (1996). Cognitive disability, misfortune, and justice. *Philosophy and Public Affairs, 25*(1), 3–33.

McNeil, J. (2000). Employment, earnings, and disability. Retrieved from http://www.census.gov/hhes/www/disability.html

McRuer, R. (2006). *Crip theory: Cultural signs of queerness and disability*. New York: New York University Press.

McWilliam, E., & Taylor, P. (1996). Pedagogy, technology, and the body. New York: Peter Lang.

Mercer, J. (1973). *Labeling the mentally retarded: Clinical and social systems perspectives on mental retardation*. Berkeley: University of California Press.

Merleau-Ponty, M. (2006). From the phenomenology of perception. In M. Lock & J. Farquhar, (Eds.), *Beyond the body proper: Reading the anthropology of material life* (pp. 133–139). Durham, NC: Duke University Press.

Michalko, R. (2002). *The difference that disability makes*. Philadelphia, PA.: Temple University Press.

Mies, M. (1986). *Patriarchy and accumulation on a world scale: Women in the international division of labour*. Atlantic Highlands, NJ: Zed Books

Miles, M. (2002). Formal and informal disability resources for Afghan reconstruction. *Third World Quarterly, 23*(5), 945–959.

Minow, M. (1990). *Making all the difference: Inclusion, exclusion, and American law*. Ithaca, NY: Cornell University Press.

Mitchell, D. T., & Snyder, S. L. (1997). *The body and physical difference: Discourses of disability*. Ann Arbor: University of Michigan Press.

Mitchell, D. T., & Snyder, S. A. (2010). Disability as multitude: Re-working non-productive labor power. *Journal of Literary and Cultural Disability Studies, 4*(2), 179–193.

Mohanty, C. T. (1991). Introduction: Cartographies of struggle. In A. Russo, C. T. Mohanty, & L. Torres (Eds.), *Third World women and the politics of feminism* (pp. 1–50).Bloomington: Indiana University Press.

Mohanty, C. T. (1997). Under Western eyes: Feminist scholarship and colonial discourse. In N. Visvanathan, L. Duggan, L. Nisonoff, & N. Wiegersma (Eds.), *The women, gender, and development reader* (pp. 79–85). London; Atlantic Highlands, NJ: Zed Books.

Mohanty, C. T., Russo, A., & Torres, L. (1991). *Third World women and the politics of feminism*. Bloomington: Indiana University Press.

Molina, N. (2006). Immigration, race, and disability in early 20th century America. *Radical History Review, 94*: 11–126.

Molyneux, J. (1987). *Arguments for a revolutionary socialism*. Chicago, IL: Bookmarks.

Moreno, J. (2002, November). Orgasms in our ears. http://www.bentvoices.org/bentvoices/moreno_ears.htm

Morris, J. (1991). *Pride against prejudice: A personal politics of disability*. London: Women's Press.

Morris, J. (1992). Personal and political: A feminist perspective on researching physical disability. *Disability, Handicap, and Society, 7*(2), 157–175.

Morris, J. (1995). Creating a space for absent voices: Disabled women's experience of receiving assistance with daily living activities *Feminist Review, 51*: 68–93.

Mostert, M. P. (2002). Useless eaters: Disability as genocidal marker in Nazi Germany. *Journal of Special Education, 36*(3), 155–168.

Mouffe, C. (1992). Feminism, citizenship, and radical democratic politics. In J. Butler & J. Scott (Eds.), *Feminists theorize the political* (pp. 369–384). New York: Routledge.

Mouffe, C. (1996). Radical democracy or liberal democracy? In D. Trend (Ed.), *Radical democracy: Identity, citizenship, and the state* (pp. 19–25). New York: Routledge.

Mullahy, John, Robert Stephanie, & Wolfe, Barbara. (2001). *Health, income, and inequality: Review and redirection for the Wisconsin Russell Sage Working Group*. Russell Sage Foundation, New York, mimeo.

Murphy, R. (1987). *The body silent*. New York: Holt Publishing

Murray, C. (1993). The coming white underclass. *Wall Street Journal*, October 29th.

Murray, C., & Hernstein, R. (1994). *The bell curve: Intelligence and class structure in American life*. New York: Free Press.

Mutua, N. (2001). Policed identities: Children with disabilities. *Educational Studies: A Journal of the Educational Studies Association, 33*(2), 289–300.

Myrttinen, H. (2004). Pack your heat and work the streets: Weapons and the active construction of violent masculinities. *Women and Language, 27*(2), 29–34.

Nakano-Glenn, E. (1992). From servitude to service work: Historical continuities in the racial division of paid reproductive work. *Signs: Journal of Women in Culture and Society, 18*(1), 1–18.

Nakano-Glenn, E. (2010). *Forced to care: Coercion and caregiving in America*. Cambridge, MA: Harvard University Press.

Navarro, V. (1984). *Crisis, health, and medicine: A social critique*. New York: Tavistock Publications.

Nibert, D. (1995). The political economy of developmental disability. *Critical Sociology, 21*(2), 59–80.

Noddings, N. (1990). A response. *Hypatia: A Journal of Feminist Philosophy, 5*(1), 120–127.

Noguera, P. (1995). Preventing and producing violence: A critical analyses of responses to school violence. *Harvard Educational Review, 65*: 189–212.

Norden, M. F. (1994). *The cinema of isolation: A history of physical disability in the movies*. Piscataway, NJ: Rutgers University Press.

O'Toole, C. J. (2000). The view from below: Developing a knowledge base about an unknown population. *Sexuality and Disability, 18*(3), 207–224

Oliver, M. (1990). *The politics of disablement: A sociological approach*. New York: St. Martin's Press.

Omi, M., & Winant, H. (1994). *Racial formation in the United States: From the 1960s to the 1990s* (2nd ed.). New York: Routledge.

Parker, G. (1993). *With this body: Caring and disability in marriage*. Buckingham, England; Philadelphia, PA: Open University Press.

Parker, L., Deyhle, D., & Villenas, S. A. (1999). *Race is—race isn't: Critical race theory and qualitative studies in education* (pp. ix, 284 p.). Boulder, CO: Westview Press.

Pascall, G. (1986). *Social policy: A feminist analysis*. New York: Tavistock Publications.

Pastrana, J. A. (2004). Black identity constructions: Inserting intersectionality, bisexuality, and (Afro-) Latinidad into black studies. *Journal of African American Studies, 8*(1&2), 74–89.

Pateman, C. (1988). *The sexual contract*. Stanford, CA: Stanford University Press.

Paterson, K., & Hughes, B. (1999). Disability studies and phenomenology: The carnal politics of everyday life. *Disability and Society, 14*(5), 597–610.

Paul, D. (1995). *Controlling human heredity: 1865 to the present*. Atlantic Highlands, NJ: Humanities Press International.

Pharr, S. (1988). *Homophobia: A weapon of sexism*. Little Rock, AR: Chardon Press.

Pillow, W. (2003). "Bodies are dangerous": Using feminist genealogy as embodied policy analysis. *Journal of Educational Policy, 18*(2), 145–159.

Pillow, W. (2004). *Unfit subjects: Educational policy and the teen mother*. New York: Routledge Falmer.

Pin-Fat, V., & Stern, M. (2005). The scripting of private Jessica Lynch: Biopolitics, gender, and the "feminization" of the US military. *Alternatives, 30*: 25–53.

Price, J., & Shildrick, M. (1999). *Feminist theory and the body: A reader*. Edinburgh: Edinburgh University Press.

Priestly, Mark. (2001). *Disability and the life course: Global perspectives*. Cambridge: Cambridge University Press.

Puar, J. K. (2007). *Terrorist assemblages: Homonationalism in queer times*. Durham, NC: Duke University Press.

Puka, Bill. (1989). The liberation of caring: A different voice for Gilligan's "Different voice." In Mary M. Brabeck (Ed.), *Who cares? Theory, research, and educational implications of the ethic of care*. New York: Praeger.

Quayson, A. (2007). *Aesthetic nervousness: Disability and the crisis of representation*. New York: Columbia University Press.

Quigley, B. (2008). Displaced poor still arriving in New Orleans as saints go marching in. Dissident Voice. Retrieved from http://dissidentvoice.org/2008/09 /displaced-poor-still-arriving-in-new-orleans-as-saints-go-marching-in/

Quinlivan, Kathleen. (2006). Affirming Sexual Diversity in Two New Zealand Secondary Schools: Challenges, Constraints and Shifting Ground in the Research Process. *Journal of Gay & Lesbian Issues in Education 3*(2–3), 5–33.

Rai, S. (1996). Women and the state in the Third World. In H. Afshar (Ed.), *Women and politics in the Third World* (pp. 25–39). New York: Routledge.

Rao, M., Nayar, K. R., Rama, B., & Priya, R. (1995). Health and structural development: Major shifts at policy level. *Economic and Political Weekly, May 20*, 1156–1160.

Rawls, J. (1998). Justice as fairness in the liberal polity. In G. Shafir (Ed.), *The citizenship debates: A reader* (pp. 53–72). Minneapolis: University of Minnesota Press.

Reid, D. K., & Knight, M. G. (2006). Disability justifies exclusion of minority students: A critical history grounded in disability studies. *Educational Researcher, 35*(6), 18–23.

Rice, P., & Waugh, P. (1992). *Modern literary theory: A reader* (2nd ed.). London; New York: Routledge, Chapman and Hall.

Rohrer, J. (2005). Towards a full-inclusion feminism: A feminist deployment of disability analysis. *Feminist Studies, 31*(1), 34–61.

Roxas, K. (2008). Keepin' it real and relevant: Providing a culturally responsive education to pregnant and parenting teens. *Multicultural Education, 15*(3), 2–9.

Russell, M. (1998). *Beyond ramps: Disability at the end of the social contract*. Monroe, LA: Common Courage Press.

Safran, S. P. (2001). Movie images of disability and war: Framing history and political ideology. *Remedial and Special Education, 22*(4), 223–232.

Sarup, M. (1989). *An introductory guide to post-structuralism and postmodernism*. Athens: University of Georgia Press.

Schlosser, E. (1988, December). The prison industrial complex. *Atlantic Monthly*, 1–12.

Scott, R. (1969). *The making of blind men: A study of adult socialization*. New York: Russell Sage Foundation.

Schepper-Hughes, N. (2001). Commodity fetishism in organ trafficking. *Body and Society, 7*(2–3), 31–62.

Shakespeare, T. (1999). The sexual politics of disabled masculinity. *Sexuality and Disability, 17*(1), 53–64.

Shapiro, J. (1994). *No pity: People with disabilities forging a new civil rights movement*. New York: Three Rivers Press.

Sherry, M. (2004). Overlaps and contradictions between queer theory and disability studies. *Disability and Society, 19*(7), 769–783.

Shildrick, M. (2005). Unreformed bodies: Normative anxiety and the denial of pleasure. *Women's Studies, 34*(3/4), 327–344.

Shildrick, M. (2007). Dangerous discourses: Anxiety, desire, and disability. *Studies in Gender and Sexuality, 8*(3), 221–244.

Shildrick, M. (2009). *Dangerous discourses of disability, subjectivity and sexuality.* Basingstoke; New York: Palgrave Macmillan.

Shilling, C. (1993). *The body and social theory.* Newbury Park, CA: Sage Publications.

Shuttleworth, R. P., & Mona, L. (2002). Introduction to the symposium. *Disability Studies Quarterly, 22*(4), 2.

Siebers, T. (2008). *Disability theory.* Ann Arbor: University of Michigan Press.

Siebers, T. (2010). *Disability aesthetics.* Ann Arbor: University of Michigan Press.

Silvers, A. (1997). Reconciling equality to difference: Caring (f)or justice for people with disabilities. In P. DiQuinzio & I. M. Young (Eds.), *Feminist ethics and social policy* (pp. 23–48). Bloomington: Indiana University Press.

Silvers, A., Wasserman, D. T., & Mahowald, M. B. (1998). *Disability, difference, discrimination: Perspectives on justice in bioethics and public policy.* Lanham, MD: Rowman & Littlefield Publishers.

Singer, L. (1989). Bodies-pleasures-powers. *Differences: A Journal of Feminist Cultural Studies, 1*(1), 45–65.

Skiba, R. J., Homer, Robert, H., Chung, Choong-Geun, Rausch, Karega, M., May, Seth L., & Tobin, Tary. (2011). Race is not neutral: A national investigation of African American and Latino disproportionality in school discipline. *The School Psychology Review* 40(1), 85–107.

Skiba, R. J., & Knesting, K. (2001). Zero tolerance, zero evidence: An analysis of school disciplinary practice. *New Directions for Youth Development2001* (92), 17–43.

Smith, B. J. & Hutchinson, B. (Eds.). (2004). *Gendering disability.* New York: Rutgers University Press.

Snyder, S. L., & Mitchell, D. T. (2006). *Cultural locations of disability.* Chicago, IL: University of Chicago Press.

Spillers, H. J. (1987). Mama's baby, Papa's maybe: An American grammar book. *Diacritics: A Review of Contemporary Criticism, 17*(2), 65–81.

Spitz, H. H. (1997). *Nonconscious movements: From mystical messages to facilitated communication.* Mahwah, NJ: Erlbaum.

Stevens, B. (2010, February). Getting emotionally naked: Notes on an activist voice.

Stevens, B. (forthcoming). CripSex: Sk(r)ewed Media Representation. In R. Shuttleworth & T. Sanders (Eds.) *Sexuality and disability research: Sexual politics, identity, access and policy.* Leeds: The Disability Press.

Stienstra, D. (2002). DisAbling globalization: Rethinking global political economy with a disability lens. *Global Society, 16*(2), 109–121.

Stiker, H.-J. (1999). *A history of disability.* Ann Arbor: University of Michigan Press.

Stone, D. (1984). *The disabled state.* Philadelphia, PA: Temple University Press.

Sullivan, A., & Caterino, L. C. (2008). Addressing the sexuality and sex education of individuals with autism spectrum disorders. *Education and Treatment of Children, 31*(3), 381–394.

Sweeney, L. (2007). The importance of human sexuality for students with disabilities. *Exceptional Parent, 27*(9), 36–39.

Taylor-Gooby, P. (1991). *Social change, social welfare and social science*. Buffalo, NY: University of Toronto Press.

Tepper, M. S. (2000). Sexuality and disability: The missing discourse of pleasure. *Sexuality and Disability, 18*(4), 283–290.

Tepper, M. S. (2005). Becoming sexually able: Education for adolescents and young adults with disabilities. *Contemporary Sexuality, 39*(9), 1–7.

Tepper, M., Whipple, B., Richards, E., & Komisaruk, B. R. (2001). Women with complete spinal cord injury: A phenomenological study of sexual experiences. *Journal of Sex and Marital Therapy, 27*: 615–623.

Thomas, C. (1993). Deconstructing concepts of care. *Sociology, 27*(4), 649–669.

Thomas, C. (1999). *Female forms: Experiencing and understanding disability*. Philadelphia, PA: Open University Press.

Thomas, M. (1992). Community based rehabilitation in India: An emerging trend. *Indian Journal of Pediatrics, 59*(4), 401–406.

Thompson, S. A. (2007). De/Centering straight talk: Queerly informed inclusive pedagogy for gay and bisexual students with intellectual disabilities. *Journal of LGBT Youth, 5*(1), 37–56.

Titchkosky, T. (2005). Disability in the news: a reconsideration of reading. *Disability & Society 20*(6), 655–668.

Titchkosky, T. (2007). *Reading and writing disability differently: The textured life of embodiment*. Toronto; Buffalo, NY: University of Toronto Press.

Torrant, J. (2002). Empire versus imperialism and the question of family labor. *The Red Critique*. Retrieved from http://redcritique.org/

Traustadottir, R. (1988). *Women and family care: On the gendered nature of caring*. Paper presented at the First International Conference on Family Support Related to Disability.

Tremain, S. (2001). On the government of disability. *Social Theory and Practice, 27*(4), 617–620.

Trimble, L. (2009). Transformative conversations about sexualities pedagogy and the experience of sexual knowing. *Sex Education, 9*(1), 51–64.

Trupin, L., & National Institute on Disability and Rehabilitation Research (US) (1997). *Trends in Labor Force Participation among Persons with Disabilities, 1983-1994. Disability Statistics Report [No.] 10*.

Turner, B. S. (1984). *The body and society: Explorations in social theory*. New York: Basil Blackwell.

Twachtman-Cullen, D. (1997). *A passion to believe: Autism and facilitated communication*. Boulder, CO: Westview Press.

UN Enable (2008). International Day for Persons with Disabilities—3 December 2008. Retrieved from http://www.un.org/disabilities/default.asp?id=109.

Ungerson, C. (1987). *Policy is personal: Sex, gender, and informal care*. New York: Tavistock Publications.

Vander Schee, C., & Baez, B. (2009). HIV/AIDS education in schools: The "unassembled" youth as a curricular project. *Discourse: Studies in the Cultural Politics of Education, 30*(1), 33–46.

Walsh, D. (2005). US war in Iraq yields a social tragedy. World's Socialist Website, from http://www.wsws.org/articles/2005/may2005/iraq-m18.shtml

Watts, I. E., & Erevelles, N. (2004). These deadly times: Reconceptualizing school violence by using critical race theory and disability studies. *American Educational Research Journal, 41*(2), 271–299.

Waylen, G. (1996). Analyzing women in the politics of the Third World. In H. Afshar (Ed.), *Women and politics in the Third World* (pp. 7–24). New York: Routledge.

Weedon, C. (1987). *Feminist practice and poststructuralist theory*. New York: Basil Blackwell.

Weeks, K. (2007). Life within and against work: Affective labor, feminist critique, and post-Fordist politics. *ephemera, 7*(1), 233–249.

Wendell, S. (1996). *The rejected body: Feminist philosophical reflections on disability*. New York: Routledge.

Wiley, D. C., & Terlosky, B. (2000). Evaluating sexuality education curriculums. *Educational Leadership, 58*(2), 79–82.

Williams, P. J. (1991). *The alchemy of race and rights*. Cambridge, MA: Harvard University Press.

Williams, P. J. (1997). Spirit murdering the messenger: The discourse of finger-pointing as the law's response to racism. In A. K. Wing (Ed.), *Critical race feminism: A reader* (pp. 229–242). New York: New York University Press.

Wing, A. K. (1997a). Brief reflections toward a multiplicative theory and praxis of being. In A. K. Wing (Ed.), *Critical race feminism: A reader* (pp. 27–34). New York: New York University Press.

Wing, A. K. (1997b). Introduction. In A. K. Wing (Ed.), *Critical race feminism: A reader* (pp. 1–6). New York: New York University Press.

Wolff, J. (2010). Cognitive disability in a society of equals. In E. F. C. Kittay, Licia (Ed.), *Cognitive disability and its challenge to moral philosophy* (pp. 147–159). Malden, MA: Wiley-Blackwell.

Young, I. M. (1990). *Justice and the politics of difference*. Princeton, NJ: Princeton University Press.

Young, I. M. (1997). Asymmetrical reciprocity: On moral respect, wonder, and enlarged thought. *Constellations, 3*(3), 340–363.

Young, I. M. (2005). *On female body experience: "Throwing like a girl" and other essays*. New York: Oxford University Press.

Young, R. (2009). *Signs of race in poststructuralism: Toward a transformative theory of race*. Lanham, MD: University Press of America.

Yuval-Davis, N. (2006). Intersectionality and feminist politics. *European Journal of Women's Studies, 13*(3), 193–203.

Zavarzadeh, M. U. (1995). Post-ality: The (dis)simulations of cybercapitalism. *Transformations: Marxist Boundary Work in Theory, Economics, Politics, and Culture, 1*(1), 1–75.

Zita, J. (1996). Review of *Making bodies, making history: Feminism and gender identity* by Leslie Anderson, *Unbearable weight: Feminism, Western culture, and the body* by Susan Bordo, *Bodies that matter: On the discursive limits of "Sex,"* by Judith Butler, and *Volatile bodies: Towards a corporeal feminism* by Elizabeth Grosz. *Signs, 21*(3), 786–794.

INDEX

structural, 16–17, 38, 42, 47, 57–8,
  89–91; *see also* Farmer, P.
voluntarism, 38, 45, 54, 160–1, 189

welfare state, 15, 45, 73, 133, 200
  and disability, 150–1, 167–9, 181–91
whiteness as property, 165–8
Williams, P., 65–6, 73, 91, 95–6,
  118, 120

see also Critical Race Feminism
Wilson, Junius, 22, 98, 104–8,
  115–18, 120

Young, I. M., 37–8, 157
Young, R., 53–4, 61–3
  see also race, as commodity
  fetish
Yuval-Davis, A., 101–2

21875522R00135

Made in the USA
Middletown, DE
13 December 2018